Playing the Other

of related interest

Reminiscence Theatre
Making Theatre from Memories
Pam Schweitzer
Foreword by Glenda Jackson MP
ISBN: 978 1 84310 430 8

Psychodrama
A Beginner's Guide
Zoran Djurić, Jasna Veljković and Miomir Tomić
ISBN: 978 1 84310 411 7

Rebels with a Cause
Working with Adolescents Using Action Techniques
Mario Cossa
Foreword by Zerka T. Moreno
ISBN: 978 1 84310 379 0

Sambadrama
The Arena of Brazilian Psychodrama
Edited and translated by Zoltán Figusch
Forewords by Adam Blatner and José Fonseca
ISBN: 978 1 84310 363 9

Focus on Psychodrama
The Therapeutic Aspects of Psychodrama
Peter Felix Kellermann
Foreword by Jonathan D. Moreno
ISBN: 978 1 85302 127 5

Introduction to Dramatherapy
Theatre and Healing – Ariadne's Ball of Thread
Sue Jennings
Foreword by Clare Higgins
ISBN: 978 1 85302 115 2

Trust and Power
Taking Care of Ourselves through Drama
Penny Casdagli
ISBN: 978 1 85302 556 3

Essays in Drama Therapy: The Double Life
Robert J. Landy
Foreword by Gavin Bolton
ISBN: 978 1 85302 322 4

Playing the Other

Dramatizing Personal Narratives in Playback Theatre

Nick Rowe

Jessica Kingsley Publishers
London and Philadelphia

First published in 2007
by Jessica Kingsley Publishers
116 Pentonville Road
London N1 9JB, UK
and
400 Market Street, Suite 400
Philadelphia, PA 19106, USA

www.jkp.com

Library of Congress Cataloging in Publication Data

Rowe, Nick, 1954-
Playing the other : dramatizing personal narratives in playback theatre / Nick Rowe.
p. cm.
Includes bibliographical references and index.
ISBN-13: 978-1-84310-421-6 (alk. paper)
ISBN-10: 1-84310-421-0 (alk. paper)
1. Improvisation (Acting) 2. Drama--Therapeutic use. I. Title.
PN2071.I5R69 2006
792.02'2--dc22

2006032988

British Library Cataloguing in Publication Data

A CIP catalogue record for this book is available from the British Library

ISBN: 978 1 84310 421 6

Printed and bound in Great Britain by
Athenaeum Press, Gateshead, Tyne and Wear

*This book is dedicated to Major Dennis Rowe and Mrs Anne Rowe,
my dear parents, whose kindness and love sustains me still.*

Contents

Acknowledgements

Thanks are due to Hazel and Rebecca who have lived the stresses and anxieties of this book over the many years of its development. Without them this would not have been possible.

I am also very grateful to Playback Theatre York who gave permission for me to conduct the research within the company. Without their support, encouragement, and skill this book would have not have been written. I acknowledge my enormous gratitude to: Di Adderley, Andy Bird, Bernard Campbell, Susanna Cunningham, Sarah Fallon, Marie Flanagan, Viv Hathaway, Louise Larkinson, Greta Mikaelson, Steve Nash, Felicity North, Louise Peacock, David Powley, Claire Smith.

York St John University have supported this work consistently, through financial means and through releasing me for study leave. I am very grateful to them. I also recognize the support of C4C: *Collaborating for Creativity*, an HEFCE-funded Centre for Excellence in Teaching and Learning at the University. Finally, I am deeply indebted to Professor Baz Kershaw whose wise advice sustained me through my PhD, which provided the basis for this book.

Special Notes

Gender pronouns

To avoid the clumsiness of using 'his/her' or 'she/he' I have used gender pronouns randomly. It will be clearly indicated if the usage of a gender pronoun is deliberate.

Playback Theatre York

Playback Theatre York has kindly given me permission to make use of examples of their work and discussions in this book. In general, and with their permission, I have used the first names of company members. There are occasions, however, when the sensitivity of the material has led me, in consultation with the people involved, to use pseudonyms.

Chapter 1
Setting the Scene

From The Playback Theatre Rehearsal: A Short Story
(Please see Appendix 1 for the full story.)

'I've got a story!' shouted Rona as she moved toward the storyteller's chair. She had to move quickly, otherwise someone would get there before her. She was determined to tell a story this week since, over the last few rehearsals, she had missed out. Either she did not think of one, or one of the others got there before her, but tonight she was going to make sure. She landed on the chair, skidding as she did so from the speed of arrival, and waited for one of the company to sit on the chair next to her.

Laura joined her and said, 'So what's your story, Rona?'

The truth was that Rona had been in such a rush to get to the chair that she hadn't totally decided. She hoped that when she got there it would be clear what she wanted to say, and now, with Laura and the whole group waiting, she experienced a moment of panic. 'I'm wasting people's time,' she thought to herself.

'It's about my father,' she said finally.

'OK,' said Laura. 'Choose someone to be you.'

Rona looked at the line of four actors sitting on chairs in front of a rack of coloured cloth. Who would she choose to play her? As her eyes moved along the group she was drawn to Bridget. It was something about the way she was sitting in the chair, slightly slumped as if pressed down by some force, a tension in her face and, unlike some of the others, not looking at Rona. It was likely, Rona thought, that Bridget did not want to be chosen, but there was something about her vulnerability, her reluctance, that drew Rona to say 'Bridget'. Bridget stood up.

'OK, so tell me about your story,' said Laura, putting her hand on Rona's knee. Rona spoke of the phone call from her father telling her that he was going into hospital. She spoke of the darkening silence that had seemed to push out everything between them, filling the space with its demanding presence.

'It made me feel cold,' said Rona, suddenly feeling cold herself. 'I can feel it now.'

'Describe it to us,' said Laura.

'It's kind of bleak and very, very empty...well, empty yes, but also lonely, bereft, like...' Rona paused for a minute. 'It's like Sunday evenings at boarding school, in November, it's getting darker and colder and there are weeks and weeks before Christmas. Dark, cold, Victorian, cheerless buildings. That's what it was like.'

Rona hadn't expected to say the last bit, but having done so she felt a little leap of excitement, an almost sexual excitement.

'OK,' said Laura. 'So what happened next?'

'My father said that he had been to the hospital and he'd had some tests and was waiting for the results – something to do with pains in his stomach. He'd never told me about that before.'

'Choose someone to be your father,' said Laura.

Again Rona looked at the actors. This time she had no doubt. 'Bruno,' she said, and Bruno sprang to his feet as if he had always known he would be chosen.

'Give Bruno some words to describe your father in this story.'

'Oh, I don't know, I think he was a little nervous, a little irritated by me going on about work...it was so strange for him to phone and he seemed ill at ease.'

Laura patted Rona's hand as she said, looking toward the actors, 'This is Rona's story of a phone call with her father. Let's watch.'

Playback theatre is a form of improvised drama in which members of an audience are invited to tell personal stories to a 'conductor' and see these improvised by a company of actors and musicians. It is a form developed by Jonathan Fox, Jo Salas and their company in 1975 (see Fox 1994; Fox and Dauber 1999; Salas 1993) and is now practised in many countries across the world. In the playback lexicon, the contributor of each autobiographical narrative is called the 'teller'. They are invited to sit on the stage and to recount their experience to a 'conductor' who, at the conclusion of the story, turns it over to the performers by saying 'Let's watch'. Playback practitioners usually work in companies and perform to a wide range of audiences. The company of which I am a member, Playback Theatre York, performs at conferences, for different professional groups, to people with mental health problems and professionals who worked with them, in health and social care settings and occasionally at events that mark significant life transitions (for example birthdays, weddings, and retirements).

Setting the Scene

I am an enthusiast of playback theatre. Over the ten years of my involvement with Playback Theatre York, I have derived enormous personal and professional benefit from telling my own stories and playing back those of others. Although it is important that the reader is aware of my enthusiasm from the outset, it is not my intention to write an apologetic for playback theatre; that would I think produce a less interesting and less relevant book. At this stage of its development a critical and interrogative approach is needed to bring into focus the pressing ethical questions raised by playback around telling, representing and bearing witness to autobiographical narratives. Playback theatre is a young discipline and quite understandably much of the writing to date has been aimed at explaining the practice, enthusiastically justifying its efficacy, or describing its development. A canon of literature which exposes the practice to critique has not yet developed. This book aims to open up some of the debates related to the telling and performing of personal stories in public places, which are often heard amongst practitioners, but have not yet reached a wider audience.

In light of this, and in order to rehearse some of these debates, I will begin with an example from the work of Playback Theatre York that, although acceptable to the teller and the audience at the time, on reflection raises significant issues related to the representation and ethics of personal narratives.

A Gift at Christmas

The performance takes place near Christmas time in the community mental health centre of a town in the North of England. The audience is comprised of about 50 people with mental health problems and the professionals who work with them. In the centre of the stage is a line of five chairs on which the actors are seated. There is a musician to the audience's right surrounded by musical instruments. An assortment of coloured fabric is hanging on a clotheshorse at the back of the stage. To the left there are two chairs; one is occupied by the 'conductor' and the other is empty and awaits the first 'teller'.

A woman in her late thirties or early forties comes forward. She tells the conductor that her story is about '...getting my daughter back on Christmas day'. Her story begins on Christmas Eve; she is sitting in the lounge of her house with her new partner, her eight-year-old daughter, her ex-husband and his new partner. They are making 'small talk'. She tells the conductor and the audience that because of her 'illness' her daughter has been living with her ex-husband. We learn that the daughter is to spend Christmas with her father – the teller's ex-husband, but as the father and his new partner prepare to leave, her daughter asks if she can spend Christmas with her mother instead.

After the initial reluctance of the father it is agreed that this will happen. The teller is clearly delighted by this and describes it as 'a wonderful Christmas present'. The conductor asks her to choose an actor to play herself. She chooses Viv, calling her 'the big woman' – she herself was large – and she chooses Greta to be her daughter. The conductor says 'A Gift at Christmas, let's watch.' While the musician plays, some of the actors collect fabric from the clotheshorse. They stand on either side of the stage facing each other. When they are ready, the music stops and one-by-one they enter the stage to form an initial tableau.

The enactment begins with this 'still tableau'. The daughter sits on one of the chairs and the ex-husband sits beside her, putting his hand on her knee. The mother stands across on the other side of the stage. They begin to make 'small talk', repeating the words 'small' and 'talk' in different combinations. The father takes his daughter's hand as they start to leave and he tells her what a great Christmas they will have together. They turn their backs to the mother and move away from her so that the diagonal between the two groups stretches across the stage. The mother speaks to the audience about how much she will miss her daughter; she begins to cry. As she speaks of how much she wants her daughter to share Christmas with her, the daughter begins to turn towards her mother and reach out toward her. The father resists this turn, pulling his daughter toward him. The daughter pulls against her father and continues to move towards her mother. The father lets her go. As mother and daughter meet they began to dance, slowly at first, but gradually the energy of their dance builds and finally they are vigorously swinging each other across the stage. The audience applaud and cheer in delight. The dance ends with a hug. The performers turn and look at the teller and await her response.

The conductor asks the teller to comment upon the enactment. She is crying as she reports that she liked the way the actors danced together and that it was 'lovely' when all the audience joined in. She seems to find it difficult to speak further. She returns to her seat, accompanied by applause led by the performers.

Although this story of *A Gift at Christmas* is not one of the most effective of Playback York's enactments, I have chosen it because it reveals what is the main subject of this book: the complexities of the performer's *response* to the teller's story[1]. It is clear that for the teller the most important aspect of this enactment was the response of the audience and the sense of affirmation that this afforded her. For her it was 'lovely' that the audience applauded and joined in her joy at having her daughter for Christmas. This validation of experience is one of the most important claims that are made for playback

1 I have chosen the term 'response' deliberately to stress that the performers' work cannot be a 'replication' or 'reflection' of the teller's story, but as a response that is inevitable influenced by complex subjective, dramatic and context-dependent factors.

theatre. The telling of personal stories and the subsequent enactment can counter that most destructive of beliefs: that we are alone in our experience. In many cases, it can provide a space for what the German playback practitioner Daniel Feldhendler calls 'a culture of remembrance' (2001, p.8).

Playback theatre can provide a space the collective remembering and the sense of validation and belonging that this offers. For example Maria Elena Garavelli (2001) has written of her playback performances with relatives of 'the disappeared ones' in Argentina; and Susan Evans and William Layman (2001) staged a playback performance for the families and friends of fire-fighters following a forest fire in Washington State. These instances, and others I will refer to later, provide evidence of the capacity for playback theatre to provide a space for affirmation and collective remembrance.

However, *A Gift at Christmas* also raises issues that are considerably more problematic. In the enactment the actors produced a kind of 'Hollywood moment' – a moment in which triumph was written unambivalently upon the narrative. When the mother and daughter danced, there was no room for ambivalence, despite all the unanswered questions that lay within the story: why had the daughter been separated from her mother? Did she stay with her permanently after this reunion? How did the father feel at losing his daughter for Christmas? Why had the mother lost the daughter in the first place? The power of the narrative of 'triumph' had such strength that we were all willing to suspend the difficult questions. After all, who could resist a 'gift of a child story', especially at Christmas? One could ask whether the performers were 'spinning' the narrative in order to produce the desired effects in the audience. There is always the risk that a story will be subverted to the needs of the listeners, or to be more politically nuanced, to the desires of those who hold the power to represent it. This is clearly an issue in playback practice, particularly since the form is designed in such a way as to give the performers a powerful hold over 'the means of representation'. Playback always raises questions about the *interpretive responsibilities* of the performers.

The vignette also raises questions concerning the relationship between the teller's narrative and the enactment. If the performers are not replicating the story, what are they doing? In what sense, if at all, can we say, as some playback practitioners do, that the performers are conveying the 'essence' of the teller's story? Would it not be more accurate to say that they are responding from their own subjectivity, desire and theatrical sensibilities to the story? What are the ethical implications if this is the case? For example, the teller did not say that she had cried on that Christmas Eve, yet the performer showed her doing so. Perhaps she did this to clarify and heighten the poignancy of the storyteller's situation and/or perhaps to dramatize her own subjective response to the narrative. In any case the performer was stepping beyond the told story and although one might argue for the theatrical efficacy of her doing so, significant ethical issues are nevertheless raised. It seems that, particularly in light of the title of this book, questions need to be asked concerning the *limitations of 'playing the other'*.

Another question concerns the nature of autobiographical narrative. The performers are not the only participants in the playback process who are responding to the presence of the audience, the tellers are also doing so. Personal stories told in public places are inevitably performed stories. It is not possible to assert a direct correspondence between the teller's experience and the narrative told in a performance. It more likely that the narrative will be inflected by the various contexts of its telling – the stories and enactments that preceded it; processes of identification that are present for the teller during the performance; the dialogue between the teller and the conductor; and the response of the audience during the telling. If it is not possible to assert that correspondence, then any supposed linear progression or straightforward translation from experience to recounted narrative and then on to its enactment is significantly complicated. We need to ask questions about what is happening to the *nature and quality of personal narratives* when they are told in public places.

A Gift at Christmas suggests that there is an intense awareness of the audience amongst both performers and tellers, and inevitably this will significantly influence the telling and performing. Although the response of the audience to the story was clearly important for the teller in my example, a critic of playback may legitimately wonder whether playback theatre can potentially debase individual experience. They might argue that the demands of the performance will force complex individual narratives into culturally familiar channels – that caricature will replace idiosyncrasy.

This vignette also poses questions about the way in which personal narratives are enacted. Why do playback performers choose to improvise? Is there something about improvising 'in the moment' which makes a significant contribution to the teller's account? On what sources do the performers draw in responding to the teller's narrative and how do their different subjective responses inflect the ongoing dramatization? Despite the difficulties of writing about the improvisational process – it is always a compromise with complexity – I will want to address these questions in the forthcoming pages.

Another set of questions surrounds the position of the teller in playback theatre. Their position as a spectator rather than as an actor distinguishes it from other cognate practices such as the theatre of the oppressed, psychodrama and dramatherapy. As is evident in my example, the teller only has a limited time to comment on the actors' work; there is usually no systematic opportunity for them to reflect at length on the enactment. This clearly places playback theatre at variance to such practices as psychodrama and dramatherapy in which a thorough discussion of the enactment it considered essential. What are the implications of *the relative lack of involvement of the teller* in playback theatre?

It is clear from what I have said here that when personal stories are told in public places, significant ethical issues are raised concerning the exposure of the tellers and the responsibility and accountability of the performers. This brief rehearsal of some of the questions raised by playback practice gives an indication, albeit sketchy, of the direction of this book. In forthcoming pages it will be necessary to set this out in more detail and with more precision. Some consideration of the history and scope of playback theatre will set these questions into a clearer focus and wider context.

Playback theatre: history and scope

Jonathan Fox, the founder of playback theatre, described the first playback theatre performance as follows:

> It is Sunday afternoon in winter, the early afternoon sky bright despite a cover of cloud. The light pours in through the big windows of the church hall, in the centre of which are placed about thirty chairs facing a line of plastic milk crates. On one side of the crates sits a collection of musical instruments. On the other side brightly coloured cloth hangs from a wooden prop tree. The voices of children resound in the hall as their parents usher them in and help them off with their coats. In a back room I am with my actors. We are facing our first performance with a new company and a new approach called Playback Theatre. It is totally improvisational. Our objective is to act out, using mime, music, and spoken scenes, the personal stories of the audience. (Fox 1994, p.1)

That first playback theatre performance took place in New London, Connecticut in the spring of 1975. The audience were friends and families of the actors, gathered together for '...improvisational theatre based simply on the real life stories of people in the audience, enacted on the spot by a team of actors' (Salas 1993, p.9).

Later in that year, Jonathan Fox moved, with his partner Jo Salas, to New York State and formed what later to be was called the 'original playback theatre company'. They performed in Poughkeepsie, a small town in the Hudson Valley, close to where, in 1936, Jacob Moreno had founded the Beacon Hill Sanatorium and had developed the clinical application of psychodrama.

Nearly a quarter of a century later, in August 1999, Playback Theatre York hosted the Seventh International Playback Theatre Conference to which 265 people from 26 different nations attended. Companies from

Australia, Japan, Austria, Hong Kong, Taiwan, the United States, Finland, Germany, France, Holland, Hungary, England and Italy performed in what was, to date, the largest playback theatre conference to be held. The growth of playback theatre is remarkable and plans for the next international conference in Sao Paulo, Brazil suggest that this will continue.

Jonathan Fox, as joint editor of the first book of essays on playback theatre wrote: 'I am...the one who first conceived the playback idea' (Fox and Dauber 1999, p.9). Fox was an actor and teacher with a particular interest in the oral tradition of pre-literate societies and a distaste for 'the competitive, sometimes narcissistic aspects of the world of the mainstream theatre' (Salas 1993, p.9). In the early 1970s, he had worked for the Peace Corps in Nepal and had been struck by the 'redeeming roles of ritual and storytelling in the pre-industrial village life of rural Nepal' (Salas 1993, p.9).

With his partner, Jo Salas, a musician and therapist, he returned to the United States where he encountered psychodrama and worked with Zerka Moreno, the widow of the founder of psychodrama, in Beacon, New York. Clearly inspired by psychodrama and by Moreno's wife, he wrote:

> What I heard from her lips, and what I witnessed under her guidance, felt like a revelation. Here was true community theatre. Here was theatre that made a difference. Here was emotion. Here was often stunning beauty. (Fox and Dauber 1999, p.10)

He experimented with improvisation and what he called 'immediate theatre' (Fox and Dauber 1999, p.9), eventually founding a small company called 'It's All Grace' in 1974 (Salas 1993, p.9). The company mainly comprised some of the parents of a small experimental school where he and Jo Salas sent their children. It was this group, which, in 1975, staged the first performance of what later was to be called playback theatre.

Fox describes his 'discovery' of playback theatre as his 'café vision'. This is elaborated by Jo Salas:

> One day, over a cup of hot chocolate in a diner, the idea came to him: an improvisational theatre based simply on the real life stories of people in the audience, enacted on the spot by a team of actors. (Salas 1993, p.9)

We should note the 'cup of hot chocolate in the diner' and query what the writer was trying to convey in this strictly unnecessary elaboration. The everyday and accessible homeliness and innocent beginning that is suggested hints at a particular perspective on playback. The act of uncovering origins inevitably involves the reading and writing of 'genesis' stories. These stories often tend to simplify – so in some way we may imagine that, back in the spring of 1975, the founders of playback faced less complexity than is the case at the present time. They often seek to convey qualities of innocence and freshness. This can be detected in the opening paragraph of this account, which refers precisely to the weather conditions and 'the light pouring in through the big windows of the church hall'. There is a sense here of bright new mornings and of epiphany. This 'genesis story' is particularly potent when, as is the case of playback theatre, there is a single founder whose life-partner has also been involved from the outset. The existence of this 'original' parental pairing is a powerful formula for myth-making and the formation of charismatic forms of leadership. I have not escaped this transferential dynamic nor have, in many cases, the playback community as a whole. Individual playback companies often operate very independently; however, at international events, where the tensions of a large organization operate, there sometimes seems to be a tendency to gather around these founding figures. In a recent interview with Fe Day, Jo Salas recognizes the problems that over-identification with a founding figure – especially a male one – have caused:

> It's such an old model of the world that there's one name, one person – and it's almost always a man... The truth is much more complex. And the truth is that Jonathan's vision was absolutely central. This was the person that we were following. It was very significant that he was someone who was both charismatic and tolerant – he held the group together. But the truth is *also* that his idea would have gone nowhere without me and the other people in the company. (Salas 2004a)

Although this has undoubtedly had a significant impact on the development of playback theatre, it is important to make two important caveats. The first is that most playback practitioners throughout the world practice in companies, which although may be affiliated to the International Playback Theatre Network operate independently, and second that playback theatre is not alone in having its charismatic founding figure; we need only think of the role Augusto Boal has played in the theatre of the oppressed and the Moreno family in psychodrama.

Soon after that first Sunday afternoon performance, Fox and Salas moved to New Paltz in the Hudson Valley where Fox could finish his studies at the Moreno Institute. During that period, fellow psychodrama students complemented the nascent playback company. The Moreno Institute contributed to the development of playback theatre, not only in providing some of the early actors but also by paying the rent of their rehearsal space for the first two years. The influence of psychodrama has continued to be crucial in the development of playback theatre; for example, the establishment of playback in Europe was made far easier by the significant presence of a psychodrama community in, for example, Germany and Finland. Jonathan Fox continued this connection, editing in 1987 *The Essential Moreno,* a collection of Moreno's writings on psychodrama, group method and spontaneity (Moreno 1987).

The Original Company performed weekly through the late 1970s and early 1980s to a mixture of regular and new audience members. Performances were also given at conferences, to schoolchildren, prisoners, the elderly, people with mental health problems and people with learning disabilities. It was clear from this that the genre was establishing itself as being available for disadvantaged groups and this has been the case throughout its history. It is clear that, from the outset, playback theatre was maintaining the psychodrama tradition from which it had partly emerged, in having a clear intention to explore the efficacious and restorative potential of the theatre form. Fox described in 2000 that the 'original playback vision' was to 'recapture that kind of ceremonial enactment in which there is no distinction between art and healing' (Fox 2000, p.14).

Fox describes the development of playback's dramaturgy within the original company:

> Our mission was to find effective dramatic forms for the enactment of any and all personal stories. We tried many different ways, some dance-like, others clowny, others psychodramatic. Over time we learned that our form demanded its own aesthetic. Some of our experiments suited the Playback approach and became part of our dramatic tradition, while others, after a hot period of discovery, turned out to be less effective and were eventually dropped. (Fox 1994, pp.3–4)

Of course, since then there have been innovations and developments to playback's dramaturgy. For example The Theatre of Spontaneity International (founded in April 1990), an international group of playback theatre performers, developed some new forms, which are still used by Playback Theatre York.

In 1980 four members of the company were invited by Francis Batten to travel to Australia and New Zealand. They performed and led workshops in Auckland, Wellington, Sydney and Melbourne. By the following year the Sydney and Melbourne companies were performing, followed by Auckland, Wellington and Perth in 1982 and Christchurch in 1984. By the mid-1980s, playback theatre was firmly established in the United States and Australia and began to develop more widely. In 1984 Jonathan Fox visited Japan, Annette Henne formed 'Playback Theatre Schweiz' in Switzerland in 1988 and Christina Hagelthorn established a company in Sweden in the same year.

In 1986 the original playback theatre company disbanded, exhausted by the constant performing and travelling, but by then playback seems to have been well established in the United States. The history of playback theatre from this date has been one of accelerating growth across the world and has been characterized by the challenges that result from responding to increasing cultural diversity and from managing a growing organization. In 1990 the International Playback Theatre Network was established and the first edition of its newsletter *Interplay* was published with an Australian, Mary Good, as editor. In Europe, Christina Hagelthorn formed The Theatre of Spontaneity International, a loose group of playback practitioners who performed together annually in a different European city.

The 1990s were clearly a period of rapid growth for the playback theatre movement. The number of companies in the United States rose rapidly and in Australia playback theatre was given considerable impetus with the establishment of the Drama Action Centre in Sydney. This centre, founded by Bridget Brandon and Francis Batten, both of whom had trained at L'Ecole Jacques Lecoq, focused on improvisation, *commedia dell'arte*, clowning and community-based theatre. It provided fertile soil for the development of playback theatre companies in Australia and New Zealand with many company members training there.

The development of playback theatre in Britain has been, in contrast to other key countries, a relatively slow process. The first British company was formed in June 1991 when Susanna Cunningham and David Powley invited Christina Hagelthorn to work with a group of interested therapists, teachers and actors in York. After this weekend, Playback Theatre York was formed. This company is still performing with nine of the original founding members; it is the company that this author joined in September 1994. The formation of a London Company followed shortly after in September 1991. At the time of writing there are 12 playback companies in Britain.

Outside the English-speaking countries, playback theatre has been developed most actively in Finland, Germany and Japan. The reasons for this are no doubt complex, but are certainly related to the presence of pre-existing psychodrama practice in Finland and Germany, and the work of key figures – Jonathan Fox in Germany and Japan, and Deborah Pearson, Robyn Weir and Christina Hagelthorn in Finland.

Rapid growth and diversification has presented considerable challenges in terms of responding to and welcoming differences in approach, while at the same time trying to maintain what is understood to be the key characteristics of playback theatre. The widening international development of playback has also caused many participants from white Caucasian backgrounds to face the complicity of their nations in the oppression of non-white, indigenous peoples. This was particularly in the case at the Perth Conference in 1997. Playback theatre grew within white, middle-class, educated communities of the Western world and, to a large extent, developed a philosophy and discourse that reflected that fact. The growth of playback within such very different countries as India, Botswana and Fiji, as well as within such communities as the indigenous peoples in Australia, and Afro-Caribbean people in the USA, has challenged the movement to respond in both its practice and discourse. Judy Swallow, one of the members of first playback group, acknowledges this challenge:

> Playback theatre has spread all over the world, and has expanded through the social and artistic visions of its practitioners. There is wonderful cross-pollination as groups meet and share new forms and ideas. Practical questions arise – inclusion/exclusion? Themes addressed overtly/covertly? How much 'quality control', and by whom? When can playback theatre be harmful? How can it be used to further justice? (Swallow 2000, p.16)

Great distances of discourse and ideology lie between that 1970s Sunday morning in New York State and the diverse playback communities of the early 21st century. Explanations and theories developed in the early days of playback theatre arose out of its white, Western and affluent beginnings and these need to be – and undoubtedly will be – challenged in order to suit the cultural and geographical diversity of contemporary practice. It may be that in some important respects playback theatre had outgrown its roots; it is hoped that this book may help in re-thinking playback for the 21st century.

Playback in the contemporary world

Playback theatre did not solely grow out of the will of a group of people in New York State – the ground for its growth was prepared by social and cultural trends in the post-war West. It emerged at the last quarter of the 20th century out of the fertile soil of Moreno's psychodrama, the experimental and improvisational theatre of the 1960s and 1970s and the shifting sands that Francois Lyotard terms the 'post-modern condition'. The picture is a complex and contradictory one, but we see trends through the second half of the 20th century that paved the way for the emergence of playback theatre. The practice joined and was fed by larger movements which emphasized:

1. The growing distrust of 'grand narratives' such as Marxism and Freudianism have led to the valuing of individual stories and experiences. Universal explanations are rejected in preference for local accounts.

2. A shading of the boundaries between the fictive and the real. There is a growing recognition that our personal stories borrow from the world of fiction and that a sharp distinction between truth and fiction is hard to sustain. This gives practices like playback theatre the chance to experiment and improvise.
3. A fascination with ordinary lives, which partly derives from democratization. It is not just the lives of the powerful that form the subject of popular culture. As we see in 'reality TV' the experiences of ordinary people are regarded as worthy of exposure.

These features of the Western world are counter-balanced by other trends, which may be seen simultaneously as both contradicting and contributing to the above. For example, the explosion in the means, speed and ease of communication enables the geographical and class boundaries of the past to be traversed and the patterns of political action to be radically altered while, at the same time, potentially homogenizing cultural and political expression. Playback theatre would not have grown at the rate it has without this. Additionally the growth of capitalist consumption has allowed a wider range of personal expression and an ideological emphasis on 'doing your own thing', while simultaneously reducing the range of options through the marketing practices of huge multi-national corporations. It could be argued that playback theatre's emphasis on acknowledging and validating individual experience has partly been stimulated by these developments.

Three examples of current playback practice

In this section I set out three examples of current playback practice in order to give some indication of the diversity of the work and its geographical spread.

1. Playback theatre at a time of grieving

On the 10th July 2001, a forest fire swept through the Chewuch River Valley, USA, after a small blaze started by an unattended campfire exploded out of control. Fire-fighters were caught out by the speed of the blaze and four were killed. On the Sunday afternoon following the funerals, the *North Central Washington Playback Theatre Company* from Wenatchee, Washington State offered a 'debriefing' performance for the entire crew who had been involved in fighting the fire. Members of the Company Susan Evans and William Layman wrote soon after the event:

> we met with crew members before the enactment to establish consensus agreements involving privacy and confidentiality. As can be imagined the Playback Debriefing was very intense as this was the

> first opportunity that the entire crew had to gather together since the tragedy. (Evans and Layman 2001)

They go on to offer some lessons they felt the company learned from this remarkable event. These include advising performers in events of a similar nature to recognize that some members of the audience will feel their presence to be an intrusion. They advise: 'playback whatever emotions you get including anger at you for being there.' They also urge that the very private nature of the work needs to be protected 'which means keeping media away from the event and being careful about how such stories are written up for public use.'

The proximity of this playback performance to the traumatic event is unusual and the company's experience is thus particularly important in understanding how playback theatre can work with recent trauma. There have been other instances of performances that follow traumatic events: for example Paul MacIsaac and Playback Theatre New York City did a performance in the shadow of the 'U.S.S. Enterprise' soon after the 9/11 attacks; and the Hudson Valley company staged a performance entitled *Stories of a Changed World* a day after the event. However what is striking about the NCW performances is the use of playback in the case of recent and very personal loss.

2. Playback theatre in Tel Aviv

The Tel-Aviv Playback Theatre was founded in 1990 by Aviva Apel-Rosenthal and it continues to offer regular performances to local people and organizations. Not surprisingly, stories of the continuing conflict in Israel are told during its performances and the company considers that they may have a role in providing a forum for the airing of these stories and for the opposing views that inevitably emerge when they are told. One of the company members, Nurit Shoshan, told me of two stories told at a recent performance that illustrate the potential of playback theatre to provide what Fox calls a 'radical social encounter' (1995, p.4) in which issues of conflict, reconciliation and forgiveness can be explored. They are stories which, in a sense, 'speak to each other' about the complex moral and ethical decisions faced by all those caught up in the violence.

In this performance held for the parents of those who had been killed during the sectarian violence, an Israeli woman told of losing her son and of the numbing grief that followed. For a year she sat at home, unable to continue with her life. Finally she decided that to improve her own situation she would try to establish contact with Palestinian parents who had also lost children in the conflict. It seems that this was an important step for her in moving on from incapacitating grief; it also was a way of her doing something to heal the divisions in her society.

Following the company's enactment of her story, a man came on to the stage and told about losing his daughter in a suicide bomb attack. Not long after she died, he read in the local paper of an Israeli pilot who had been given instructions to fire a missile at a house thought to contain suicide bombers. The pilot, knowing that the house was likely to contain women and children, could not use his weapon. On reading this the teller described his anger at the pilot for sparing the life of the person who may have been responsible for the death of his daughter.

In both these stories the tellers, the audience and the performers are faced with the complex ethical dilemmas that are always thrown up in times of conflict. The desire for forgiveness and reconciliation in the first story is set against the understandable anger in the second. As Nurit Shoshan told me, the audience and the performers can empathize with these contradictory feelings described by the tellers. The work of the company provides a vivid example of how playback theatre may provide a space for exploring contradictory ideas and opposing accounts – and perhaps most importantly – a means through which they can be acknowledged.

3. Mixing castes: a playback company in Chennai, India

In Chennai, South India, Cyril Alexander and the Sterling Playback Theatre Group have performed regularly in the villages, beaches and social care organizations around the city. The company is unusual because of its composition; its members include different religions, castes, ethnic groups, and people of different socio-economic status. This was important to the group's founders, Cyril explains:

> Because Sterling Playback theatre has members from different backgrounds, the group process is different, the group members will know about the differences and they will learn how to work with difference. In this way differences are helping the group members to grow and develop new things. (Alexander 2003)

The mixed composition of the company is important because they often hold performances where issues of difference and inequality are important to the audience. For example, the company performs for mixed groups of Muslim, Christian and Hindu people, and through the structure of a playback performance aims to create 'a platform for inter religious dialogue'. The company have also been doing work in a children's jail in Chennai.

Clearly, accessibility is an important issue for the company. This is evident not only in the make-up of the group, but also in their choices of venue. They are prepared to hold their performances in villages, beaches and in local institutions. In light of this they have adapted existing playback forms and developed new ones in order to work with groups who, for example, surround the stage or who are more likely to come and go as the performance develops.

An overview

In this book I aim to address some of the questions identified earlier in this chapter and to raise more as they arise in the analysis of playback's practice. In Chapter 2, two interrelated themes will be considered: the ethics of telling personal stories in public places and the concept of *openness*, which I will propose is a key feature of successful playback performances. Playback performers and audiences are often acutely aware of the risks attendant to telling personal material in a public place. In this chapter I will open up debates around the ethics of playback and consider some of the criticisms which have been directed at the practice. At this stage no response or apology will be offered, the aim will simply be to air these important debates since they open up the questions that surround the practice of dramatizing personal stories in public places. In later chapters I will consider these as they arise in relation to specific aspects of playback practice. Closely related to this, I will discuss the kinds of stories and performances that seem to constitute successful playback events. The term *openness* will be employed to denote a kind of playful indeterminacy and ambivalence that characterize certain stories and effective playback performing.

It is one of the aims of this book to establish firmly that the types of stories and performances that are possible in playback theatre are always profoundly influenced by context. The tellers' decision concerning what to tell and the performers' choices do not take place in a vacuum, but are always inflected by personal and collective history, cultural associations and practices. In Chapter 3, I will substantiate this claim by looking in detail at the impact a sense of place has upon teller and the performers. I will look at how expectations of the event may be influenced by cultural context and by information received by audience members and performers. As an audience gathers for an event, complex clues are given concerning its nature and the role the audience will play. This is particularly important in playback theatre where the audience's participation is crucial to its success. In Chapter 3 I will also be interested in how the particular configuration of the space shapes audience expectations and thus influences their decisions concerning which stories to tell.

In Chapter 4, I examine the nature of the autobiographical narrative told in playback theatre performances. I am particularly keen to bring into question the notion, often employed in playback discourse, of the 'essence' of the story. To pre-suppose that the teller's story has an essence is to suggest that it is a stable entity uninflected by historical and performative contingency. To pre-suppose this tends to prevent us from recognizing that each time the story is told it will change in response to the differing audiences and the personal necessities acting upon its teller. To maintain an idea of the teller's story as having an essence also masks a recognition that the past is, to a large extent, created in and for the present; we tell stories to serve our present needs and in response to the demands and promptings of the context in which they are told. This is no mere academic point: if we refigure our understanding of the story told in performances then what is happening in playback theatre is refigured.

To understand this *Lifegame* can provide an interesting contrast. *Lifegame* is a format devised by Keith Johnstone in which one person is invited to tell their life story and see that enacted. The programme notes inform us that the aim of *Lifegame* was

> to talk to someone about their life, improvise scenes based on the stories they tell, find out 'how it was' and maybe as we are watching remember how it was for us. (The Improbable Theatre Company 1998)

The striking similarities and differences to playback theatre are interesting and provocative, particularly in relation to the phrase to 'find out how it was'. Certainly the performers were aiming for as much verisimilitude as they could with the teller's memories, to the extent that he was asked to lay out the scene for the actors and given a bell to ring if the actors were particularly 'close to the truth' and 'a buzzer' if they were off the mark.

Playback theatre does not give that kind of control to the teller, or to put this another way, actors in playback have a great deal of freedom in developing the enactment. If it is not helpful to conceive of playback actors playing back 'the essence of the story' or 'to show it how it was' – as the performers of *Lifegame* seek to do – then what are playback performers offering? The answer to this question is, in many ways, central to this entire book. The performers do not portray essences or replicate the past, rather they respond to the teller's narrative within the dramaturgy of playback. That response, as I shall detail in later chapters, is never more than wholly human and, I would argue, the more interesting for that.

In Chapter 5, I will consider one aspect of playback's dramaturgy in some detail: the frequent use of the image and the symbolic. In playback there is a clear and marked juxtaposition of the 'telling' and the 'enactment'. The former is delivered in a verbal and relatively 'literal' style; the latter draws on a wide array of theatrical, imagistic and figurative devices to play the story. Fox claims that playback theatre permits a 'different kind of dialogue' within the performance; I will examine this claim and suggest that the use of the figurative and symbolic in playback's dramaturgy has the effect of permitting *openness* within and between the personal stories told. The teller's narrative – already inflected within the conductor/teller dyad and by the performative nature of its production – becomes an open field of association, reference and allusion. The teller's narrative is opened up to the play of the performers.

In Chapters 6 and 7, I will look in detail at the performers' response to the teller's story. In Chapter 6 I will be particularly interested in what is going on in the minds and bodies of the performers as they prepare for the enactment that will follow and what thoughts, impulses, images and ideas motivate the performers toward dramatic action. It will become apparent that actors in their listening and subsequent response need to find, to quote one of the actors, 'a world half-way between self and character – a no-man's land, a half-way place'. On this 'narrow ridge' between self and other they are able to draw on subjective promptings as well as on the details of the story. The performers' response is a complex one, drawing as it does on a range of impulse and influences that are perhaps impossible to fully describe. But that difficulty of description should not lead us to assume that some mystical or magical processes are at work: the performers' response always remains fully human and ultimately understandable.

In Chapter 7 I will look at improvisation in playback theatre. I will propose that the fact that the work is improvised is important and will suggest that improvisation can challenge predictable and settled versions of personal and cultural narratives and loosen established cognitive schemas. When the performers improvise with the teller's story, they create a more open and porous work that can loosen the grip that one 'take' can have. The notion of 'in betweenness' will be explored further in this chapter, and there will be an analysis of the tensions performers need to maintain in their work in order for it to do justice to the teller's story while at the same time animating it with something new and surprising. However we need to be cautious of attributing too much to spontaneous improvisation, and in this chapter I will qualify and nuance the contention that the performer's response emerges out 'the spontaneous moment'. The performers do not plan the enactments beforehand; nevertheless they are based on certain patterns of response that are developed through rehearsal and previous performances. As Barthes wrote of any text, the performers will draw on 'bits of code, formulae, rhythmic models, fragments of social language' (Barthes 2000, p.183). Their work perhaps can never be freshly minted and 'unique'.

In Chapter 8, the playback ensemble will be considered. I will propose that the sustained company life in which most performers practise playback theatre is crucial in protecting both the players and the teller from the excesses of an improvised theatre form. It is the ensemble which provides the conditions for risk-taking in performance and which allows a kind of safety net if the performer loses his way. Additionally, by providing a space within which performers can rehearse their own stories, the company offers a means through which they can experiment and explore the difficulties, sensitivities, and pitfalls of playing the other.

In Chapter 9, the ethics of playback theatre performing will be considered. I will attempt to raise questions that go to the heart of the playback and bring into question the ethical responsibilities of the performer: what are the limitations of the playback actor? Can we play a teller no matter how culturally 'strange' to us? If we accept that our performances are always influenced by our culture and ideology, then is it ethically acceptable to represent another? Can the performer ethically assume the power of interpretation over another's story? I go on to consider what an ethics of playback performing may look like and propose principles that may protect the performers and audiences from some of the risks of telling and performing personal stories in public places.

Jonathan Fox has argued that the 'ultimate purpose of playback theatre' is to promote a 'radical social encounter'. In Chapter 10, I will examine to what degree it is possible to regard playback as a tool for social intervention. Amongst playback practitioners there seem to be three main claims that support playback's capacity to intervene politically and socially, namely, that playback provides an opportunity (i) for marginalized groups to tell their story; (ii) for opposing voices to be heard, and (iii) for groups and communities to remember collectively and create/recreate their own history. I will exemplify and discuss these claims and then go on to think through two interrelated criticisms of playback practice in relation to its credentials as a tool of social intervention. These first, are that the lack of involvement of the teller in the dramatic action significantly reduces his or her interpretive control over how the story will be represented and second, that the structure of the event does not allow the participants to question the decisions of the performers. While accepting these criticisms as ones that playback practitioners should take seriously, the chapter will conclude with a proposal that playback theatre provides a space in which the story can be opened up in order that the teller and the other spectators can see that what happened to the teller (and thus potentially to all of us) may be represented (re-presented) in other ways. To put this another way, I will suggest that effective playback opens the story up to multiple levels of reflexivity so that performers, spectators and teller can see its 'workings' – that they can view how it is represented and so how it might be represented differently. This, I will suggest, is a key means through which playback theatre can have political and social impact.

Limitations

All written accounts of theatre practice are inevitably limited. This is especially the case for improvised theatre. Theatre is a live event, taking place in the here and now; attempts to preserve its 'liveness' run into significant difficulties. Memory of the performance decays quickly and forms of written, video or audio recording cannot retain the vivacity of the moment. The particular contexts of the event, namely, the perceptual sets of the participants and the particular patterns of meaning that emerge during the performance, cannot be preserved. Specifically, playback theatre derives its energy through relationships in the here and now, relationships between performers, spectators and tellers. Our memory of these relationships is always partial (Clifford 1986) in both senses of the word – it records only 'part of' any experience and it is always and unavoidably subjective.

The scope of this book is also significantly restricted by the limitations of the writer. Although I refer briefly to playback practice in other companies and countries, this book cannot cover the liveliness and variety of practice across the globe. A thorough and detailed account of this work still needs to be written.

One further limitation needs to be noted. In this book my experience and interest has largely concentrated on the issues and experiences of the playback actor. The reader will not find a thorough consideration of the work of the conductor – or indeed of the musician – in this book. With reference to the conductor, whose role is crucial in receiving the teller's story, this is a significant omission and the book should be read in the light of this. Having noted this, however, the title suggests my particular concern – the ethics and possibilities of playing the other – and it is hoped that I will be forgiven for concentrating on this area of playback practice. Readers interested in the role of the conductor should refer to Salas' *Improvising Real Life: Personal Story in Playback Theatre*, Fox's *Acts of Service*, and Fox and Dauber's edited book *Gathering Voices: Essays in Playback Theatre.*

Chapter 2

Openness and Ethics

In the evening following what we felt was a particularly successful performance, the company were eating together. A discussion developed concerning the last story of the show. A man had come on to the stage unsure of what his story was, but knowing that he had been moved by the previous one. The story he eventually told concerned the death of his mother, the loss of his father in early childhood, and communication with his mother at a séance. He began to cry as he told this, so much so that without invitation his wife came up on stage to comfort him. We discussed our concerns about the ethics of allowing the man's vulnerability to be so publicly revealed. We worried that we may have manipulated this situation. One member of the company argued that it was 'therapy without boundaries' – without the protection and continuity of the ongoing therapeutic relationship. It is a discussion we have had regularly over the years. I would suppose that many other companies have had these kinds of discussions.

The truth is that, to some extent, we hope for these kinds of stories in playback theatre. But, as is clear here, we also feel some unease when they are told. What are the characteristics of these stories? What is the unease we feel? What does it mean to talk about playback theatre as 'therapy without boundaries'? Does this epithet have any truth to it? What are the ethical implications of asking for personal stories to be told in public places? In this chapter I will attempt to address these questions. It will not be possible to reach any conclusive answers, but hopefully the discussion will introduce some key issues that will be addressed in different ways throughout this book.

As playback practitioners what do we hope for in a playback theatre performance? Put simply, we aim for personal stories to be told which are significant to the teller and the audience. We hope that the actors and musicians will be able to 'add something' to the story, so that tellers and spectators will see, hear, and feel something that may be surprising or that may be an acknowledgment of something that has been concealed. We hope that this surprise and acknowledgement will stimulate new stories that may not have been told otherwise. We hope therefore for a kind of fluidity or *openness* in the performance so that stories and the truths they reveal can be examined, explored, reflected upon and perhaps changed. The act of telling in public can, of course, in itself produce change and re-evaluation, but the practice is designed to expose the story to the particular energies that are available through dramatic improvisation.

Openness is the term I have chosen in this book to denote the fluidity that constitutes effective playback theatre. I do not mean to use the word in its common usage, however. When openness is referred to as a desirable objective in playback performances, I do not necessarily mean the openness of significant self-disclosure or emotional catharsis. I am using the word rather like Umberto Eco (1989) does when he talks about the 'open work'. He is thinking of art work which has an unfinished quality that invites elaboration and exploration. Playback stories and enactments can have that quality of openness to them; they can invite expansion, investigation and playful engagement. In the following sections the nature of open stories and open performing will be considered. In subsequent chapters some of the qualities of a performance that allow openness or inhibit it will be examined.

All this talk of openness may produce unease in the reader. Isn't this just 'therapy without boundaries'? In the second part of this chapter the significant ethical concerns raised by playback practice will be introduced and acknowledged. Those worried about the ethics of playback tend to make two main points: the first is that something is happening in the wrong place – it is inappropriate to call for personal stories in public places – and the second is that playback involves the manipulation of the teller for the purpose of spectacle. These are significant criticisms, and should be taken seriously. They crop up throughout this book as the ethical and epistemological problems of playing the other are addressed.

Openness: open stories

Probably the most difficult and challenging stories to enact in playback theatre are those with a clear structure and narrative direction, the kind of stories that have the quality of having been told before. For example, it can be difficult to play a detailed story of a journey that leaves out the subjective experience of the teller, or an articulately told and well-crafted anecdote, or a story in which the teller is careful to distance herself from it, or a story which has a 'punch' line that produces laughter or shock during the telling. It may seem surprising that it is the well-crafted stories which present more problems rather than, say, those with disorganized narratives. They are difficult for the performers, because they allow little room to respond or elaborate. The story has been told in such a way that it appears that there is little more that can be added through dramatization. The audience already know where the story is going and how it will end; they have already heard the punch line. It can be difficult for the actors to find a way to play the story without disappointing the audience. They need considerable skill to add anything new. To some extent these stories are a response to the apprehension of telling a personal story in a public place. Out of an understandable need for defence, these stories are 'closed'. They don't leave very much room for the actors to open them up to exploration and elaboration.

These kinds of stories are often told at the beginning of performances when the levels of anxiety are high. They are common in large venues where audience members do not know each other, or in small settings where unease is produced through the unfamiliar intimacy. They are told when audience members are not sure of each other, or when the spectators detect anxiety and uncertainty amongst the performers. A note of caution needs to be sounded here however: I do not mean to suggest that these kinds of stories are unwelcome in playback performances. They often have the function of warming up the audience and the performers and, perhaps more importantly, they can produce emotional effects in the audience that lead on to stories that have more potential for exploration through playback. The 'problem' of these stories lies with the performers and the conductor, not with the audience. However they are not stories for which playback is best suited. It is to those stories I now wish to turn. Consider these two stories:

1. The Sisters

About halfway through a performance to an audience of health professionals and academics interested in personal narrative, a woman came on stage to tell a story. She began by saying that she was not sure what she wanted to tell, but that she had been thinking through the day about a forthcoming reunion with her estranged sister. She talked about the incidents that had caused the rift in their relationship and her hopes for their meeting. She also talked about their closeness when they were children. When asked by the conductor, she said that she wanted to see what had happened and the anticipated reconciliation.

2. The Glass Door

(C = conductor and T = teller)

C. How long ago did this story happen?

T. About one month ago.

C. Tell us something about yourself at the time of this story.

T. Cool and trendy...well I wasn't really. I had been to America and had met lots of people. I was back at College and going to the bar. I was wearing really weird clothes...orange glasses. There was a group of boys in the trendy bar...

C. A trendy bar...was there a not so trendy bar?

T. Yes (laughter). There was this group of boys I was trying to impress...and one boy in particular! I pushed at the glass door to get in the bar and fell straight through it. There was no glass in the door! Someone said 'Maybe you should try wearing glasses'. I felt such a fool!

C. Choose someone to be the guy you were trying to impress.

(T chooses an actor)

C. What was his name?

T. (laughing and looking rather embarrassed) James...

C. And some words about James.

T. He's really cool, he's in the 'in crowd'.

C. This is T's story of falling through the door. You watch...

Both these stories in their different ways give the performers a great deal of room to work in. The story of *The Sisters* presents the actors with the possibility of exploring the archetypes of sister relationships and the broad sweep of time allows a counterpoint between how it was then and how it is now. The idea of 'reconciliation' gives the actors and the musicians a chance for imaginative creation. *The Glass Door* at first glance seems rather like one of the 'closed stories' I have referred to above. But, one could suggest, it is really a story about feeling foolish and being humiliated; it offered the actors an opportunity to explore the dynamics of social embarrassment that are familiar to us all. It also may have provided a prologue or overture to stories that came later in the performance. Both of these stories are 'open' because they allow development and elaboration on the part of the performers.

In playback theatre an 'open story' is one which leaves room for the performers to explore and elaborate. I prefer the term 'open stories' to what is sometimes called 'deep stories' in playback discourse. The problem of 'depth' as it refers to personal stories is twofold: first, it implies high levels of evident personal disclosure that are not necessarily appropriate or desired in a public performance, and second, the idea of 'depth' implies a judgment concerning the story which is often very difficult to make. There are stories in playback which on the 'surface' appear simple accounts that give little away of the emotional world of the teller, but which, in the context of the performance and of the other stories told, can have a significant impact. We cannot make a judgment about the 'depth' of a story without doing a disservice to intentions of the teller. The notion of open stories avoids these problems by focusing on the *impact on the possibilities available* to the performers in the subsequent enactment.

The notion of the 'open story' bears some similarity to what Umberto Eco calls an 'open work'. In his analysis of contemporary art forms, Eco looks at work which leaves the completion of the artwork to the performer or to the audience. He suggests that these works are unfinished and possess 'a halo of indefiniteness' that makes an open work 'pregnant with suggestive possibilities'. He goes on to say that an open work 'sets out to stimulate the private world of the addressee so that he can draw from inside himself some deeper response that mirrors the subtler resonances underlying the text' (Eco 1989, p.9).

For Eco, open works are characterized by their 'suggestiveness', 'ambiguity' and unfinished nature. Open stories in playback have similar characteristics: they invite the performers to continue them. Although open stories often lead to more interesting enactments in playback theatre, I am not suggesting that in themselves they are necessarily desirable. Stories in playback emerge out of the context of their telling and there are occasions when the conditions are not suitable for stories which invite the exploration of the performers and self-disclosure on the part of the teller. I am not using the term 'openness' in the sense of 'honesty' or 'frankness'. A high level of self-disclosure is not a defining characteristic of the 'open story'. Rather, open stories are ones that are incomplete – one might use the term 'loose' here – and thus invite the performers to explore and elaborate upon them. They are stories which do not conclude dialogue but *open it up*.

The characteristics I suggest for open stories are as follows.

1. Open stories tend to have a looser narrative structure and seem to emerge or be discovered through the act of telling. The teller has not decided the precise shape of the story before she comes onto the stage; but as she begins to talk to the conductor it begins to take shape.
2. Open stories possess a degree of self-reflection apparent in their telling – the teller in some way is aware of the provisional and constructed nature of the story they are telling. In other words there is a sense in which the teller is aware that the story could be told differently and is curious to know what the conductor, the audience and the performers will make of the story.
3. There is often a degree of self-disclosure in 'open stories'. There is a sense in which the teller is taking a risk by telling this story in this context. I do not however wish to suggest that 'openness', in the sense that I am using it, is synonymous with 'honesty'.

4. Open stories are not necessarily ones in which there is a high degree of expressed emotion. The expression of emotion in a public performance is dependent on cultural and personal factors; it does not necessarily indicate significant self-disclosure.
5. Open stories often employ or invite symbolic exploration. The teller may make use of metaphor, or the way in which it is told may suggest that to the performers.
6. Open stories invite the response and experimentation of the performers.
7. Open stories often have the quality of being unfinished. They are not neatly tied up, but leave room for elaboration.

As we have seen open stories tend to produce an open response from the performers. If the story is told in a 'spirit of openness' then the performers are more likely to respond in that way. The opposite is also true: if the performers' response to the story is 'open' it more likely to produce open stories. It is to that response that I now wish to turn.

The performers' response

During rehearsal the teller talked of her sense of loss at the death of a close colleague. She spoke about how difficult it was to imagine that she would never see him again. Viv, cast as the teller's actor, sat stage left with a drum in hand and said simply, 'I knew a man,' then as the funeral developed onstage, 'I once knew a man who opened doors for me'. Then at the end as the body leaves the mourners, Viv says:

> We say it with smiles, we say it with tears.
> We say it in minutes, we say it over years.
> And yet we have no other word than this...goodbye.

Later Viv told me: 'the poem is a dreadful misquote of an actual poem that I wrote in my little quotation book when I was about 14/15 years old. The last line is (I think) correct, but the rest I just cobbled together as best I could. It's a bit of a blur. What is interesting to me is the fact that I thought at that tender age that there would be a lot of 'goodbyes' ahead. On my mum's flowers at her funeral I simply wrote 'goodbye'. It really is the only word.

In his discussion of Walter Benjamin, Peter Brooks tells us that an autobiographical narrative is a gift. It is:

> an act of generosity to which the receiver should respond by an equal generosity, either in the telling of another story...or in the comment-

> ing on the story told, but in any event by the proof that the gift has been received, that the narrative has made a difference. (Brooks 1994, p.87)

In Chapter 1, I suggested that performers do not play the essence of the teller's story, but rather that they responded to it from their own subjectivity, partiality and through the dramaturgy of the playback form. I agree with Brooks that the generosity of the teller's story calls for 'equal generosity' as 'proof that the gift has been received, that the narrative has made a difference'. This is perhaps the first and most important duty of the actor or musician: to show that the 'gift' of the story has been received. The performers aim to do this through their response. This, I think is evident in the example above. Viv responds from her own memories and makes use of these to enact the teller's story.

The performer's response does not always succeed and sometimes tellers feel that the performers have not listened to their story. In Poland, for example, Playback Theatre York performed a woman's story about being caught up in a crowd of football fans. We played it for laughs. It was clear at the end that the teller felt we had missed showing the fear she felt at being in the middle of the crowd. The conductor asked us to do it again. Perhaps out of our anxiety of playing to a Polish audience for the first time, we had not listened to her properly. Or perhaps we were too keen to entertain the audience. What is clear is that in any enactment, the teller needs to receive the impression that their story has been 'received' by the performers. Their response must demonstrate this in some way. Of course, as the title of this book suggests, this raises all sorts of ethical issues that will emerge in the forthcoming pages. For now I want to sketch out what are some of the general characteristics of the performers' response to the story, characteristics which I hope will demonstrate the complexity and provisional nature of that response.

First, the performers' response will always be '*partial*'. I take this word from the writing of the anthropologist James Clifford and mean it in both senses: as both 'committed' and 'incomplete' (Clifford 1986, p.7). He was referring to the writing of ethnographic accounts, yet his notion of 'partial truths' applies equally well to the playback performer. The performer will from his subjectivity emphasize those aspects of the story to which he is, for what ever reason, committed or attracted and inevitably make choices that will render the enactment an incomplete version of the story told in the performance. Walter Benjamin's comment in relation to storytelling applies equally to the playback enactment. He writes: 'traces of the storyteller cling to the story the way that handprints of the potter cling to the clay vessel' (Benjamin 1970, p.92).

Second, the performers' response will always be *profoundly influenced by context.* In each of the different environments in which playback theatre is performed, different takes on what is considered 'public' and 'personal' will be negotiated and established. This is a dynamic process: performers and spectators will be engaged in a constant negotiation and re-negotiation of what can be revealed in a public place. The nature of the autobiographical narratives and the subsequent enactments will always be inflected by these complex considerations. The performers' work will also be influenced by the stories and enactments that preceded it; processes of identification that are present for the performer during the performance; the dialogue between the teller and the conductor; and the response of the audience during the telling and the enactment.

Third, the response of the performers is almost always *intra- and interpersonally polyphonous.* It is the product of multiple voices and perspectives working together. There is no authoritative playwright in playback theatre; it is what Jonathan Fox calls 'non-scripted theatre' (Fox 1994). The enactment develops out of the interplay of many 'voices'. Each performer will bring different perspectives to the enactment. Each performer will also be aware of many internal impulses and points of view that might direct their action. There is no authoritative version of the story; it is brought together by the democratic collaboration and interaction of multiple points of view: a process inherent in improvisation that Keith Sawyer calls 'collaborative emergence' (Sawyer 2000).

If we accept the players' response as partial, contingent and polyphonous, then the idea of their playing the essence of the story seems highly problematic. Whatever develops after the conductor says to the audience 'Let's watch' is far less stable than that. However what does happen when the actors are working well is that they *open* the story up. By 'working well' I mean that the performers are working openly. They make themselves available to the affective, somatic and cultural possibilities suggested by the story, just as Viv does in the example above. The *open performing* has many of the characteristics of open stories:

1. When the actor is performing openly, she tends to allow the action to emerge or be discovered through the act of performing. The actor does not decide what she will do before she comes onto the stage, but allows the enactment to emerge through improvisation with the other actors and the musician.
2. Open performing is characterized by close ensemble work. Performers work together to produce the enactment. There is no one actor who controls its overall direction.

3. In open performing the actor or musician often have a high level of personal commitment to the story and their involvement in it. They describe feeling empathy and personal connection to the teller (see Chapter 6).
4. There is often a degree of self-disclosure in open performing. There is a sense in which the performer is taking a risk in their performance.
5. Open performing produces work that is, in some way, unfinished, allowing the teller and spectators space to attribute their own meaning and interpretations to the work.

The response of the performers in playback theatre is always and only a human response to another's story. The performance can be wonderful, generous, risky and inspired, but it is *never more than human.* As such it can heighten awareness of the means and the narrative structures we employ to represent experience. It is axiomatic of the current interest in 'narrative therapy' that we can be trapped, as well as validated, by our own stories. Effective playback loosens the 'ties' of the story, opens up other possible interpretations and reveals the means through which we make sense of our experience.

The story has been told in such a way that it invites exploration from the performers, who in turn produce work which opens the story up to different perspectives. To put this another way, I would say that openness in telling and performing liberates the teller and spectator from the tyranny of the *closed, fixed viewpoint.* Stories can enslave individuals and communities; the playback process at its best opens these stories to investigation and playful restructuring. These arguments will be substantiated in the forthcoming chapters. For now as a kind of 'taster' for my idea, consider this proposal from the psychoanalyst Christopher Bollas. He speaks about the central importance of play in psychoanalysis. His point resonates with the notion of 'openness'.

Bollas is concerned with re-thinking Freud's notion of free association – a process which Freud saw as being an important vehicle toward 'truths' inaccessible to the conscious mind. In his re-framing of the relationship between the therapist and patient, Bollas asserts that the fundamental agency of change in psychoanalysis is not the discovery of truths; rather it is the free associative and playful discourse in the relationship itself. He writes:

> If unconscious thinking is too complex to be grasped by consciousness, if one person's unconscious can communicate with another's unconscious mind only by playing with it, then psychoanalysis is a radical act – freeing the subject from character restraints and

> intersubjective compliances through the naturally liberating and expressive medium of free association.... The fundamental agency of change in a psychoanalysis is the continuous exercise of this freedom, which ultimately deconstructs and disseminates any narrative action...and establishes in place of the morality of the thematic a dissembling spirit that *plays the self into myriad realities. All along, what has seemed to be the means to truth – free association – is the truth itself...* (Bollas 1995, pp.69–70) [my emphasis]

Having rejected the notion that playback performers replicate the teller's story, or convey its essence or offer authoritative interpretations, I want to explore the proposal that playback can provide a space for 'free associative discourse' that opens up the teller's narrative by exposing it to the multiple perspectives of the performers. Effective playback performances are ones which permit openness in telling and performing. In subsequent chapters I will consider the conditions for open stories and open performing and will propose the notion that effective playback allows a kind of open *play* with the teller's story.

Ethics and playback theatre: listening to its critics

I am aware that my claim for the importance of openness in telling and performing raises significant ethical issues. Playback theatre always does this; performing personal stories told in public spaces is bound to throw up questions of privacy and exploitation. It raises questions about the problems of playing the other and the potential manipulation of the tellers who offer their stories. It may seem strange to devote a section of an early chapter to playback's critics; however this book aims at looking at the complex ethical issues raised by the form. It is not my aim to rebut criticism or to write an apologetic, but rather to open these issues up for examination and discussion and debate. Arguably we learn more about our practice from its critics than from its supporters, and it is in this spirit that this chapter is written. Perhaps because playback theatre is such a risky venture for performers there is little robust criticism of the work. When there is, it may tell us something important about how playback contravenes or challenges contemporary practices and mores.

In Britain – and I daresay in other Western countries – playback theatre contravenes common theatre conventions. By asking audience members to tell a personal story in a public place, the form breaks the usual rules of theatrical gatherings. Theatre events do not usually invite audience participation; indeed to do so is often likely to produce significant anxiety amongst spectators. In most Western theatre, the boundary between stage and auditorium is rarely crossed and the audience role, although essential for the success of the event, is confined to socially defined contributions such as applause, laughter and silence. Inviting audience members to share autobiographical material publicly in what resembles and is designated by the performers as a theatrical event is, at the very least, to introduce ambiguity into the minds of spectators unfamiliar with playback theatre.

Playback theatre, as some of its critics point out, does not offer the carefully constructed boundaries of the therapy space, yet it invites participants to tell personal experiences. It does not invite the usual responses of theatre audiences, but instead suggests that the performance will not be possible without their contribution. Spectators might ask: what kind of public place is being created here? What responses are required from the spectator? What kinds of stories is it 'safe' and appropriate to tell in this public place? It is hardly surprising that many audience members speak of their tension in the early moments of the performance.

Not surprisingly, critics have responded to these concerns through correspondence with the company. There are two related concerns: the first is that a public performance is an inappropriate place to ask for personal stories to be told, and the second is that the tellers are being manipulated for entertainment and spectacle.

Some years ago, Playback Theatre York received two letters from audience members who had attended a performance to an audience of users of mental health services and local professionals. The two correspondents were psychotherapists. Their letters follow a similar theme, which may be summarized as a concern about the 'framing' of the playback event and the psychological safety of the participants. The first correspondent complained that some tellers were left weeping after the performance of their story and that the enactments had been done for 'entertainment'. For this writer it was almost unthinkable to consider the sharing and enactment of personal stories in a public setting as entertainment. It was clear that the writer believed that something was happening in the *wrong* place. The second correspondent also shared her concern about the telling and enacting of personal stories in public places and wondered what kind of event she was attending which although suggestive of therapy does not possess the 'therapeutic boundaries'.

Another criticism some years later picks up on this theme. Elinor Vettriano (1999), having attended the International Playback Theatre Conference, writes, 'I found myself questioning the safe nature and validity of this form of theatre'. She goes on to wonder whether there is the 'safe container' of dramatherapy present in the playback theatre practice and asks important questions about the form. In the same article, Maggie Morgan asks the same questions, writing:

> In certain 'contained' contexts, Playback could have a most effective role. Questions need to be asked, however, about boundaries and even accountability. It is an artistic form worth much more than being an up-market Oprah Winfrey show. (Vettriano 1999, p.9)

It is clear that these correspondents felt that they had attended an event that did not possess the 'boundaries' they believed to be important when personal stories are told. More than that they felt that the performers were, perhaps salaciously, making use of this confusion of categories; that the tellers, at best, were not fully informed about the nature of the event and, at worse, manipulated into providing personal stories for 'entertainment'. These are very serious criticisms of the form. Are the boundaries between the personal and public so blurred in playback performances that it constitutes a psychologically unsafe environment? Perhaps some tellers feel as I did after telling a story during rehearsal:

Through telling the story I am over-exposed. I over-stepped my own privacy. Revealing what, at that moment, was not safe to reveal, I opened a wound, perhaps to appease, to please, or to be seen – and then I could find no way to close it. One of the other actors said to me 'People will only tell stories that they feel safe to tell'. Is this true? Is it not possible that tellers will find themselves stumbling into saying more than they wished to say, or more than they had expected?

Is the risk too great? Is it too much to hope for the openness I have described in this chapter? Is playback just another example of the exploitation of the individual's desire to be seen no matter what the cost that is so evident in TV shows like *Big Brother* and *Oprah Winfrey*? In order to address these questions it is first necessary to understand what is going on in playback performances. How do place, the dynamics of telling, the dramaturgy of playback, and the nature or playback acting and improvising shape the telling of personal stories in public places? Once that analysis is conducted the ethical questions raised here and the possibilities for openness can be reconsidered.

Chapter 3

Personal Stories in Public Places

The Rats

The performance took place in a community mental health centre in the North of England. Before it began, I was sitting in the audience talking to a woman about the forthcoming show. I asked her what story she might tell. She told me about a recurring dream of being attacked by rats in her bed. The rats start to bite her; she calls out, but when her mother comes into the room the rats bite her as well. In the dream she always wakes up terrified. I said to her that if she wanted to, she could tell this story during the performance.

Much later, when the conductor invited the next story she stood up and came forward on to the stage area to applause from the audience and the actors. I felt a mixture of dread, excitement and some responsibility. I had suggested to her that she could come forward to tell the story and, I thought, she had taken up my suggestion and done so. It did nor occur to me then that she might be making up her own mind about telling the story? She began in a nervous and rather timid fashion to tell the dream she had told me. I was aware of her vulnerability and of my anxiety at what would happen. As the story unfolded I was aware of the conductor trying to find a redeeming end to it. She asked questions like: 'When you wake up are there any things that make you feel better?' and 'Is there an ending to the dream that you would like to see?' To both of these questions the teller said 'No'. It was clear, I think, that she just wanted to see the dream. The teller was asked to cast herself in the dream and she chose C. For her mother she chose M (a worker in her Centre). The rats were then cast as a chorus by the conductor.

The action begins with C holding a cloth as if it were a pillow. The music conveys a rising sense of foreboding. The rats are far stage right. The mother attaches a long piece of elastic to her daughter and moves stage left holding the other end and a grey cloth. As the action continues we see the dream begin to move across the sleeper's face. The rats begin to call to the dreamer and move toward her.

I felt a shiver of fear as the rats began and I looked toward the teller to see her reaction, I saw her trembling and nodding her head. The rats begin to circle the dreamer and she became increasingly terrified; they call out to her, using her name and calling, 'We are going to get you'. She calls out for her mother who moves toward her gathering in the elastic as she does so. I remember thinking that this was not how the teller described it. She had said that her mother entered and the rats started to bite her too. What impulse had led M to change the story? This was an act of interpretation beyond the story told by the teller.

Mother comforts her daughter saying, at first, that everything is alright and later, that she must learn how to stand up to the rats. Mother demonstrates by shouting at the rats to go away; they retreat a little. She places the grey cloth between her and the rats and shouts to them that they must not 'cross the line'; she then takes a large hand drum from the musicians' table and says 'This is how you do it!' She bangs the drum. The dreamer shouts 'I can't' repeatedly, before taking the drum and rather timidly, at first, beating it. The rats retreat slightly; encouraged by this she beats the drum more loudly; the rats retreat further. A look of triumph grows on her face and she says 'I can do it, I can do it'. The rats begin to come closer again and again she beats the drum.

As this was happening I watched the teller,[1] she seemed to be totally absorbed; there was a smile on her face, as if enjoying the defeat of the rats. Nevertheless, we had changed her story. The action ended with the dreamer repelling the rats one more time with growing confidence and the mother looking over with pride. They all turned to the teller, to indicate the end of the piece.

The conductor asked the teller if that was the way it was, and if there was anything in the story that was particularly strong for her. She said it was good when the actor beat the drum to get rid of the rats, but she said 'I can't do that'. The conductor thanked her for her story and she returned to her seat to applause. The conductor asked if there was anybody in the audience who also had frightening dreams. A number of people nodded and I put up my hand to tell of a dream that I used to have of insects crawling all over me. Another person in the audience described a nightmare she had regularly.

Personal stories in public places

Usually Playback Theatre York is very keen to avoid trying to find a 'happy ending' to a teller's story. There are plenty of examples in the company's history when they have enacted the story with the same emotional force with which the teller told it. It is clear that in this example the particular circumstances of the performance – the venue, the audience, the fact that one of the actors was a worker at the Centre (M), the fearful and psychotic-like

1 The fact that the audience can see the teller watching the story is a key aspect of playback theatre.

nature of the story – may have persuaded us to find a resolution not provided by the teller. The episode emphasizes the key role played by context (venue, audience composition and pre-existing relationships) in the decisions made by the performers. It is clear that the conductor and the performers were being influenced by the nature of the venue and by their own perceptions of such a place.

In the last chapter I stressed the *humanness* of the actors' response; in this chapter I will consider in some detail how *context* influences decisions about telling and performing – how perceptions of place shape what happens on stage in the auditorium. I will analyze the impact that perceptions of 'public place' has on the disclosure of personal stories in playback theatre, and I will be particularly interested in how 'place' can inhibit or encourage the telling of open stories and its 'bedfellow', open performing. I will demonstrate how a complex range of factors influence the spectators' decision about the kinds of stories they will tell in different public places.

I use the term 'public' here fully recognizing its ambiguity and contingency; that the nature of what is construed of as 'public' is a dynamic process dependent on expectation, perception and negotiation. Despite the ambiguity of the term, its usefulness for my purpose lies in the tension between the public and the personal which is, I will suggest, a key characteristic of a playback performance. Alongside the manifest telling and performing of personal stories there is always the question: what can be told here? In Chapter 10 I will explore this tension in more detail.

How the individual spectator and the audience answer this question and how they draw the line between the personal and the public will be mediated by a complex interplay of subjective, relational and environmental factors operating in and around any particular venue. The spectators' personal and cultural history, their perceived and actual relationships with other participants, and the configuration of the space and context, will all influence how they interpret the event and thus shape their decisions concerning what is appropriate personal disclosure.

I will contribute to the debate initiated in the last chapter concerning the ethics of telling in public places by suggesting that playback theatre 'dramatizes' this tension between the personal and the public, drawing attention not only to the conventions of personal disclosure that may be ascribed to certain spaces, but also to the implications this may have for the private and cultural domains that lie outside a particular performance. In other words what I am suggesting is that playback theatre is not just about the telling and dramatization of personal stories, it is also concerned with, and sometimes a challenge to, *accepted views concerning the boundaries* between the personal and the public.

In order to make sense of what happened during the telling and performing of *The Rats*, it will be important to look at how context shapes playback events.

Space

In his analysis of space Henri Lefebvre writes:

> Vis-à-vis lived experience, space is neither a mere frame, after the fashion of the frame of a painting, nor a form or container of a virtually neutral kind, designed simply to receive whatever is poured into it. Space is social morphology… (Lefebvre 1991, p.95)

In relation to human experience then, space does not exist prior to the social processes that construct it. Space is not a container in which human relations take place but it is rather, as the geographer Doreen Massey puts it, 'the product of interrelations' (Massey 2005, p.9). This is no mere academic point. It suggests that space, far from being a neutral frame, is formed and changed by the actions of those who interact with it. One could say that spaces bear the imprint of those that inhabit them. With reference to theatre spaces then we can go along with Richard Schechner when he writes that '[T]heatres everywhere are scenographic models of sociometric process' (Schechner 1988, p.164). Theatres are, to some extent, maps from which we can 'read' social processes at work. To look closely at theatre spaces and how they are organized is likely to reveal far more than the 'merely' spatial. An analysis of the spaces constructed by playback theatre companies for their performances is likely to tell us something about the intentions of the performers and the responses of the spectators. It is important to adopt a broader definition of 'place' than merely the physical environment in which a playback performance occurs. I am suggesting a notion that may be better termed 'context', since it seeks to convey all the subjective, informational, and environmental factors that build towards a spectator's perception of a particular performance.

A note of caution needs to be sounded however. As Massey points out, we limit our conception of space if we consider it solely a representation from which social processes can be mapped. To do so she argues eloquently, is to 'tame the spatial into the textual and the conceptual; into representation' (Massey 2005, p.20). Especially in the theatre, space is livelier – more plastic – than that: space itself is shaping the work of the performers and the responses of the audience. Despite this caveat, however, tracing the construction of playback spaces will illuminate some of the processes that influence the spectator's decisions about telling personal stories in a public places.

Before the event: the horizon of expectations

Susan Bennett writes that 'theatre audiences bring to any performance a horizon of cultural and ideological expectations' (Bennett 1997, p.107). She argues that we cannot regard the audience's 'horizons of expectation' as fixed; rather these shift in response to the complex influences that act on the spectator as they anticipate a theatrical event. In this section I will explore this process, aware that such expectations will significantly influence the audience's reception, the roles they assume during the performance, and their sense of collective identity.

CULTURAL FACTORS

All audiences bring to a performance culturally inscribed expectations of what constitutes a theatrical event. These will be influenced by socio-economic and geographic factors as well as by personal history and experience. Personal and social histories of theatre-going are bound to influence what audience members come to expect from a performance. There is however an additional dimension as spectators anticipate the performance; they will arrive with expectations and conventions concerning appropriate levels of public self-disclosure that are profoundly inflected by culture and personal history. Past history and socio-cultural 'rules' concerning what is appropriate to reveal in public will always be at work in performances.

To a large extent, the notion of what is private and what is acceptable to reveal in a public place are always socially and culturally defined. Consider for example Fadwa El Guindi's claim that Western notions of privacy are closely related to the Western constructs of 'individualism and individual rights to property' (El Guindi 1999, p.82) whereas Arab ideas are 'relational and public' (El Guindi 1999, p.82). I cannot comment on the veracity of this claim, but it does nevertheless suggest that broad cultural and ideological forces are at work when personal stories are told in public places. Socio-economic class, cultural and religious belief and geographical factors are certain to influence the boundaries of privacy in a public space. It is perhaps the case that cultural notions concerning mental health were at play in the way the performers approached *The Rats* story. It was clear that the performers in *The Rats* were certainly aware of this in the decisions they were making. After the performance I spoke to the conductor; her language suggests an awareness of context that may not have been present at another performance:

> We were all quite anxious; there was a level of anxiety about how fragile are the ego strengths here in the audience. It was a terrifying dream...and perhaps the actors were feeling my nervousness...

However, one needs to be careful not to over-determine the cultural and socio-economic factors that influence the audience's expectations. Although for example the British are often seen as reticent when it comes to the display of personal feelings in public, it would be a mistake to build this into a general rule concerning the behaviour of British audiences. No audience is a homogenous group; complex subjective, cultural and environmental factors will be at work to mediate broad national characteristics. In considering any playback theatre audience, one must always be aware of the risk of cultural stereotyping.

NEGOTIATION WITH THE HOSTS

The negotiation with the hosts of a performance usually takes place on the telephone or by e-mail some months beforehand. The company are particularly interested in the size and composition of the audience, the performing space, and the aims that the host has for the event. Usually the host will fund the performance and they may ask for certain themes, related to the wider event or to the institution, to be explored. Most performers do not rely on playback for their income – although the Brazilian Sao Paulo company is an exception in this respect – and this means that economic concerns are less influential in shaping the way that the company works than may be the case in professional theatre companies. There are exceptions: for example when Playback Theatre York was asked to perform for British Airways in 1998, the relatively large fee and the clear and forceful wishes of the funders to create a kind of 'Hollywood ending' for their employees caused the company to adapt their work quite considerably. This episode will be discussed in more detail later in this chapter.

Most theatre companies need to carefully select a repertoire to attract a particular audience (Bennett 1997, pp.117–9), whereas playback companies are not under this pressure. Nevertheless, it is likely that the wishes of the hosts, their understanding of the purpose of the event, and their thoughts on the nature of the audience will affect the performers' work and their capacity to perform openly. In turn, it is probable that the audience will detect this and, in response, make decisions concerning their own level of personal involvement.

TIME AND PLACE

'Everywhere', Richard Schechner writes, '...theatre occurs in special times in special places' (Schechner 1988, p.161). Time and place are crucial issues in determining the audience response to performance. As Raymond Williams has written, the most common kind of signal of an art work is its 'occasion and place' (Williams 1981, p.131). In the case of playback theatre different occasions and places will lead spectators to construct different kinds of public places and thus inform their decisions concerning levels of personal involvement. This will have a significant bearing on the openness of telling and performing.

It is unusual for playback to take place in venues solely designated for theatre. Most performances of Playback Theatre York are 'embedded' in host institutions (such as mental health day centres) or in wider events (for example, conferences or training days). This is a crucial factor in the construction of the audience and their sense of collective identity. The company are usually visitors rather than hosts; inevitably this has a bearing on the dynamics of relationships in the performance. It is common for audience members to know each other, to be familiar with the venue, or to be responding to issues that are pertinent to the institution or event in which the performance is embedded. For example, the location of the performance within a venue familiar to the audience is likely to lead to pre-existing patterns of social interaction being replicated to some extent in the performance; this will significantly influence the nature of personal disclosure considered appropriate. In *The Rats* the actor cast to play the mother of the teller was a worker within the centre. She knew the teller and had worked with her. It is perhaps no coincidence that she was chosen to play the teller's mother and, as the actor told me later, there was no doubt in her mind that her previous knowledge of the teller was influencing how she performed the story.

Spaces are always defined against the territory that surrounds them. A space is given meaning by that which lies beyond it. Specifically, a theatre space is shaped by the particular cultural and geographical attributes of what lies outside its boundaries. In playback theatre, the dynamic between inside and outside can be crucial in determining the type of public space experienced by the spectator and thus their decisions concerning personal disclosure. In turn, the nature of the personal stories told in a performance will influence the spectator's 'take' on the cultural spaces that lie inside and outside the theatre space. A performance which takes place in a hotel function room for example, will partly be shaped by its cultural geography; the way that economic and social activity are defined through the use of space will have a bearing on how public theatre space is conceived. Furthermore, the nature of personal disclosure in this particular space is likely to lead to a reassessment of what constitutes the public domain beyond the performance itself.

The timing of a performance can also have a bearing on degrees of openness in performing and telling. Since most performances are embedded in institutions or wider events, it is much more common for venues to be either at the base of the commissioning host or at the site of a wider conference or training event; it is also common for these performances to take place during the day to accommodate the particular audience. There are exceptions: for example, the Sydney Playback Company hold monthly evening performances in a local drama space, nevertheless it remains common that performances take place at host venues and at times designed to be suitable for the anticipated audience. Aside from the logistical ease of locating events at places and times suitable to the audience, there are perhaps two further related reasons why companies do so. They are reasons I would suggest that are closely related to a desire amongst playback practitioners to render the event in some way efficacious:

1. Holding performances at convenient places and times expresses a wish to reach audiences that may not usually be able to access this kind of theatre – what Bennett calls the democratization of theatre through geography (Bennett 1997, p.128). The desire to bring playback theatre to marginalized groups or, as Fox puts it, to 'those who suffer or are not heard' (Fox and Dauber 1999, p.196) is an important factor in understanding the genre.
2. Theatres are, as Schechner tells us, 'maps of the cultures where they exist' (Schechner 1988, p.161) and thus their geographical location carries ideological loading. Playback's preference for non-traditional theatre venues is a desire, shared with other non-traditional theatre groups, to 'escape the tyranny of architectonic grandeur and its aesthetic and ideological implications' (Elam in Bennett 1997, p.136).

PRE-SHOW ADVERTISEMENT

In the practice of Playback Theatre York, as the audience enter the space they will often discover the company brochure placed on their seats. With regard to shaping expectations of purpose it would have read:

> Playback theatre is community theatre, where the real moments, dreams and stories of the audience are spontaneously improvised. With the help of our conductor you can tell your story: choose the actors to play the parts and then sit back and watch as it is brought to life by our company of actors and musicians. Sometimes people come with stories they want to tell and, sometimes, stories are inspired by the performance. Sometimes people come simply to watch. This positive and enjoyable process demonstrates that everyone's story is worth telling. Stories can be hilarious, humdrum, tragic or joyful – any moment, however small, can make a playback story. (Playback Theatre Brochure 2002)

This provides some indication to the audience of what to expect in the forthcoming performance. It also alludes to the possibility that the performance will be efficacious ('positive and enjoyable') and it reveals a democratic desire for audience involvement (everyone's story, however small, 'is worth telling'). Playback theatre practitioners tend to suggest to the gathering audience that the performance is, in some way, intended to be efficacious. The pre-show advertisements and the invitation to tell stories suggests that their telling enactment may bring about personal and social change or, in some way, promote personal insight. Playback theatre adopts practices and holds certain desires with regard to the audience which point toward some kind of healing potential in performances. These indications of the performance to follow will play a part in shaping audience expectation and contributions.

Before the performance begins, it is common for audience members to discuss and ask questions about what will happen and what will be expected of them. It is likely that as they read the brochure they will be trying to decide what may be appropriate to tell in this space. Their nervousness is not surprising in light of the unfamiliarity of the event that is about to take place.

Gathering

As the spectators gather for the performance, there will be a series of signals to shape their expectations and thus their reception of the event. If theatres are 'scenographic models of sociometric process' then particular social relationships in performances may be 'read' back from the ways that the audience are guided as they gather and are subsequently placed in relation to the stage, the performers and each other. In the case of playback theatre, it is a gathering process that is likely to suggest to spectators that their participation will be encouraged, and that there will be some fluidity across the stage/auditorium boundary. It is also likely to point to the constructed and extemporized nature of the event to follow, and thus draws attention to the means of representation at work in the performance.

In most cases playback audiences will be invited into the space when all the preparations are completed; spectators will find as they gather in the space that the lights are up and they are able to see each other. They have an opportunity to observe each other and to finesse their expectations of the performance and make decisions concerning their own level of psychological safety. This will be crucially affected by the size of the audience and their familiarity with each other, any interaction with the performers, the view they have of the stage and, crucially, the integrity of the boundary between the theatre space and the outside.

AUDIENCE SIZE AND COMPOSITION

Audience size and composition will be an important factor in determining the kind of involvement spectators will feel able to make. A larger audience who do not know each other, for example, are likely to make very different decisions with respect to their involvement than a small and familiar group. For an audience comprising of 80–100 conference delegates who may not know each other or be familiar with the space, it is likely that there will be less attention paid to who is 'allowed' to enter the performance and, since playback is not usually performed in dedicated theatre spaces, there may be problems with sight-lines and acoustics. These concerns, together with the need to 'entertain' a large audience, tend to produce a less intimate performance – one more directed to humour or to clear, unambiguous representations. The 'public' nature of these performances often means that the prospect of telling a 'personal' story is daunting. Stories tend to be those which have a clear narrative and structure which can often leave less 'openness' for the performers to explore. In general, not surprisingly, as audience size and unfamiliarity to each other increases, so the levels of personal disclosure and identification decrease; it is likely that there will be more concern about how far the story will 'spread'; the stories tend to become more closed, structured and narrative-driven; and performers tend to take fewer risks in pushing the enactment beyond what was actually told to them. It is far less likely in larger performances that the enactments will be questioned or that the tellers will be invited to discuss them.

ENTERING THE SPACE

As spectators enter the space it is common for them to be *greeted by the performers*, who will introduce themselves, encourage conversation and apprise them of what to expect in the forthcoming performance. In a small gathering it may be possible for the performers to meet most of the audience; in a large one this will not be possible. This 'mingling', as the York Company calls it, is designed to promote audience participation from the outset, begin processes of identification between actors and spectators, and give the performers an opportunity to 'read' the makeup of the audience. It may also suggest that the audience will be able to view 'actor' as well as 'character' during the performance; this is likely to maintain awareness of the constructed nature of the theatrical event and as Schechner suggests, that this kind of self-reflexivity is indicative of a desire to render the theatrical event efficacious in some way. The size of the audience will be a significant factor in determining the effect the pre-performance meeting with performers will have on the way spectators interpret the nature of the space.

As both Schechner (1988) and Bennett (1997) argue, this gathering process is crucial for transforming a group of individuals into an audience.

In playback much of this process is designed to prepare the audience for the particular kind of involvement required during the performance, one that requires them to move back and forth from spectator to active contributor. Occasionally a playback company will forgo this gathering phase, for example, the Sterling Playback Theatre group in Chennai, Southern India, regularly perform on local beaches to passers-by who may join after the performance has begun or leave before it is completed. However, most companies seem to conduct these early moments in similar ways in order to prepare the audience for the particular kind of involvement required in playback.

VIEWING THE ACTING SPACE

When the spectators are seated they have the opportunity to *view the acting space* and this will provide further clues to the forthcoming performance. In structuring the relationship between the performers and spectators, playback companies almost always create a recognizable 'proscenium' arrangement. In the rehearsal room and in performance they look to arrange the audience seating so that it faces a rectangular space (sometimes elevated) bordered at the back by a wall and arranged as already described at the outset of this thesis. The stage area is clearly identifiable. Unlike many script-based theatre performances, what is on stage is not a foretaste of the fictional world to be represented in the play. Although, as Schechner (2002, pp.160–1) points out, in the history of theatre illusionistic stage sets are the exception, nevertheless the non-fictive nature of the playback set is likely to carry a message for the spectators as they take their seats and wait for the performance to begin. One might say that the space points rather more to the performative aspects of the forthcoming show than to the representational ones. Although space can never be neutral or free from social mediation, what they see is an open performing area that awaits the arrival of the performers and, they may deduce, the enactment of their stories. That the performance may not yet be 'planned' and that it may be partially dependent on their involvement is likely to produce anxiety or anticipation in the audience and influence the way they interpret the nature of the public space in which they are gathering. It may be that the non-representational nature of the space prepares the spectators for what Bruner calls the 'subjunctive mood' (Bruner 1990, p.53). The openness of the playing area may suggest to the teller an attitude of uncertainty, receptiveness and fluidity.

AT THE EDGES OF THE SPACE

In psychotherapy and other therapeutic practices where personal stories are disclosed, there is commonly an emphasis on the psychological safety provided by a rigorously maintained spatial *boundary* (Clarkson 1995, p.48).

It is considered crucial that the space is free from intrusion and activity at its edges, so that the client feels safe enough for personal disclosure and catharsis to take place. Playback theatre performances vary considerably in the degree to which they allow movement around or across the threshold of the theatre space. This variable is likely to influence audience decisions concerning the nature of the public space. In general it is likely that activity at the boundary of the theatre space will influence, and be influenced by, the nature of the event taking place, the existing power relations amongst audience members, and the audience size. As I will exemplify later, activity at the threshold is a symbolic indication of the kind of public place that has been created. If, as psychotherapists maintain, the preservation of clear boundaries are essential for personal disclosure, then the activity that takes place at the edges of a playback event will contribute to the kind of decisions the audience make concerning their level of personal disclosure.

To conclude: in each of the different environments in which playback theatre is performed different takes on what is considered 'public' and the 'personal' will be negotiated and established. This is a dynamic process; performers and spectators will be engaged in a constant negotiation and re-negotiation of what can be revealed in a public place. To invite audience members to recount autobiographical narratives in public places is always likely to invite a process of evaluation concerning the psychological safety of doing so and the nature of the public space in which it is to be told. The nature of the autobiographical narratives and the subsequent enactments will always be inflected by these complex considerations. The degree of the openness of the stories and the performing will be highly dependent upon the factors that have been outlined.

In order to exemplify these processes I will now briefly consider four different playback venues. An analysis of a playback rehearsal, a performance to a small audience, a show in a mental health agency and at a large conference event will enable me to illustrate some of the theoretical issues identified in the previous section. I will not systematically deal with all of these issues for each venue; however, I will be particularly interested in how different venues, audiences and host agencies influence the performance and the decisions spectators make concerning the stories they tell.

Four performances

The rehearsal

Playback Theatre York meets to rehearse for a day once every two months; rehearsals usually take place in the rooms of a public institution such as a college, hospital or gym. The rooms are not usually dedicated performance spaces; therefore some rearrangement is required to make it suitable for playback. This is not an event open to others; intrusions are discouraged;

non-company members are only allowed to attend after discussions and with the agreement that they take a full part in the rehearsal. This is largely because, in common with other playback companies, the group rehearses by staging enactments based on the personal stories told by its members.

The carefully protected privacy of the space provides the opportunity for company members to risk significant personal disclosure. This is also supported by the long-standing relationships that exist between company members. Close friendships that have extended over 15–20 years in some cases create an intimacy that allows both personal disclosure and the open expression of emotion. We might say that this is the least 'public' of the performance spaces being discussed here, in the sense that tellers do not feel so acutely that they are 'going public' with their stories; they are fairly certain of the limited dissemination of their story and of the supportive response of the audience. This intimacy can make it difficult for new members to join and the level of personal disclosure can, in my experience, sometimes be unsettling. Nevertheless, rehearsals often provide the most favourable circumstances for open stories and open performing; both tellers and performers are more likely to permit the stories to be opened up to exploration and experimentation than is usually the case in more public performances.

Stories told in rehearsal often have a different quality than they have in performance. The sense of privacy and psychological safety in rehearsal makes it more common for tellers to recount experiences that are driven less by narrative than by 'a feeling' or by a nebulous sense of discomfort. The 'openness' of their story invites the performers to explore its meanings and significance through improvisation and interaction with each other. The 'events' that would usually 'signpost' the direction of the improvisation are less apparent and the actors are more free (than they would be with a story with a clear narrative direction) to open the story up to a play with meaning.

Additionally, because of the relative psychological safety in rehearsal, the performers are more prepared to experiment and take risks with the story. In rehearsal, in my experience, it is more likely that performers will feel safer to explore the performative aspects in an enactment than they would in a more public performance. This is likely to lead to the kind of play with meaning which, I argue, is a key characteristic of effective playback.

The intimacy and familiarity in rehearsal make it more likely that the tellers will express their dissatisfaction with an enactment. It is not uncommon for the performers to replay it in response to this; this is a rare event in a public performance. However the wish to re-do an enactment is driven as much by issues of 'quality' as by the teller's feelings that their story has not been satisfactorily played. Rehearsals give an opportunity for company members to discuss their work at length and this can sometimes expose a tension between the teller's wish to explore personal material and the company's need to rehearse and improve the quality of their work.

The rehearsal space is therefore a very particular kind of public space: one which is more likely to permit open stories and the associated willingness of performers to pay attention to the performative aspects of an enactment. In rehearsals, not surprisingly, there is more room for performative exploration and experimentation with the meanings that may be attributed to the teller's story. For the participants, in my experience, the intimacy of rehearsals often leads to a re-evaluation of the levels of disclosure and vulnerability that may be possible in other places; work and personal relations are often reassessed in light of the particular space created in rehearsal. In a performance to a small audience some of the intimacies of the rehearsal remain, but concerns about personal disclosure create a very different space for the telling of personal stories in public places.

The small 'intimate' performance

Often Playback Theatre York is invited to perform to a relatively small audience (15–30 people) who wish to explore a particular theme or a shared set of experiences; the company regularly stage performances for General Medical Practitioners (GPs), for example. These performances are part of a wider training event and usually take place in a hotel function room in the evening. This produces a particular kind of audience: the 'delegates' are at a hotel, away from home, they have just had dinner, they are not with their usual work colleagues and they may therefore be able, to some extent, to relinquish their professional roles. However, as they arrive at the performance and meet the performers they will discover that they are expected to contribute stories from their professional lives; this is not the kind post-dinner entertainment that sometimes takes place at professional conferences. The work of the day is not over; it continues after dinner. This is likely to produce some ambiguity – not to say ambivalence – in the minds of the spectators.

It is not uncommon in these performances for members of the audience to draw attention to a perceived similarity with 'therapy' or 'psychotherapy' – an impression produced presumably by the invitation to tell personal stories, the small size of the audience, and the expectation that stories will be re-interpreted in some way. Considering their professional role, it is likely that the audience remain acutely aware of the consequences of telling a story and of the uncertainly of how widely their words will be disseminated. Any determination of the public nature of this space therefore is ambiguous and this can produce both anxiety and jocularity. It may be that the audience remain unsure about what kind of public event they are attending. On the one hand, certain cues suggest 'entertainment' (after dinner events are usually considered entertaining), on the other hand the associations with psychotherapy suggest another and perhaps conflicting kind of event. This ambiguity is present in many playback performances. In this event it can be reflected in the stories told: some reveal the vulnerabilities and stresses of the work of a GP, while others seem, on the surface, to be humorous incidents designed to amuse the audience and perhaps break the tension.

Although audience members may not know each other, their shared professional background and their small number can permit stories which disclose professional vulnerabilities and perceived failings. However the small size of the audience can sometimes produce discomfort. Susan Bennett makes this point generally: 'When a theatre has very few spectators, the sense of audience as group can be destroyed. This fragmentation of the collective can have the side-effect of psychological discomfort for the individual which inhibits or revises response' (Bennett 1997, p.131).

The 'sense of audience as group' is partly established by the boundaries created between auditorium and stage and between the theatre space and the surrounding environment. In these small performances the audience are very close to the performers; there is often no clearly marked physical boundary between the stage area and the audience seating. This is likely to increase the psychological discomfort of the spectators and to render the nature of the public space ambiguous. If spectators have not attended a playback performance before, they may for example be anxious that they will be required to perform. In these small performances the entry to the theatre space remains intact: there are usually no exits or entrances throughout the show.

With their carefully protected outer boundaries, proximity of the performers and small audiences, these performances bear some similarities to playback rehearsals; they certainly can produce significant self-disclosure. However, the ambiguity concerning the nature of the public space introduces an element into the performance that is not usually present in rehearsal. In an event that seems to be neither quite theatre nor quite therapy, questions are raised and dramatized about what personal experiences can be revealed safely in a public space; questions that are likely to resonate beyond the performance itself. In my next venue for analysis – a mental health centre – these questions remain, but are inflected differently by context and expectation.

A performance in a mental health centre

The performance in which *The Rats* was told took place in the dayroom of a community mental health centre. The venue was located near the city centre, although access was limited to professionals, and those who had been accepted as members of the centre because of recognition of their mental health problems. Mental health establishments carry particular kinds of cultural and historical associations that are likely to shape the reception of a playback performance. They are places that often exclude the general public to either offer 'asylum' to its users or to 'protect' the public from the imagined dangers presented by people with mental health problems. They are places which often attract pejorative unofficial nomenclature, a sure sign that they produce unease in the general population. The theatre space at this event therefore would carry associations as much by what lay outside it as by what took place inside.

The room where the performance took place was a familiar space that had been transformed for the performance; this is likely to have signalled a change from routine to the audience, and perhaps suggested the potential for a transformation of everyday relationships and identities. However familiar spaces just as often suggest familiar patterns of relationship and holding a performance at a venue so loaded with ideological weighting may well trigger pre-established roles and patterns of interaction. To a significant degree it is likely that spectators came to this performance with expectations and roles partly defined by the institution in which it was held. In an establishment designated as a place to promote personal change, it may have been presumed that the performance would be directed to that end. This may stand in contrast to a playback performance at a large conference, for example, which may be anticipated as one which will focus on the conference theme and provide an entertaining diversion from the main event. These contrasting expectations are likely to influence the nature of personal disclosure and the audience sense of collective identity.

To a certain extent these expectations shaped the split in the audience roles: between mental health users who would be expected to tell their stories, and professionals who may not. Users of the centre attended the performance by virtue of their role as people who had experienced mental health problems, while professionals attended as providers of therapy and specialist support. These roles would have significantly influenced the degree to which the different groups would be prepared to reveal personal material. A pattern of personal disclosure may be hypothesized here: by and large, the users of the service would expect – and be expected – to tell their personal experience to professionals, but not expect that disclosure to be reciprocated. This 'pattern' is likely to have been replicated – and occasionally challenged – in the performance.

Pre-existing roles may also influence the kinds of story told; it is likely that certain types of stories, particularly those related to mental health problems, would be regularly told to professionals and would be framed within the particular understandings present in mental health contexts. Because of their understanding of their professional responsibility, professionals may be protective of users and may attempt, for their 'safety', to limit the kinds of stories that would be safe to tell in a public space. In the performance it is likely that these patterns of personal disclosure would be continued.

This performance produced interesting dynamics in relation to the boundaries of the theatre space which were likely to have influenced the audience's decisions concerning their psychological safety. Perhaps because the space was a meeting room which the members and staff of the centre were accustomed to entering and leaving informally, there was continual activity around the one doorway into the theatre space. People entered and left regularly to, for example, have a cigarette or answer the phone. Boundaries in psychiatric institutions are often contested sites that are in the control of professional groups and, although the movement in this agency seemed relatively free, it is interesting to note that there seemed to be a preponderance of staff at the doorway, 'guarding', as it were, the exits and entrances. There may have been another reason for their presence there; in a cultural event that did not clearly mark social hierarchy, it may be that it was a means of marking their separation and difference from the centre's users. It seems that the boundary to the theatre space was employed as a symbolic marker of power and status relations. It is likely that this activity at the doorway influenced decisions concerning the nature of the public space and therefore the extent of personal disclosure that was possible there. Throughout the performance there continued to be activity around the door that is likely to have reduced the sense of psychological safety in both the audience and the performers.

The large conference venue

Large conference venues produce a different kind of public event. The size of the audience, their unfamiliarity with each other, the distance of many of the spectators from the stage, and the likelihood of regular activity at the doorways often produces a sense of being in a public space where significant self-disclosure seems inappropriate. Spectators tend to tell less open stories that have the well-crafted quality of having been told before, or they prefer to be less personal, telling stories which could be seen to apply to the audience as a whole. Because the performers are concerned with projecting their voices and with overcoming the difficult sight-lines in large venues, the work tends to be less intimate and more declamatory. They are less likely to be responsive to each other during the enactment and in general 'open performing' is more difficult to sustain.

At a hotel near Heathrow Airport in December 1998, Playback Theatre York staged a performance to about 100 'middle managers' of British Airways. Their line-managers had asked the company to contribute to a day designed to prepare the staff for the changes that were soon to be implemented. Unusually the company were to be a part of a day which had a definite desired end-point summed up in their hope for a 'Hollywood ending', in which the anxieties about change (which were to be aired earlier in the day) would be replaced by excitement and anticipation of the future. The fee was considerably larger than the company were used to, and it is likely that this led the company to accept rather uncritically the managers' remit. There is no doubt that the nature of public disclosure was inflected by the audience's awareness of the presence of their managers and the particular corporate ethos of the organization.

This was a public space 'monitored' in some way by the BA management. The types of stories they told, their level of personal disclosure and the performers' response were all coloured by this awareness. The BA performance emphasized the contingency of autobiographical storytelling in playback performances: politics and power are always influencing to some degree the audience's construction of public place. In performances with large audiences, these dynamics may be more difficult to address than in small gatherings where the pressures to conform are less marked. The BA performance was an interesting one because it challenged company members to review the political and ethical status of their work. It suggested that playback theatre could be employed to serve purposes that are not necessarily in line with the performers' political or ethical orientation, and that the telling of personal stories in public places is not a universal and unequivocal 'good'.

Concluding remarks

Gaston Bachelard observes that 'all really inhabited space bears the essence of the notion of home' (1994, p.5). In the space created for a playback performance the imagination of the spectator draws on her memory of similar places in order to make sense and to make safe. The stories told in playback are always shaped by this, and in their turn, shape public space. What is remembered and brought to mind in a performance is always being shaped by place and context. A sense of place is then further created by these memories. The performers are not immune to this process: as *The Rats* vignette shows, a sense of place will always have a significant impact on the conductor, actors and musicians. As the performance unfolds, their work will be altered and defined by that sense of place.

In general we can argue that stories where 'the sense of risk is palpable' are more likely to be told in smaller more intimate and 'protected' spaces, where the size and the familiarity of the audience allow self-disclosure, and where 'the politics of the space' do not inhibit certain types of stories being told. However, this is not always the case: 'intimate' public spaces can, as we have seen, produce a sense of fragmentation of the collective and reduce the audience's feeling of psychological safety. What is clear, however, is that stories in playback are products of the place in which they are told, a conclusion which renders the notion of the 'essence' of the teller's story problematic. The 'openness' of the stories told and the subsequent enactment are profoundly influenced by the audience's sense of place. In the next chapter I will explore this further, analyzing the nature of memory, autobiographical narrative and the 'performing' of personal stories in public places.

Chapter 4
Narratives and Memory Work

In his novel *Nausea*, Jean-Paul Sartre writes that 'a man is always a teller of tales, he lives surrounded by his stories and the stories of others, he sees everything that happens to him through them; and tries to live his life as if he were recounting it' (2000, p.61). Playback theatre is clearly organized around the stories of members of its audiences; therefore some consideration of the nature of narrative will be important if we are to understand the peculiar *performed* stories told in playback. In this chapter I will also look at the complex relationship between memory and narrative so eloquently expressed by Nabokov when he writes that 'the supreme achievement of memory is the masterly use it makes of innate harmonies when gathering to its fold the wandering and suspended tonalities of the past' (cited in McConkey 1996, p.271). Before doing this, however, I begin with a story of my own which will form the basis of much of the discuscion that follows.

The 'teller': *The Red Coat*

In September 1998 my father died. With my mother and two brothers, I was at his bedside through the last hours of his life. As his breathing became more laboured and we wiped away the foam that kept gathering at his mouth, we talked about his life and, in clumsy ways, spoke about our feelings towards him. It was the first time we had all been together without partners and children for over 30 years, and I was aware of the old battles, long forgotten, but still capable of animating and distorting the relationships between us.

Dad died slowly, but seemingly without pain. Over the last hour he seemed to stop breathing many times and then would take one further breath – something that I remembered from my nursing days to be called 'chain-stoking'. The gaps between these breaths gradually lengthened until finally he was silent. My mother held his hand and with a look of terrible and unbearable pain, asked each of us where we thought he was now. Struggling for some sort of answer, but refusing to repeat some neat formulaic answer, I said, finally, 'I don't know'.

After a short while, I went downstairs to see how my seven-year-old daughter was and to tell her that my dad had died. As I walked outside into the quiet residential street I saw Rebecca in the distance on her bicycle, easily visible in her red coat, which seemed radiant in the bright sunshine. A neighbour stood across the road, smoking, I went over to him and asked him for a cigarette. He lit it for me, being, for a moment, the father that I had lost. Together we stood smoking watching Rebecca's exuberance – the scintillating redness of her coat against the deep blue sky, the sharp late September air brightening the image.

I told her that 'Papa' had died and asked if she would like to see him. She said she would and we went upstairs. She sat on my knee, by his bedside, holding me tight as we talked about what had happened.

I wrote this passage in March 2001, two and a half years after the death of my father. By coincidence it was written on the day of my daughter's tenth birthday. Having written it, I went to collect her from school with a feeling of calmness, almost of completion. For a moment I felt better disposed towards the world.

The autobiographical narrative and playback theatre

Stories are ubiquitous in playback theatre; indeed, the autobiographical narrative and its dramatization give the practice its organizing focus. This chapter is devoted to the 'personal story' and its characteristics, as they seem to emerge in a performance. The aim of this chapter will be to destabilize the notion, often present in playback discourse, of the 'essence' or the 'heart' of the teller's story. I will propose that such a conception suggests an 'essential' story existing beyond mediation and contingency. It suggests, and this is important for our understanding of playback theatre, a story which, in some way, could be replicated or *mirrored* by the performers in their enactment. It will be my proposition that it is misleading to conceptualize playback theatre in this way because it denies the relational, negotiated and context-rich nature of playback performances. It denies the humanness of the response and fails to recognize that the past is, to a large extent, created in and for the present. If the story has an 'essence', it is a fluid and dynamic thing that is always being created to serve the moment and the place.

In this chapter I will discuss the complex relationship between memory, narrative and the self. I will propose that the veracity of autobiographical narrative is inevitably inflected by the need for coherence, intelligibility and reparation of the past. As seems clear from *The Red Coat*, the relationship between my 'experience' and the story I wrote in March 2001 raises profound questions relating to the nature of memory and its representation. It is not possible to maintain that there is a direct correspondence between the experience of the teller and the narrative they tell. Instead what we must conceive of is a cumulative process of mediation that begins with the experience (as I sat at my father's bedside I was already developing the first 'drafts' of the story) and extends onwards through subsequent 'tellings' to (and after) the enactment. Indeed it may plausible to suggest that this process begins before the experience (I had anticipated my father's death and to some extent had created a story of how it would be). Playback theatre can be seen, then, as intervening in and inflecting this, perhaps endless, process of *mediation*. Such a conception requires us to re-think playback. Rather than viewing the performers as capturing the 'essence', we must see them as entering into what Annette Kuhn (1995, p.107) calls 'memory work'. A complex process she argues 'is potentially interminable: at every turn, as further questions are raised, there is always something else to look into' (p.5). To conceptualize playback as an intervention in ongoing memory work is to re-figure the practice as one of many representational responses to the complexity of experience rather than as a final 'essential' version; playback theatre can be seen in this way as pointing rather more to the future than to the past.

The re-thinking of playback performing as a response to, and an intervention in, the teller's ongoing 'narrativization' rather than as a replication of some essence of their story is further strengthened by the proposition that playback theatre stories are particular sorts of narratives that derive from the means of their production. It is not possible to regard stories told in playback theatre performances as existing independently of the act and location of their telling. They emerge through a complex process of dialogue between teller and conductor and what's more that they are told within, *and* with a view, to performance. Such an argument recasts playback stories as contingent and context-dependent entities embedded in complex interactions. The delivery of the teller's narrative is *performative* in the sense that it draws attention to, and is inflected by, the circumstances of its telling.

Homo Faber: narrative and the self

> It was a stormy night in the Bay of Biscay and his sailors were seated around the fire. Suddenly the crew said, 'Tell us a story, Captain'. And the Captain began; 'It was a stormy night in the Bay of Biscay...'
> Ciaran Carson, *Fishing for Amber: A Long Story* (cited in Kearney 2002, p.1)

In the last quarter of a century there has been an increasing interest in the autobiographical narrative and its function in conferring coherence, intelligibility and identity. This has been apparent within psychology (Bruner 1990; Sarbin 1986), philosophy (Kearney 2002; MacIntyre 1985;

Polkinghorne 1988) and in psychotherapy (Brooks 1994; McLeod 1997; Toukmanian and Rennie 1992).

The notion of 'Homo Faber' or the 'motivated storyteller' (Hermans and Hermans-Jansen 1995) may, perhaps, be best introduced through the work of the philosopher Alisdair MacIntyre. In *After Virtue*, MacIntyre is concerned with the 'liquidation of the self into a set of demarcated areas of role-playing' (1985, p.535). He rejects the idea of a self as a mere accumulation of social roles. Instead he posits, 'a concept of self whose unity resides in the unity of a narrative which links birth to life to death as narrative beginning to middle to end' (1985, p.536). The self is unified through and by narrative.

He argues that it is 'natural' to think of the self in narrative mode and that narrative is 'the basic and essential genre' for the characterization of human action. For MacIntyre, this privileging of the autobiographical narrative is an *ethical* imperative. He proposes, as Bruner has done in psychology, placing the individual's idiosyncratic accounts at the centre of philosophical analysis.

He goes on to propose that narrative provides the primary means through which human beings achieve 'intelligibility'. He also argues, as Sartre does in the quotation that opens this chapter, that we imagine ourselves as characters in a story whose identity is formed through the creation of narrative. He writes 'personal identity is just that identity presupposed by the unity of the character which the unity of the narrative requires' (MacIntyre 1985, p.548).

Narrative is, according to MacIntyre, the organizing principle of human identity. Human beings are, from this point of view, on a 'narrative quest' for intelligibility, identity and teleological closure. It is a compelling vision of the organizational power of the narrative; however it does seem to be in danger of reifying that narrative as a structural and organizing progenitor of the self. This would lead us into the same problems that accrue if we maintain the notion of a transcendent self. I would agree with Greimas when he writes 'Narrative structures do not exist *per se*, but are a mere moment in the generation of signification' (Greimas 1991, p.293). A 'mere moment': autobiographical narrative structures are provisional and dynamic; they are drawn into the process of remembering and constituting identity. Rather than giving narrative the status of providing overall organizing authority, perhaps they are best seen, as Barclay suggests, as improvisational acts in the fluid creation of subjectivities or, as he calls them, protoselves. He writes that '...autobiographical remembering is largely an improvisational act. Accordingly, the improvisational activities that are characteristic of autobiographical remembering – for example, ongoing justifications of fleeting feelings in and between people – create *protoselves*, or remembered selves in the making' (Barclay 1994, p.70).

Lyotard's conception of the contemporary self is similarly a dynamic and evanescent one. He writes that the self

> does not amount to much, but no self is an island; each exists in a fabric of relations that is now more complex and mobile than ever before. A person is always located at 'nodal points' of specific communication circuits... Or better, one is always located at a post through which various kinds of messages pass. (Lyotard 1984, p.15)

In this conception, the self is not transcendent, nor has it vanished into Baudrillard's hyperreality (1983); rather it is, as Holstein and Gubrium argue, *'first and foremost, a practical project of everyday life'* (2002, p.70) [my italics]. The self is a constant and ongoing project of self-construction and 'reparative reconstruction'. The self is not merely a 'sea of images' (in Holstein and Gubrium 2002, p.61), but is engaged in the pragmatic exercise of constituting itself within the discourses and actions of everyday existence. Playback theatre through its invitation to 'perform' a story and to view its enactment intervenes in this process of self-creation.

Reparative reconstruction

The past is unrecoverable. The events I describe at the opening of the chapter can only ever be the traces of what really happened. The last hours of my father's life, recalled so much later, cannot reclaim the lived experience. What remains are visual, acoustic and linguistic images – the red coat, the brilliant sunshine, the white foam that gathered around his mouth, the sound of his last breath, the strange phrase 'chain-stoking', which seemed so appropriate to a man who had been brought up in smoky pre-war London and whose pipe-smoking is one of my abiding images of him.

From these images a narrative has been created and refined over time. It has been a narrative told many times, that has gradually formed into a shape that somehow carries the existential weight of that time for me. I am reminded of what David Powley, one of the members of the York Company, said about a story told in a playback theatre performance we were discussing. A story he said is 'a ship that carries us across a sea of pain'. Or, as Cox and Theilgaard (1987, p.24) write of metaphor, it is able to 'carry the existential weight' of loss. Annette Kuhn puts this well when she writes:

> Although we take stories of childhood and family literally, I think our recourse to the past is a way of reaching for myth, for the story that is deep enough to express the profound feelings we have in the present. (Kuhn 1995, p.1)

As soon as my father died my task was one of 'remembrance'. Not only to remember, and so to commemorate him, but also to find a way to invest the bare events of his dying with significance – a significance fitting to mark the death of a man on whose knee I sat to watch *The Lone Ranger*, and whose thumb was exactly the same shape as mine. The events of that Sunday in September do not seem enough for me; they needed to be infused with something more. They needed poetic images, a narrative – a shape that gives me pleasure and even a sense of being at rest.

This is my story, it marks who I am; I was there, and this was *my* father. My story is ground on which I can stand and on which I cannot be easily contradicted. This narrative, which undoubtedly will be endlessly rewritten, identifies me – as much as the similarity of my thumbs to my father's thumbs does. In writing this story and telling and retelling it, am I not engaged in what Mark Freeman calls 'rewriting the self'? (Freeman 1993).

The task of remembrance establishes a sense of the continuity of self. This continuity for Wyatt is 'as much a *reparative reconstruction* as it is an elementary condition of remembering' (1986, p.199). Intense anxiety may occur when this sense of continuity is thwarted and the past appears fragmented into a disparate series of events without coherence. One might argue that the act of remembering, particularly through narrative is, to borrow a phrase from the psychoanalyst Murray Cox (1978), a 'compromise with chaos'. It may be considered as an attempt to bring coherence to the disordered, topsy-turvy nature of experience and so 'author' the self as continuous and unified. In writing this story of my father's death, two and a half years after the event, I continue a process of 'reparative reconstruction', a process that began as soon as he died (if not during and before) and which, I imagine, will continue on into the future. One might argue that each rewriting of these memories further fictionalizes the memory, replacing the inchoate flux of the experience with a 'workable' personal myth, capable of carrying the affective weight of that time and, in some way, commemorating my father.

Poetry drugs the dragon of disbelief

The story enacted

The Red Coat was written some two and a half years after my father's death. It seems to have performed an act of remembrance in the course of my bereavement, but it is also a story that was partly shaped by telling the story of my father's dying day at a playback rehearsal in early October 1998 – only weeks after the event itself. I had arrived at the rehearsal uncertain whether I was emotionally ready to perform but very keen to tell my story. I told the actors about the red coat and cast Susanna to be Rebecca. This actor, swathed in red cloth, circled the stage throughout the enactment, making a very strong impression on me, to such an extent that this is now the only part of the enactment that I remember. The performance altered my memory of the event, or at the very least, pushed to the foreground the red coat aspect of it. Subsequent retellings have always stressed that aspect, arguably far more forcefully than would have been the case if I had not viewed that performance. This has altered my narrative, giving me an image that previously did not have the resonance it now has. It is clearly the case that the performance has, amongst other things, contributed to the fictionalizing of one aspect of the story – literally reinforcing what I later discovered to be fictional – that the coat was pink and not red.

These processes of remembrance serve the present and future as much, if not more than, the past. Raphael Samuel puts it succinctly when he writes that 'the past is the plaything of the present' (Samuel 1996, p.429). Furthermore, for this task of remembrance to be achieved, the precise veracity of the narrative is not the priority. For example, when I showed this passage to my wife, she told me that Rebecca's coat was pink rather than red, albeit a very bright pink. Perhaps surprisingly, this does not destroy the efficacy of the narrative for me. The vivacity and the 'passion' of 'red' is what are required for the story. On the borderline between life and death, the colour must be red – pink will just not do.

It is clear that we cannot rely on any naive notion of a direct correspondence between primary experience and autobiographical narrative. Must we, therefore, treat personal story with scepticism, as being closer to fiction than fact? Must we condemn the autobiographical as mere anecdote? As Bruner (1990) has argued this has been the often-undeclared strategy of academic psychology throughout the period when behaviourism and later behavioural-cognitivism held sway. The veracity of memory, of course, has always been regarded with scepticism in psychoanalysis, which looks for the evasions, the resistances, the repressed and the symptomatic in the patient's recollection of the past. In psychoanalysis desire is always interrupting accurate recall. Can we ever trust memory?

Recognizing, as Michael Ventura does, that 'memory is a form of fiction' (Hillman and Ventura 1993, p.22) does not invalidate it. Rather it recasts memory as 'an interpretative act the end of which is an enlarged understanding of the self' (Freeman 1993, p.29). Annette Kuhn writes, 'As the veils of forgetfulness are drawn aside, layer upon layer of meaning and association peel away, revealing not ultimate truth, but greater knowledge' (Kuhn 1995, p.5).

'Memory work' which is always in one sense fictionalizing may deepen an understanding of self and other. As can be seen from my *Red Coat* story, it involves a 'rewriting of the self' that looks as much to the future as to the past. The child's red coat shimmering in the autumn sun points to a faith in what the future may hold. As Mark Freeman asks, are autobiographical narratives not '...rooted in a kind of faith, in what it might mean to live well – a faith that, however labile and transient, we cannot live without?' (Freeman 1993, p.49).

In light of this, according to Donald Spence the task of the therapist becomes one of enabling the patient to achieve 'a kind of linguistic and narrative closure' (Spence 1982, p.137) in which the therapist becomes more of 'a pattern maker than a pattern finder' (p.284) engaged in an 'artistic struggle' (p.294). He approvingly quotes Isenberg, 'poetry drugs the dragon of disbelief' (p.269).

Peter Brooks (1994) asserts that there is increasing agreement that psychoanalysis is a 'narrative discipline'. He writes that the psychoanalyst is concerned with enabling the patient to arrive at 'a recomposition of the narrative discourse to give a better representation of the patient's story, to reorder its events, to foreground its dominant themes, to understand the force of desire that speaks in and through it' (Brooks 1994, p.47). One could make a plausible case, I think, that one of the aims of playback is to 'foreground' the story's 'dominant themes' and to understand and enact 'the force of desire that speaks in and through the story'.

Personal stories give playback theatre its organizing focus. The form is built around the telling of a series of stories throughout the performance. As we have seen, these stories are altered through the act of telling and dramatization and, as we shall see later, these stories are also altered by the act of being told *in and for* a performance. In that sense it is clear that playback intervenes in the memory work of teller and the audience. Stories about our experience always leave much unsaid; there are always gaps and omissions. There are limits to what personal narrative can carry.

The limits of narrative

The creation of autobiographical narrative involves a loss. Because 'narrative truth' conforms to its own needs for 'good form', coherence, intelligibility and closure (Abbott 2002), it will always have a tendency to omit or edit out that which cannot be held by it – especially when told in public places. Narrative is always a compromise with the inexpressible and its representation always involves loss. As Peggy Phelan puts it: 'when writing about the disaster of death it is easy to substitute interpretations for traumas. In that substitution the trauma is tamed by the interpretative frame and peeled away from the raw, "unthought" energy of the body' (1997, p.5). Narratives are purposeful acts; they are designed to convey something. In doing so they often omit that which is not immediately relevant. I did not, for example, recount in *The Red Coat,* the drawing of an army officer on the wall of my father's bedroom, which evoked so strongly in me a sense of 'cruelty' that I attribute to the army life that I was immersed in as a child. I did not do so because that was part of another story – a story of old battles, long forgotten, but still capable of animating and distorting relationships in the present. This was not the story I had chosen to tell.

Trauma limits the possibility of autobiographical narrative. As Peggy Phelan writes, '[T]he symbolic cannot carry it: trauma makes a tear in the symbolic network itself' (Phelan 1997, p.5). Narrative, as an interpretative act, may perhaps be seen as an inadequate substitute for trauma. Phelan quotes Blanchot (1986): 'The danger is that the disaster should acquire meaning instead of body' (Phelan 1997, p.17). Trauma can perhaps be said to be marked deeply in the body – carried viscerally in the tissues and sinews and unavailable for representation. As the memory psychologists, Lucy Berliner and John Briere (1999), suggest memories of traumatic and emotionally-laden experiences may be partially encoded 'at the somatosensory level, as opposed to more exclusively at verbally mediated levels' (Berliner and Briere 1999, p.9).

The *limits of narrative* may mark the *limits of what is possible* in playback theatre. Usually playback theatre conductors ask for tellers to come to the teller's chair to tell stories; they are therefore asking for memories that have, in some way, undergone processes of narrative patterning. This clearly limits the possible material that may be handled. By contrast, drama and dance therapists, for example, may work through the body and so perhaps permit a broader range of expression. Phil Jones writes that through dramatherapy a client can '...explore the relationship with their body in terms of the problematic memories and experiences with which their physical self connects' (Jones 1996, p.164). A client may encounter, through a dramatherapy exercise, memories that are, at first, only accessible through the body, perhaps later finding some verbal expression for them. In playback theatre this kind of 'embodied discovery' is not available to the teller, largely limited, as she or he is, to oral expression. The requirement for verbally expressed autobiographical narrative from the teller in playback theatre acts as a limit to the possible modes of expression open to him or her. In playback theatre, it is the performer who encounters and embodies the teller's narrative – we might say – for or in the place of the teller. This marks a key characteristic of playback theatre practice, the consequences of which will be explored in forthcoming chapters. It is the performers' *body, and personal and cultural memory* that stand in for the teller. Of course this raises significant ethical issues; nevertheless in doing so it may be that they can, when playback is at its best, enrich the narrative with images that offer the teller and spectator glimpses of that which cannot be represented in narrative form. Performing bodies may find images for memory encoded at the somatosensory level.

Autobiographical narratives in playback theatre performances

Narratives told in playback theatre performances are forged by the circumstances of their telling. They do not arrive as autonomous entities ready and complete, to be delivered in the performance. They are inflected by context, the dialogue between teller and conductor, by the fact that they are performed in the presence of an audience, and by their tendency to draw upon other texts.

To explore this further I offer a verbatim account of a story told during a performance of Playback Theatre York to drama students and staff at a drama college. In fact it was the performance that followed the rehearsal at which I had told *The Red Coat.* Because of my 'raw' feelings, I chose not to perform at that event and so I had the opportunity to record in writing the dialogue between the teller and the conductor as it was spoken. It is not an exact transcript, but was written out in full after the event. The vignette has been chosen because it illustrates the complex, reflexive and dialogic characteristics of personal narratives told in playback performances. In the story we find the teller concerned about the impact the telling may have upon the audience as he remembers the effect the telling had in the earlier drama workshop. The particular kind of public place created here – a student/staff group known to each other located in a familiar college venue – may have played a part in producing a story that reflexively draws attention to its effect upon the listeners. A group of students and staff may be highly aware of the impact their words are having and how that might affect their continuing relationships. In any event the sense of guilt that the dream provokes and reveals heightens the levels of reflexive awareness and performativity in the telling.

The dialogue takes place between the conductor ('C') and a male teller ('T') in his early thirties.

The Dream of Murder

The telling begins with the conductor asking the teller to choose someone to play him. He chooses one of the actors.

C. When did this story take place?

T. A long time ago. Well it is about a dream that I had about a year ago – no more like six months ago. Although the dream is based on something that happened in real life.

C. Tell us something about you at the time of the dream.

T. I was enjoying the first year as a mature student. I had transferred from English and Computer Studies to Drama and I was really enjoying it.

I had a lot of energy. I told this dream in a drama workshop and people were terrified by it. I'm worried I might terrify the audience.

Before the dream, about 10 or 12 years before, when I was perhaps (I'm giving away my age here) 23. I was in the town where I had been a student and happened to be reading the newspaper, I came across a small article about a friend of mine and it said that he had committed suicide. I was really shocked and it was worse because our friendship had not ended on good terms. After that I couldn't get him out of my mind, I saw people in the street who looked like him...someone who had the same haircut or clothes and I thought it was him.

C. Choose someone to be your friend.

T. Could the actors choose someone?

C. I would prefer you choose.

The teller points to one of the actors.

C. Tell us about your friend.

T. He was called David. He was wild.

C. Are you wild?

T. I'm a tempered version of him. He looked like me. We had a close connection.

C. A close connection. OK. Tell us about the dream.

T. It is the middle of the dream. I can't remember the beginning. I know in the dream that I have killed him. I know what it is like to kill someone. I pull out my jumper from the washing machine – it is covered in blood.

C. How did you feel?

T. I feel remorse and terror. I could commit murder. I remember that we did not part on good terms. I woke up shocked. It is with me now. I know what it is like to kill someone. I am worried. I have the inside view of a murderer.

C. OK. This is T's story of a dream. You watch.

It is clear that the teller's narrative is not totally under his 'control'. First, the events emerge through the conductor's questioning. For example, the conductor asks such questions as 'When did this story take place?' or 'Tell us something about yourself at the time of the dream'. It is clear that the events are evoked in dialogue with the conductor. Second, the plot is co-authored between the conductor and teller. For example, the conductor's question 'Are you wild?' introduces the possibility that there is some mirroring between the teller and 'David' and so plots into the narrative inter- and intra-psychic dynamics that were not previously explicit. Therefore, as Bakhtin argues:

> Meaning does not reside in the word or in the soul of the speaker or in the soul of the listener. Meaning is the effect of an interaction

> between speaker and listener produced via the material of a particular sound complex. It is like an electric spark that occurs only when the two terminals are hooked together. (Bakhtin 1994, p.35)

Bakhtin's insights are important for us here since, for him, meaning does not emerge in the 'personalist' sense that 'I own meaning' – a concept that is 'deeply implicated in the Western humanist tradition' (Clark and Holquist 1984, p.9) in which the individual can control and have ownership of the meaning they wish to create. Bakhtin argues that meaning is created in dialogue and so 'I cannot own meaning, but only do so in dialogue with others'. An acceptance of his ideas has a profound effect on the way that playback theatre is conceptualized. It brings into question the notion of the teller as an independent self-transparent originator of meaning and questions the possibility of the independence of their story. Instead of a story 'owned' by the teller, the playback theatre story becomes not only a jointly created text but also a text that is created in relation to other texts – an 'intertext'.

Following the work of Barthes (1967) on intertextuality, Kristeva's reading of the work of Mikhail Bakhtin on the dialogic and the 'languages of heteroglossia' led her to develop further the notion of intertextuality – one that has proved enormously fruitful in literary studies. Bakhtin stressed the dialogic nature of all human communication and had argued that 'all utterances are heteroglot in that they are functions of a matrix of forces practically impossible to recoup' (Bakhtin 1981, p.428). Kristeva developed this further, asserting that any text is 'constructed as a mosaic of quotations; any text is the absorption and transformation of another' (Kristeva 1980, p.66). A text therefore, may not be understood as a hermetically sealed unit existing independently of other texts. Instead we must conceive of complex fields of interrelationships in which texts always 'refer' to other texts. Roland Barthes asserts that 'the quotations from which a text is constructed are anonymous, irrecoverable, and yet already read: they are quotations without quotation marks' (Barthes 1979, p.77). This 'loosens up' the notion of text to such a degree that we must conceive of any text as an 'open dynamic playground' (Cancalon and Spacagna 1994, p.1) in which allusion, unacknowledged quotation, pastiche and complex associations are at work.

This notion of intertextuality renders the position of the author (and thus the playback teller) problematic. He or she can no longer be regarded as having a single, unitary presence. The authority of the author and the attempt to search for his or her intentions and motivations is considered by Barthes to be a project not only condemned to impossibility but also inclined to impose single, stable meanings to texts. As he famously writes:

> We know now that a text is not a line of words, releasing a single 'theological' meaning (the message of the Author-God) but a multi-dimensional space in which a variety of writings, none of them original, blend and clash. (1989, p.116)

The search for the author behind the work becomes a futile one and the refusal to assign a single, ultimate meaning becomes, for Barthes, an 'anti-theological activity' and a 'truly revolutionary one' which refuses 'God and his hypostases – reason, science, law' (Barthes 1989, p.116).

This clearly places the teller's narrative in playback theatre in a different light. We must now regard the teller's narrative as a complex matrix of signifiers and codes, which refers, quotes, and alludes to other texts. It follows that the authority of the teller and the attempt to reveal 'essences' or ultimate meanings becomes deeply problematic. Once we have relinquished the notion that the narratives told in playback are independent entities owned by their tellers and unaffected by the nature of their production, then we may begin to see them as *negotiated and contextual* creations.

There seems to be a tension in playback discourse between an understandable and ethically driven wish to capture 'the heart of the story' and be 'loyal to the teller' on the one hand, and a recognition that stories are created in performance contexts on the other. There is a paradox here: the right to self-definition of the teller needs to be acknowledged and respected while simultaneously recognizing that it is constantly being re-negotiated in relationship with conductor and audience. One could argue that such apparent incommensurables dynamize the playback event. Few tellers would be prepared to contribute their stories if they felt that they were just grist to the mill of the conductor's and actors' playful interpretations, but neither would it be so interesting if the teller's narratives were so hermetically sealed that they could not be prised open for negotiation within the playback process. It is a tension that gives *frisson* to the playback event that is energized by the telling personal stories in public places.

The performance of the playback narrative

The autobiographical narratives in playback emerge both *as* a performance and *within* a performance. This is clear in *The Dream of Murder.* The levels of reflexive awareness are complex. The teller tells of a dream; his response to that dream; his memory of the last meeting with his friend; the impact this particular dream on the 'drama workshop' and, perhaps, the impact the telling is having on this audience.

The dream 'shocked' the teller and as he says, 'It is with me now'. The dream works in a complex relationship with the teller's memory of his last meeting with his friend that had 'not ended on good terms'. Despite the shock of the dream and the impact it had when he told it previously, he still decides to tell it here. The teller is clearly aware of the impact this story of the dream has had on others in the workshop and he may well be anticipating the impact it will have on the present audience. Gergen writes 'as narratives are realized in the public arena, they become subject to social evaluation and resultant moulding' (Gergen 1993, p.222). If performance is always *for* someone, as Carlson suggests (1996), then the teller is, in playback, performing for those assembled, for him or herself and, perhaps, for those who are absent but who, in some way, have a significant relationship to the story.

In *The Dream of Murder*, the teller begins with the dream and the effect that that has upon the people in the drama workshop and with his worry that this story might similarly terrify the audience. By doing this perhaps he seeks to heighten our interest and raise our expectations. By doing so he certainly introduces a certain *frisson*. This is heightened when later he concludes the story with the climactic: 'It is with me now. I know what it is like to kill someone. I am worried. I have the inside view of the murderer'. His statement – 'It is with me now' – has the effect of collapsing the distance between the dream and the present moment. If it is with him now, then he is suggesting that perhaps it is 'present' to the whole audience. It is a rhetorical device aimed at heightening the tension. In following this with 'I know what it is like to kill someone. I am worried' he suggests that he may be struggling now, again bringing the dream closer to the present moment of telling. And then finally, 'I have the inside view of the murderer' might be considered rather melodramatic. He has a keen appreciation of the effect he is having upon the audience. The recounting of the story is a highly self-conscious and reflexive act in which the teller has an acute awareness of the impact upon the spectators and the performers.

We may not only see the telling *as* a performance but also something that is taking place *within* a performance. That is it takes place *within* a performance and is, crucially, directed *towards* performance. Because of the ways in which the conventions of playback have been developed, the teller will usually be aware that the telling of his story will be followed by a performance. As is clear in *The Dream of Murder*, the casting of significant characters in the story will interrupt the narration. It is clear also that, by and large, the choices concerning whether to cast a character, or not, are ones made by the conductor. In the following passage, Salas writes about the purpose of these interruptions by the conductor in the course of the telling. In doing so she reminds us again of the co-creational nature of the emergence of playback stories:

> Soon after Carolyn starts telling about her dream, I stop her. 'Carolyn, hold on a moment. Can you pick one of the actors to play you in the story?'

> My interruption has at least two functions. One is that my request immediately takes her story into the realm of co-creation with me and with the actors. From now on, as she continues telling, she – and the audience – will be picturing the action that is going to take place in a minute or two. The other purpose of my interruption is to convey to her that I am there to guide the telling of her story. It's a gentle assertion of the conductor's authority – essential for both safety and aesthetics. (Salas 1993, pp.712–72)

It is clear from this passage that the role of the conductor in co-creating the teller's narrative is a crucial one. Salas suggests that it is the task of the conductor to draw the story 'into the realm of co-creation' with the conductor and with the actors. It is, therefore, in one important sense, no longer, as it were, in the sole possession of the teller, but becomes 'raw material' (or more accurately 'cooked') for a performance. The teller is required to relinquish some control over her narrative in order that it may be shaped towards performance.

Deborah Pearson, an experienced playback conductor from Australia, takes the performative nature of the teller's narration in another direction by emphasizing the role of the audience. She encourages conductors to place themselves so that they are as much in contact with the audience as with the teller. She warns against entering into an intimate dialogue with the teller that 'excludes' the audience. Speaking about the relationship between the teller, conductor and audience, she worries about the 'propensity [of the conductor] to have intimacy only with the teller, so the audience is always on the outside'. In an interview in Australia in 1998 she explained this approach to me:

> One of the things I have developed in my work…is to try and unravel the story with the audience, so that when the conductor is working with the teller, she is having an ongoing dialogue with the audience. Not in a trite sort of way – like 'Who else has been to York?' – but real meaningful dialogue so that the audience can start to get involved in their own story rather than just be voyeuristic on the teller's story. (Pearson 1998)

Pearson's recommendations suggest that she is concerned with creating a *transitive relationship* between audience and narrator in which the teller's narrative will be inflected by the spectator's own identifications and, *vice versa*; the audience's own stories will be being 'rewritten', as it were, in response to the teller's. Her wish that the audience should not be 'voyeuristic on the teller's story' calls for a level of dialogue which will, perhaps, permit multiple perspectives to inflect the individual narrative.

Performed narratives

When personal stories are told in public places, perhaps it is inevitable that narratives are inflected by the circumstances of their telling. Relinquishing the notion of the original story may enable performers to

> be ready to receive every moment of discourse in its sudden irruption; in that punctuality in which it appears... Discourse must not be referred to the distant presence of the origin, but treated as and when it occurs. (Foucault 2002, p.125)

Adam Phillips proposes that the alternative to believing in an authoritative, original version of the individual's story is 'that there are just an unknowable series of translations of translations; preferred versions of ourselves, but not true ones' (Phillips 2002, p.143). He goes on to argue that in psychoanalysis 'the only good translation is the one that invites retranslation; the one that doesn't want to be verified so much as altered' (Phillips 2002, p.146). In psychoanalysis – and I would argue in playback theatre – one is not referring back to some original, but forward to a new translation: a new, but never final, version. The performative nature of telling in playback theatre opens up gaps and excesses in the narrative that evade representation and provide opportunities for the performers. Perhaps then the name 'playback' is misleading; if it wasn't such a clumsy title perhaps we should call it 'play-forward' instead.

The Red Coat revisited: concluding remarks

It is now eight years since my father died. What story would I tell now? My argument in this chapter would suggest that any story would serve my present needs and always be inflected by the circumstances of its telling. The red coat is as Phil Mollon (1998) might say 'an illusion' designed to defend me from the terrible finality of death. Recognizing this as I write today in the spring of 2006 I make 'hazy' connections between 'chain-stoking' and 'pipe-smoking' and think of the cigarette I smoked with the neighbour across the road. I wonder if my continuing desire to smoke is in some way related to this – a means of filling the loss with smoke?

I think also of the smoke-blackened London of my father's youth. I have no direct memory of this London except through historical archives and film, yet its images remain a potent means of accessing him. Cultural and popular memory seems to play an important part in constituting personal memory, as Annette Kuhn writes 'as far as memory is concerned, private and public turn out in practice less readily separable than conventional wisdom would suggest' (Kuhn 1995, p.4). Playback performers step into this process of personal and collective memory work. It is likely that they too will possess public memories of pre-war London. It may be that the image of smoky London will also have personal resonances for them which they bring to bear on an enactment of this current story. In enacting these they expand my memory allowing me to find spaces beyond the particularity of my own story. The silence of grief remains but, in some way, it finds its place in our collective history and, as importantly, it is refigured in ways that change memory, self and, perhaps, the spectator.

Like the red coat these images written over and over again – as in a palimpsest – fill a gap that can never be filled. They constitute memory work into which playback performers have intervened and added a new but never final version. However as I shall argue in the next chapter they do so with an abundance of means of representation. Narratives in playback theatre are told primarily through language, but the performers can contribute acoustic, visual, spatial and theatrical images that can significantly extend the teller's memory work.

Chapter 5

A Very Different Kind of Dialogue: The Symbolic in Playback Theatre

Tell all the Truth but let it slant –
Success in Circuit lies.

Emily Dickinson, '1129', *The Complete Poems*,
ed. Thomas Johnson (Faber and Faber, 1970), p.506

In order to mark the end of a conference of psychodramatists, Playback Theatre York was asked to perform to an audience of about 80 delegates who recounted their experience of the weekend. The following sequence describes the telling and the early stages of one of the enactments and it will be used to exemplify some of the discussion in this chapter.

Mary's Story

The teller, 'Mary' (a pseudonym) described her feelings before she came to the conference. She told us that often found these events anxiety-provoking and as she packed her suitcase to go to the conference, she resolved to be less anxious, less 'defended' and to try to take a full part in the conference. With this resolve she attended her first workshop. As it began the leader told the participants that he had decided to do something different than previously advertised. This change of plan shook Mary's confidence and determination to be less anxious. She went into the coffee break determined to put on what she called her 'armour' before returning to the workshop. When she did return the leader announced that he had decided to revert to his original plan.

When asked to do so by the conductor, Mary cast Viv to play herself saying, 'I knew I wanted her to play me'. The conductor asked what it was about Viv that made her choose her and the teller replied that it was 'her stature, she looks safe and strong and she's a survivor. She looks like she has been through it herself'.

[Viv said later to me that she knew that she would be chosen and she was pleased. She said, 'I felt like I grew in stature a bit by being chosen.']

The enactment

'Mary' began the action, carrying a large number of cloths, centre stage. She folded a piece of white cloth saying:

'Yes, black and white, I will need these,' and packed it into her case.

'I know what I want to get out of this conference; I'm clear about that...'

'Mary' then picked up a bright blue cloth, looked at it closely and then said,

'No, I don't think I'll take that!' She threw it aside. The audience laughed.

Later Viv told me the following: 'I had an instinct around her not being glittery. She chose me, and I *knew* she would choose me. When she spoke about me, it was as if she knew me, and what I've been through. In my mind was a line that I thought I might use at some point and that was, "a lot of surviving but not much thriving". I remember a few years ago reading a book, which said something like "Yes you have survived but have you thrived?" Because she chose me, this phrase was going through my mind and black and white seemed to me to be more about surviving than thriving. I didn't think of this at the time, but I went through a time a few years ago when the world seemed black and white and had no colour. I was chucking out the bright glittery colours here because, for me, survival seemed about black and white. She had a stark way of looking at the world. These cloths were aspects of her and how she operated and how she looked at the world.'

I wonder why I was moved when Viv told me this. It was the integrity of her description of course, but it was also my own recognition of the way playback acting can be. There is no doubt that playback can be an encounter with one's own story through the teller's. But to return to the story:

'Mary' picked up a roll of white elastic and wrapped it around her fist and gestured as if she were wearing boxing gloves. The audience laughed loudly. 'Mary' looked up at the audience and said:

'You think they're boxing gloves, don't you – they're not!'

Viv told me:

'I had not intended that they would be boxing gloves. She had talked about armour and I thought the elastic would be useful, later – perhaps to wrap around myself, like we do sometimes! It was difficult to manage because it was all tangled up, so I wrapped it around my hands and then became aware that the audience thought it was boxing gloves. They felt a bit like that to me too and I began to punch with them. I felt that the audience were close and involved with what I was doing and so I was telling them that they may be wrong in their assumption and, as Mary, I was saying, "Yes, I may have armour, but I'm not going to fight".'

'Mary' continued to pack; she held up a piece gold cloth towards the audience wondering aloud if she should take it to the conference. She then turned it around revealing that on the other side it was black. She said 'Yes, I'll take this; I can always wear it inside out'.

Having clearly completed her packing, 'Mary' stood centre stage, alone with a pile of material in her arms and waited. After some time one of the uncast actors (Sarah) stepped forward saying:

'Welcome to the workshop, for the first part could everyone get their blue cloths'.

Sarah told me:

'I had watched the cloths being packed or discarded earlier, there was a dim thought, not a prepared thing, about things being thrown away. I was aware that the blue cloth had been discarded and it was a "fragment" that I held on to. I knew something would come of it. The blue cloth was like a seed – this happens a lot in playback – someone throws out a seed, some grow and some don't. In speaking this line, I consciously wanted to imply through my tone of voice that everyone would of course know about the blue cloth. In bringing it in this way, I left a space for Viv to be with her "lack". I knew she'd step into it; that she'd accept the offer and make something more from its moment.'

'Mary' looked down at the cloths she had brought to discover she did not have a blue one. There was loud and sustained laughter from the audience.

For the remainder of the enactment the disparity between the fabric brought by Mary and those required by the workshop leader was explored. This was the master metaphor that carried the story forward. The vignette carries some important insights into the process of playback performing – the use of the actors' own history, the emergence of an idea – and these will be considered in later chapters. For now however I want to concentrate on the use of the fabric and more generally what I will loosely call 'the symbolic in playback theatre'.

In this sequence it is clear that the pieces of fabric carry multiple meanings – they are polysemic. They 'stand in for' the clothes Mary is packing for the conference; they are representative of her psychic preparation; and later the blue cloth accumulates significance as that for which the teller had not prepared. 'Blue' comes to represent the gap between her preparation and what actually happens in the workshop.

Before looking at the symbolic in more detail it will be helpful here to consider the use of fabric in playback theatre performances. It is usual that the playback stage will include a rail or 'tree' of fabric, 'chosen for their colours and textures' (Salas 1993, p.58), although some companies have decided to dispense with them altogether, because they feel that they clutter the stage (Salas 1993, p.59). The fabric has an indeterminate quality and a versatility that makes it useful for symbolic use. The range of movement, shape, colours and textures that the fabric affords perhaps explains its ubiquity on the playback stage. Salas writes:

> we've found through experimentation that the less structured the cloth props are, the more expressive and versatile they can be. With the audience's imagination already engaged, a piece of fabric can be a convincing bride's dress or an animal skin. Usually, the fabric pieces are most useful as mood elements rather than as costumes... More experienced actors use the fabric props very sparsely, usually for mood or to concretize an element in the story. (Salas 1993, pp.58–9)

Returning to *Mary's Story*: the sequence gives us an insight into the development of the systems of codification in one particular playback theatre performance. It is clear that the fabric is working as more than 'mood elements'; they are beginning to accrue a range of signifying properties. The actor is playing with a distinction in her own mind between 'black and white' and 'glittery' – the former signifying 'surviving'; the latter 'thriving'. She does not, however, inform the spectators of these developing codes. For the spectator a range of possible 'readings' are available. There is, therefore, a certain ambiguity and polysemy in the way that Viv's work with the fabric develops and this is particularly evident when she wraps the elastic around her hands and makes as if to fight with them. The actor is, to some extent, playing with the audience. She is taking advantage of the fact that the audience already know the story and so are 'reading' the action in that knowledge. Salas recognizes this when she suggests that because the audience's imagination is already engaged a piece of fabric can become 'a convincing bride's dress or an animal skin'. The knowledge of the story frames and contains the spectators' reading of what is happening on stage. Viv is teasing the audience with these expectations. The audience was, as she says '*close and involved*' with what she was doing and so she revels with them in the play of possible meanings that her actions might signify. Watching the enactment will be more interesting if expectations are challenged and surprises are possible. Gaston Bachelard writes that 'the entire life of an image is in its dazzling splendour' (1995, p.xxxiii) and later: 'At the level of the poetic image, the duality of subject and object is iridescent, shimmering, unceasingly active in its imagination (p.xix). Viv is taking the audience to that point where the image becomes 'shimmering' and 'unceasingly active'. Ambiguity and lack of certainty allow the images to puzzle, surprise and challenge. In this example the fabric, far from 'cluttering the stage', plays a crucial role in carrying 'meaning'.

The literal and non-literal

The preference for 'non-literal' portrayal of the teller's story is a dominant theme in playback theatre discourse. For example, Playback Theatre York stresses the importance of 'not being literal' and of playing the story 'metaphorically'. Also a criterion for successful playback is often considered to be the degree to which performers eschew a 'literal' performance. The late Francis Batten, an experienced playback theatre teacher and practitioner, told our company after watching us perform at the British Association of Psychodramatists Conference in April 2001, that the company 'were excellent at doing the non-literal' and went on to say that he encourages the groups that he trains to 'work metaphorically'. In another example, Jo Salas writes of 'serious mistakes' in some playback acting. 'Brand new actors in their innocence do not think of anything but the literal, while sophisticated actors know how to move fluently and clearly between the literal and symbolic action on stage' (Salas 1999, p.26).

Not surprisingly considering the difficulty of its definition, 'literal' is being used here as shorthand for a complex of ideas that guide performers. Stern (2000, p.43) suggests three uses of the term 'literal'. First, as something that is clear and unequivocal and lacks ambiguity. Second, as implying the 'empirical' and 'factual', and suggests a certain epistemology in which a distinction may be made between 'the literal truth' and other, perhaps more figurative or rhetorical, ways of speaking. Finally, it is common to use 'literal' to denote that which is precisely transcribed, copied or reproduced.

The distinction between the literal and its antonyms is difficult to maintain. Even the 'plainest' speech often relies on hidden or unacknowledged metaphor and metonymy. Richard Rorty tells us that the distinction between the literal and the metaphorical is the distinction 'between familiar and unfamiliar uses of noises and marks' (Rorty 1989, p.17). He goes on to describe the 'career' of the metaphor:

> it will gradually require a habitual use, a familiar place in the language game. It will thereby have ceased to be a metaphor – or, if you like, it will have become what most sentences of our language are, a dead metaphor. (Rorty 1989, p.18)

Any stable definition of 'literal' is, therefore, clearly problematic: first, because the term is used in very different ways; second, because it is very difficult to speak 'literally' without the use of trope; and finally, because its synonyms – such as plain, unembellished or truthful – often carry ideological and value-laden associations.

The use of the phrase 'literal' seems to be used as a shorthand in playback discourse to describe an enactment that is factual, unambiguous, lacking in symbolic or figurative devices and that may give a 'word-for-word' or 'event-by-event' representation of events. As one member of the York Company said, in a 'literal' playback enactment, 'What you see is what you get': a certain 'plainness' and a lack of the twists, turns, displacements and condensations of the figurative are implied. In playback the injunction to work 'non-literally' may simply be an encouragement to explore a range of theatrical and musical styles, genres and conventions. It is, I would suggest, also about the wish for an excess or abundance of twists and turns that is called for when actors seek to 'portray the story non-literally'.

In this chapter I am using the symbolic loosely to refer to the process, defined by *The Collins Concise Dictionary* (1988) as something that 'represents or stands for something else, usually by convention or association'. Of course most theatre is symbolic since actors and objects 'stand in for' that which they represent. However more precisely I am referring to the performers' choice to substitute one set of signifiers with another, or to 'condense' a number of complex ideas into one metaphor. Consider the use of the fabric in Mary's story, or this example taken from a performance of the Sydney Playback Theatre Company in July 1998:

> The story is told by a man who recounted when, in his youth, he regularly drank too much, took illegal drugs, and got into fights. This period in his life ended when he was arrested and beaten up by the police. The actor cast as him began by taking centre stage and making the sounds and movements of a crowing cockerel. The use of the cockerel continued through the enactment as the police arrived outdoing the younger man with their louder and more vigorous crowing.

In both these examples, a new signifier is chosen to stand in for ones used in the teller's story. In *Mary's Story* the fabric works to convey Mary's anxiety, her preparation and her choices. In the Sydney example the cockerel stands in for the young man's 'cockiness'. Why do the performers choose to effect this substitution? A number of reasons may be suggested why playback theatre practitioners wish to incorporate the figurative and symbolic into their enactments. Each of these reasons emphasize the role the figurative plays in creating performative openness.

1. In therapeutic discourse the most familiar argument for the figurative and metaphorical is that such non-literal means allow the representation of thoughts and feelings that may be inexpressible or be too painful to communicate through more straightforward means. 'The metaphor' Cox and Theilgaard write, 'offers a haven, an asylum for those whose experience is too sharp to disclose – yet too painful to contain' (1987, p.112). In playback theatre, the use of the symbolic may sometimes work to shield teller, audience *and* performers from the full 'reality' of the story.

2. Gaston Bachelard writes of the 'poetic power' of the image. A power that can touch us deeply before thought intervenes. The image, he tells us, 'has touched the depths before it stirs the surface' (Bachelard 1994, p.xxiii). And once received

 > It takes root in us. It has been given us by another, but we begin to have the impression that we could have created it, that we should have created it. It becomes a new being in our language, expressing us by making us what it expresses; in other words, it is at once a becoming of expression, and a becoming of our being. Here expression creates being. (Bachelard 1994, p.xxii)

3. The image, for Bachelard, is before cognition. It is not a representation of something else, but emerges from the depths of being intact as it were and ready, through its expression, to create self. This perspective has implications for playback, since it suggests images are not merely representative devices but have iridescent being.
4. Individual experiences are of course unique; but they also have collective meaning and relevance. It is likely that *Mary's Story*, for example, had elements with which many of the delegates could identify. The use of the symbolic in playback enables the performers to draw the teller's story away from its particular and idiosyncratic detail and so give the audience and the teller an opportunity to enter into closer identification with it on the one hand, and appreciate its wider contextual relationships on the other. The symbolic in playback can loosen the story's particularity and enable the audience to recognize its shared features.
5. In relation to this, as I will argue in Chapter 9, the symbolic can work to protect the actors and tellers from the dangers of over-identification. It opens up a gap between character and actor that enacts the inevitable 'failure' of all playing the other. This stresses the ethical use of symbolic: the inability of the actor to fully stand in for the teller who sits watching is made visible by transposing the story into symbolic form.
6. The figurative and symbolic can often surprise. In doing so it can cast the story in a more unfamiliar light. The actor's choice of the cockerel, for example, produced surprise and delight in the audience and also may have led them to see the story a little differently. Viv's play with the audience around the 'boxing gloves' is another example. On this point Stern quotes Aristotle:

 > Liveliness is specially conveyed by metaphor, and by the further power of surprising the hearer; because the hearer expected

> something different his acquisition of the new idea impresses him all the more. His mind seems to say 'Yes, to be sure, I never thought of that.' (cited in Stern 2000, p.275)

7. It may be that by deploying a wide range of devices – metaphor, symbolism, visual images, rhyme, rhythm, unfamiliar uses of sound – playback can surprise and render the teller's story less familiar. I am arguing here that the symbolic *works to promote open performing.*
8. Symbols are 'pregnant' with meaning and can bear multiple interpretations. Umberto Eco expresses this clearly speaking of 'their vagueness, their openness, their fruitful ineffectiveness to express a final meaning' (Eco 1984, p.130). As he goes on they stand for 'a nebula of alternative and nevertheless complementary contents' (p.161). They are suggestive and invite associations: the fabric in 'Mary's' enactment, for example, accrued a range of different meanings as the piece developed.
9. The symbolic can emphasize the subjective aspects of the teller's story. Playback's dramaturgy employs means of 'symbolization' that bear some relation to dreams and unconscious processes. To some extent it mimics the unconscious world; playback theatre enactments seek to match, or resonate sympathetically with, the processes of memory and the dream which both make active use of the symbolic.

This list will require substantiation in the following pages; however, it is not my intention to deal with each claim in turn – this would compound the reductive problems that are always inherent in listing. One further comment needs to be made with regard to the list. The reader may notice that there is an apparent contradiction between the claim that the symbolic in playback leads to both a heightening of the subjective *and* a step away from the particularity of the teller's story (2 and 5 above). It may be that this apparent contradiction holds an important insight concerning the playback process: that it works around and across the borders between self and other.

The primacy of the signifier

We should imagine the spectators and the performers watching and listening to 'Mary' and seeking to make sense of the emerging enactment. For each person there is a gradual emergence of meanings as the piece develops. Indeed these emergent meanings apply to the actor also; she probably has no clear idea where the action will take her, and instead she 'discovers' the next action through her interaction with the cloth and the audience response to what she is doing. This is probably what Sarah means when she says that the blue cloth becomes a 'seed'. The seed was planted when Viv, as Mary, rejected the blue cloth during her packing; Sarah then 'allows' it to grow as a possible idea and sees her opportunity to use it when she decides to take of the role of the workshop leader. Jacques Lacan's notion of *the primacy of the signifier* will provide a useful tool for understanding this process. I quote a lengthy section to illustrate his argument.

> As a rule, we always give precedence to the signified in our analyses, because it's certainly what is most seductive and what seems at first to be the dimension appropriate to symbolic investigation in psycho-analysis. But in misrecognizing the primary mediating role of the signifier, in misrecognizing that it is the signifier that in reality is the guiding element, not only do we throw the original understanding of neurotic phenomena, the interpretation of dreams itself, out of balance, but we make ourselves absolutely incapable of understanding what is happening in psychosis. (Cited in Dor 1997, p.44)

In his analysis of Poe's story *The Purloined Letter*, Lacan demonstrates his argument for the primacy of the signified. The characters in Poe's story are 'made to act' in response to a letter, received by the Queen. Each character acts according to their desire to discover the content of the letter, devising secret and complex plans to acquire it. Lacan suggests that the letter may be considered the signifier and its contents, the signified. It is the letter, the signifier, which mobilizes the characters – they are acting in response 'to the intolerable nature of the pressure constituted by the letter' (Lacan 1988, p.207). In the same way one may argue that the performers in the above vignette are mobilized by the 'signifier' (the cloth) and follow where it leads. I note, for example, that Sarah's intervention as the workshop facilitator is prompted by her observation of the blue cloth being discarded by 'Mary'. It became a 'seed', a 'dim thought' and 'a fragment to hold on to'. Sarah put this in another way, a way that seemed strange to me at first but now seems to make sense. She said that the blue cloth 'floated into my stomach'. Her metaphor suggests that she 'ingested' the signifier. The properties and possible significations of the blue cloth were working 'inside' her; she was allowing the signifier to loosen from the signified, or to use Bachelard's language the image was allowed its full iridescence.

In my example, we can argue that it is the coloured cloths, as signifiers, that begin to 'govern the network of signifieds'; that they begin to become the 'guiding element' of the enactment. This is illustrated, for example, when Sarah talks about the blue cloth as a 'seed'. In other words the actors (and the spectators, as they follow the development of the piece) begin to follow the logic demanded by their symbolic encounter with the cloth. This counter-intuitive assertion complicates the straightforward assumption that the actors are primarily concerned with the representation of the teller's story. It is my experience, as we shall see in later chapters, that performers often respond as much to the symbolic associations that develop in the course of the enactment as to the teller's story: acting in playback theatre is characterized by a tension between the act of representation of the teller's narrative and the performers' 'encounter' with each other and with the symbolic.

Time, place and dialogue on playback theatre

In order to exemplify the theoretical assertions I have made in the following sections I will consider the ways in which time, place and dialogue are 'performed' in playback enactments.

The representation of time in playback performances

In everyday conversation we often make a distinction between the chronological and the subjective passage of time. We might say for example that an event 'only lasted five minutes, but seemed to go on forever'. Our experience of the passage of time is one way through which we 'measure' the subjective impact of an event upon us. For example, during a performance, a teller described a car journey he made after hearing that his young daughter had disappeared while playing at a friend's house. The journey he told us 'stretched out forever'. That gave clues to the actors about how to represent that car journey. In common with other forms of theatre, playback performances compress and stretch out the passage of time to represent our subjective experience of it and to point to the affective loading attached to the events on stage.

COMPRESSION AND DILATION OF TIME

The French dramatist d'Aubignac wrote in 1657 that a 'Dramatic Poem' has two sorts of time – 'the true time of the Representation', that is the time of the performance itself, and the time of the 'Action represented' (in Brownstein and Daubert 1981, p.72). This simple division will be helpful in analyzing how playback enactments deal with time. In terms of d'Aubignac's first division, playback enactments are often shorter than the telling and usually no longer than seven or eight minutes – a period of time largely dictated by the wish to hear a range of different individual's stories. It is almost always the case that playback enactments involve a considerable compression or, to use the psychoanalytic term, a condensation of time. The events represented are usually of much greater duration than playback's enactment. Occasionally the opposite is the case and playback performers will stretch or dilate time. A teller may recount, for example, a moment of realization, or epiphany or terror, which in chronological time was very brief but which the performers may draw out to explore its subjective/experiential texture.

This compression and dilation of time, although certainly not unique to playback theatre, has important implications: it directs the spectator's attention to the *subjective* experience of time – how the passage of time is represented in memory and in dreams. Our memory of the passage of time is notoriously unreliable. In memory, as in the dream, time does not elapse evenly but jumps forward or dwells at length on a particular episode. Memory compresses, elides or dilates time according to the interests and preoccupations of the 'rememberer'. Through the compression or dilation of time, playback theatre enactments seek to match, or resonate sympathetically with, the processes of memory and the dream.

SEQUENCING

Not only does playback 'play' with the duration(s) of time and but it also does so with its *sequencing.* In playback's discourse, a 'literal' enactment would be said to be one in which the performers follow closely the chronological sequence of the events in the teller's narrative. It is interesting that for Playback Theatre York, one of the most difficult types of story to enact is those that follow a clear chronology. The Company often gives these stories the generic name 'travel' or 'action' stories, stressing the linear nature of the story's narration. An example of this kind of story follows. It was told during a performance to General Medical Practitioners. The audience had been attending a conference entitled *The Arts and GP Practice.* The audience members – between 30 and 40 in number – were largely unknown to each other before the conference; however they had worked together throughout the day using drama to explore professional experience and this may have influenced the level of personal disclosure.

I have written this up from two perspectives: 'the performer' and 'the reflecting actor'. 'The performer' is written in the present tense and aims to capture the performers' experience inside the enactment. The 'reflecting actor' is a kind of first draft of the reflections that pass through the actor's mind during and after the event.

ON THE EDGE

This vignette illustrates the way in which playback performers seek to avoid the linear presentation of events (see Box 5.1). They leave out, for example, the arrival of the aeroplane; they do not point clearly to the departure of the boat or to the arrival in the harbour.

Box 5.1 Avoiding the linear presentation of events

The 'performer'

The teller begins by reminding us that earlier in the performance, when the audience had been invited to give titles to stories they might tell, he had called out the title, 'On the Edge'. *He recounts how, a few years ago, he had flown into Newfoundland. The plane needed to circle the airfield a number of times because of thick fog before landing. As the weather 'closed in', he boarded a boat with a group of fellow travellers intending to visit the ice floes. The weather worsened steadily, it became increasingly cold and ice began to close in on the boat. He tells us how they became progressively more frightened as it became clear that the leader of the expedition could not find a way out of the closing ice. With thick fog and the imminent threat of nightfall, they finally found a way through the ice, returning, with huge relief, to the 'haven' of a small harbour.*

The performers confine the action to the boat, which is indicated to the audience by a piece of elastic stretched into a triangular shape with the teller's actor placed downstage, at the apex of the triangle – suggesting the prow of the boat. As the danger increases the apex is stretched forward toward the audience. There is an increasing threat that the actors holding onto the other sides of the triangle will not be able to hold on. The loosening of the elastic and the return of the protagonist to the other actors, upstage, convey the arrival at the harbour.

The 'reflecting actor'

The problem for the performers in this kind of narrative is how to preserve the sense of progression in the story (from the anticipation of adventure to danger to the safety of the harbour) without a linear representation of the events.

Playback enactments do not have the burden of 'telling the story', since that has already been accomplished by the teller. They must add something or elaborate upon some aspect of the story. The audience may also have experienced the 'threat'. At this point it is possible that they may be struck by the loosening elastic.

What is interesting is that this playback enactment, like most others, tends toward loosening the narrative from what one might call its particularity. This loosening of the story from its particular circumstances may be possible in playback theatre for two reasons. First, the story has already been told and so the performers are, to some extent, released from the task of representing the events in order to tell the story. Second, playback narratives emerge within the context of the performance as a whole. For example, the *On the Edge* story followed a short story from another member of the audience about the impact of listening to a reading of *The Perfect Storm* that afternoon.

In addition, these doctors were attending a course on 'The Arts in GP Practice' and some had spoken about how the proceedings had challenged them and made them think about their practice. It is possible that they may have felt, in some way, 'on the edge' and so this story may have been resonating for them beyond its particularities? The 'threat' of the loosening elastic as it was stretched out towards them may have contributed to a sense of being 'on the edge'. This loosening of the 'literal' signification of a particular story seems to be a property of playback's dramaturgy. Compressing or dilating time as well as altering the sequencing of events may partly achieve such a loosening.

SIMULTANEITY

One further characteristic of playback theatre's treatment of time is that of simultaneity. It is a relatively common feature of the genre that it will present two time frames simultaneously. For example, a childhood episode recounted by the teller may be presented alongside an adult commentary upon it. The 'adult actor' may watch herself, for example, as a child playing with her brother and comment in some way upon the action. This device involves a considerable complexity of gaze for the viewer. Since the teller is always visible to the audience in this simultaneity of time frames, the spectator may view the teller re-viewing herself re-viewing her memory. This complexity of simultaneously available time-frames draws the spectator's attention to act(s) of memory and the representation of experience. It promotes a high degree of reflexivity. The spectators have available to them a range of 'points of view', each of which allows insight into the act of representing the past. The spectator is offered a series of 'meta'-positions but in doing so is paradoxically reminded that there is no panoptic position from which all may be omnisciently viewed. The importance of these multiple viewpoints will be discussed in Chapter 10 when it is proposed that this feature of playback is important in understanding its political purpose.

Playback's tendency to compress or dilate the duration of time, alter sequencing and present simultaneous time-frames, renders an unequivocal reading of meaning in the performance problematic. The spectator becomes aware of the choices made by the actors and of the processes of interpretation that inevitably are involved in the responses to a personal narrative. It supports an argument that playback theatre is concerned with exploring and playing with hermeneusis (the processes through which we make sense of personal experience).

The representation of place in playback theatre

The improvised nature of playback as well as the relatively bare stage makes it impossible for playback performers to achieve a verisimilitude of setting.

The ice floe off Newfoundland in *On the Edge* cannot be represented naturalistically. Of course the task for the spectator is considerably eased because they have already heard the story and know that the events took place in Newfoundland. Nevertheless it is clear that the performers eschew naturalistic means of indicating location. What is of interest here is the way in which the particularities of the environment are drawn into symbolic relationship with the story. Before I examine in detail this characteristic of playback theatre, a brief comparison with psychodrama may be useful.

There are significant differences between playback theatre and psychodrama in the way that the stage is set. In psychodrama the director will usually ask for a clear and detailed description of the environment in which the protagonist's story took place. Care will usually be taken to clarify this for the protagonist, the other actors and the audience. Take, for example, this vignette given as an example of psychodrama practice by Eva Roine:

> Protagonist: I stood by the window watching my father walk along the road toward the house. I knew he was angry and that I would have to account for what I had done.
>
> Director: Does your father come into the room where you are?
>
> Protagonist: Yes, and when he does, I turn around and want to run away.
>
> Director: What does the room look like? Describe it in detail. Where is the door, the window? Is there anyone else there? (Roine 1997, p.127)

This careful geographical orientation is, by and large, absent in playback theatre. The actors themselves make the decisions about how the stage space will be used. This leads, in my experience with Playback Theatre York and in my observations of other playback companies, to a more figurative use of space and relationships within that space. To take Roine's example, in playback theatre the room into which the father walks may be denoted by a single piece of cloth on the floor or the actors might create a shelter, which then is invaded by the returning father. The actors may choose to locate the action in a metaphorical space: a womb, an animal's burrow or a child's playhouse. These decisions would be arrived at, without discussion, in light of the whole story given by the protagonist. If, for example, the teller describes her relationship with her father as one of oppressive power, then this will influence the staging decisions made by the actors.

The ways in which the location of the teller's action is drawn into a symbolic exploration of the story is a relatively common aspect of playback's dramaturgy. This is apparent in the *On the Edge.* All the action takes place on what the spectators may suppose is the boat. However this boat, created by elastic stretched into a triangular shape, is introduced in such a way that it suggests a tension between the excitement and adventure of personal risk and the opposite impulse toward personal safety. It may be that the actors were led to this exploration by the stories that preceded *On the Edge.* One member of the audience had, for example, spoken about the risk of performing in front of his fellow GPs at a workshop that immediately preceded the performance. Additionally, it may be that the 'risk' to the audience, introduced by the stretching elastic may have not only represented the particular story, but also dramatized the sense of risk in the audience.

It seems, therefore, that in playback theatre the actors have a considerable degree of artistic freedom given to them by the form. They are more likely to create a *mise-en-scène* illustrative of either their own interpretation of the psychological and social dynamics of the event or, if provided by the protagonist, of her internal representation of it. This 'symbolization' of place is also evident in *On the Edge.* The physical environment in which the action takes place accumulates symbolic properties as the piece progresses. While the 'telling' is primarily conducted through *verbal* means, the performers in the 'enactment' have a far wider range of systems of symbolization available to them. It will be interesting to consider this further through an analysis of the verbal in playback enactments. It may be instructive to consider, for example, what happens to the teller's words as they reappear in the enactment.

Dialogue in playback theatre

> To a significant extent, drama in playback theatre is not conveyed with words. In fact, the entire thrust of the performance is to take the verbal rendition of experience and translate it into not-so-verbal drama – the dramatic part of the performance is permeated with non-linguistic elements – so much so that playback has often been described as a kind of mime. The process of this particular kind of story dramatization has a hypnotic effect on the audience; they are taken away from their normal rational–intellectual responses. (Fox 1994, p.39)

> It is not a question of eliminating spoken language but of giving words something of the importance they have in dreams. (Artaud 1998, p.191)

There is a tendency, within playback discourse, to favour non-verbal communication over verbal, and, in so doing, to suppose a link between the verbal and the 'rational–intellectual'. A criticism that members of Playback Theatre York often make of their work is that 'it was too verbal' or that 'we talked too much'. We sometimes talk about a 'flight into words' and note that this is often a sign that we are not 'warmed up'. This injunction to avoid words is more complex than it first appears. Playback does not, in its practice, eschew words, rather it uses them in ways which contrast with the usual narrative 'rendition of experience' that was evident in the 'telling' of the story. In practice playback does indeed give words 'something of the importance they have in dreams'. The following examples will illustrate my point and will recall Lacan's notion of the primacy of the signifier, particularly since the slippage of the signifier from the signified is especially evident in dreams.

REPETITION AND THE PRIMACY OF THE SIGNIFIER

This vignette is drawn from a performance that took place to an audience of professionals working in health and social care. The story concerned a woman who was gradually deteriorating from the effects of Alzheimer's disease. The teller, who had been a very close friend of this woman, described how distressed she was at seeing her friend's deterioration. Only two actors were cast – the teller's actor and her friend with Alzheimer's disease. The rest of the actors formed a chorus and commented upon the action. The chorus began to play with the word 'lost':

'I've lost my...'
'I have...'
'I've lost...'
'I'm lost.'
'Lost'
'I'm lost...'
'I have lost my memory'
'I have lost my...'
'I have lost my friend'.

There are two important points to note here. First, that the chorus build up the phrases, repeating them in different ways for emphasis. This type of repetition is common in playback theatre enactments. Second, the chorus is playing upon the word 'lost', exploring its different possible meanings to progress the enactment. The word 'lost' has at least three meanings in this extract – being lost, losing memory and losing a friend. The signifier 'lost' begins to slip and slide as the actors play with it and, for me, there is a poignancy in allowing the word 'lost' to encompass both the loss of memory and the loss of a friend. The slippage of the signifier permits a dream-like process of 'condensation' in which, as Freud wrote, 'collective and composite figures and...strange composite structures' (Freud 1995, p.61) are created. This process of condensation is, as Lacan points out, analogous to the metaphoric process of signifying substitution (Dor 1997). In an analogous fashion to metaphor, in condensation:

> the latent elements that present shared characteristics fuse together [lost my friend and lost my memory], so that they are all represented on the manifest level by a single element [lost]. This is how the composite characters, collective figures, and neological composites that inhabit our dreams are made. (Dor 1997, p.59)

EMERGING DIALOGUE

There is another aspect to the dialogue of playback theatre that gives it 'something of the importance it has in dreams' and that is the fact of its *improvised emergence.* Lacan tells us that 'the anchoring point' in dialogue operates so that the signifier is prevented from sliding away, as it were, from the signified. For Lacan, in dreams and in psychotic experience, the anchoring point is loosened or absent, so the signifiers gain primacy. I would suggest that because playback dialogue is improvised within ensemble, there is a certain loosening of the anchor between the signifier and the signified because its direction is not under the control of one person – it is emerging through polyphonic encounter. Consider this piece of dialogue taken from a story in which 'Mike', now married and with young children meets an 'old flame' and looks back, somewhat regretfully at 'what might have been'. The actor playing Mike is running a piece of long white cloth through his hands as he contemplates the time that has passed.

Mike: So much stuff (running white cloth through his hands).

Laura: Show me (stepping downstage and directly addressing the audience). I wonder what it would have been like?

Mike: O God, yes.

Laura: Is it a bit stupid then? It's a long time ago.

Mike: One could have...

Laura: Life takes its turns and...

Mike: ...and goes on this and that path.

Laura: If I'd turned another way.

Mike: But just supposing, just supposing, just supposing. You really turned me on you know.

Laura: I know.

In this sequence the 'usual forward-moving, speaker–listener/listener–speaker, turn taking system' (Aston and Savona 1991, p.64) of conversation is subverted. Through a combination of dramatic asides ('I wonder what it would have been like'), repetition and short incomplete sentences, the actors convey a sense of longing and regret. Their lines seem to drift off into wistful yearning. Their reflections are interrupted when, after 'Mike' says, 'You really turn me on you know', an uncast actor leads the wife, 'Rachel', across the diagonal.

The actors are improvising this sequence together; they are picking up on each other's cues:

Laura: Life takes its turns and...
Mike: ...and goes on this and that path.

They are also making their own 'offers', initiating ideas to develop the 'conversation'. The above has not been pre-planned or rehearsed, and this has, at least, two important implications for an understanding of dialogue in playback theatre. First, one might ask the question: if these lines do not come from a text, how are they created? Or to ask a question often posed by audience members after a performance: how did you know what to say? This is a complex question and I will consider it in more detail in later chapters. The performers, one would suppose, draw from personal experience, from an understanding of the teller's story and from a cultural storehouse of similar kinds of stories. They 'accept offers' (Johnstone 1981) given by other actors and respond to cues given them by fellow performers. They do so with sufficient openness and spontaneous engagement to allow the enactment to 'emerge' rather than to be determined by a pre-existing plan.

Second, dialogue in playback theatre is generated as the performers respond to the 'here and now' exigencies of the stage environment. Instead of ignoring the 'extra-textual' problems that performers often face on stage it is relatively common for playback performers to make use of them. To some extent, dialogue in a playback theatre enactment is 'discovered' or 'encountered' in relationship. It requires the actors to maintain a high level of awareness in the here and now and to be able to respond spontaneously to the changing circumstances of the performance. As there has been no opportunity for the actors to explore what impact the text may have on the audience or on other performers, as there would be for actors working from a dramatic text, the actors are discovering the impact of their words only as they speak them. They discover this from the reaction of the other actors, the audience and from the impact the words have on the developing action.

But, as playback actors often say, words can be a kind of avoidance, a distraction or a refusal to enter into the teller's story. Enactments are sometimes criticized for relying too heavily on words. Words are ubiquitous; they may easily lose their currency. A descent into cliché and stereotype is a constant possibility in improvised dialogue, since the paradox remains that in improvising speech it is difficult to avoid stock phrases and formulaic routines: in responding spontaneously it is difficult to be fresh. Cliché might be seen as language that has lost its vibrancy and texture through repetition. Dialogue in successful playback maintains that vibrancy and texture through a willingness of the performers to play with the signifiers and to allow verbal sequences to emerge through relationship and encounter.

Ethical concerns: getting lost in the symbolic

> There can be a danger in going too far in the direction of abstract representation. Above all we need to see the story. If the actors launch themselves into the stratosphere of symbolic action, the essential particularities of the teller's story can get lost. The meaning of the experience can only express itself in the actual events of the story, where it happened, when, who was there, what did they do and say. (Salas 1993, p.61)

Salas' warning is a wise one for playback performers. The performers can get lost in the 'stratosphere of symbolic action' and lose touch with the teller's story. This happens in playback performances sometimes, usually when the actors have not listened to the story or the story is unclear or it is not 'grounded' in real life events. This danger is surely behind the experienced playback performer Peter Hall's statement that effective playback maintains 'a tension between literal truth and poetic truth', as he explained to me during a meeting in Australia.

Performers need to freely enter into play on stage in order to explore the possible meanings, associations and references suggested by the story, but this can raise significant ethical issues. Are playback actors just messing around with the teller's story, throwing the pieces of the jigsaw in the air, scrambling its pieces, holding up one piece to the light for close inspection, totally ignoring other pieces – placing pieces together in ways that were not suggested by the original? There is a steady space to which the performers need to return: it is the teller's story, to which they must remain 'loyal'. That is the 'original' that will prevent the performers 'drowning' or being lost in the 'stratosphere of symbolic action'. Despite the fact, as we have seen in Chapter 4, that the teller's story is dependent upon associations, references to other texts, unreliable memories and the particular context of its telling, it remains the solid ground on which the teller's need to maintain a foothold.

Concluding remarks

In this chapter I have explored the use of the symbolic in playback theatre enactments. My suggestions point toward the conclusion that the substitution on one set of signifiers by another, the play with signifiers and the consequent surprise and ambiguity that are produced contribute to *openness* of performing and telling. This openness, as I will continue to propose through this book, is designed to open up new horizons – to open up new ways of making sense of our experience. Playback is far more than the replay of the past it is the re-figuring of the past to release us from its power to control the present and future.

Chapter 6

On 'The Narrow Ridge': The Performers' Response to the Story

From The Playback Theatre Rehearsal: A Short Story

(Please see Appendix 1 for the full story.)

Bruno felt he was bursting. His heart was thumping hard and he had a sick feeling. He knew Rona would choose him and he knew what he would do. Well no, that wasn't quite true. It would be more accurate to say that he had no worries about what he would do. An insistent energy would carry him. Amanda's music was feeding that energy, viscerally changing Bruno, and he used it to find his place on the stage. He dragged one of the chairs into the centre of the stage, and drawing himself in as tightly as he could manage, he sat on the chair and waited. He knew that the other actors would be forming a tableau around him but he couldn't see anything; they must all be behind him. He could hear, but not see, movement. It went silent and, it seemed to Bruno, rather dark. They too were waiting, he guessed.

There is a directional instruction that the company had often spoken about. It was that if, as an actor, you do not know what to say it is often effective to say how you are feeling at that moment because it is probably related to the character you are playing. Remembering this, Bruno said,

'I can't see you, it's dark here. Where are you?'

Enclosed tightly, as he was by his arms and by the hardness of the chair, Bruno waited. It seemed to him that his words were spreading a cold darkness across the stage and, he guessed, were freezing the actors. He felt a moment of panic. 'They don't know what to do with this,' he thought.

However, he was determined to stay with it, to wait. He could hear movement in the darkness, a quick movement across the stage to somewhere in front and to the left of him. There was silence and then a sound, he wasn't sure, but it was as if someone's lips were moving, mouthing sounds with no words.

There was something terrible about this sound and, in the darkness, he felt, for a fleeting moment, a terrible emptiness. The sound had a nightmarish quality, like a child calling for help through sheets of impenetrable glass. He could hear some movement too and he imagined grotesque, spastic movements.

He called out, 'I can hear you! Do you need help?' The sound continued, oblivious to his call. He repeated, 'I can hear you! Do you need help?' There was no response.

A voice whispered in his ear, 'Can you not hear her? She needs your help.' Bruno experienced a shock; he had been so caught up in that sound in the darkness that he had totally forgotten about the other actors.

'Open your eyes; look at her,' continued the voice.

Bruno couldn't open his eyes. If he did everyone would see him, and he couldn't bear the thought of that.

'I can't, she'll see me,' he found himself saying.

'What will she see?' asked the voice which he now identified as Lawrence. Bruno didn't know, or at least, he couldn't find the words for it. He felt exposed and suddenly aware of Rona and Laura watching him. He felt he was holding things up, he worried he was boring everyone. It seemed all of a sudden, rather boring, self-indulgent and not very good theatre. He had forgotten Rona's story and was now somehow playing out his own. Almost unbearably the face of his daughter formed in his mind – that terrible look of accusing pain that she had given him when she first went into hospital.

With a massive effort of will Bruno said, 'I've been to the hospital today, I've had some tests.'

He opened his eyes. What surprised him first was the light. The harsh light of the church hall seemed so merciless, so terribly everyday. It hid nothing and so showed nothing. He then saw the source of those strange mouthing sounds: it was Bridget. Of course, he knew it would be her, but nevertheless he was surprised. He was surprised by the presence of her – a vulnerable presence, looking at him, present, sensual, alert.

'Why didn't you tell me before, Dad?' said Bridget.

'I didn't want to worry you, it may be nothing – and there's no point worrying about things that may never happen,' and warming to a theme which suddenly occurred to him and struck him as characteristic of Rona's father, he continued:

'Don't worry! Smile, it may never happen! You've got to keep going, no point in worrying, you'll make yourself ill.'

For the first time Bruno was aware of Rona. He heard a sound like a sigh or a stifled laugh. He then realized that Bridget was angry with him.

'Smile…that's what you always do…so much talking and smiling, you never listen, do you? You never listen…'

'Whoa, hold your horses. Wait one doggone minute.' Where this came from Bruno had no idea, clichés were piling up, one upon the other, and Bruno seemed to have no control over them. He was still in the chair, but was now leaning forward, his hand reaching out towards Bridget to silence her.

He wondered if he should go over to her but he rejected the idea. There had to be that space between them. It was filled with tension, longing and fear.

Then Bridget turned toward the audience.

'He always does this, he silences me, not by force but by a kind of tenderness...' She searches for the words. 'Everything is so fragile...the fear that if I speak I will break him, destroy him – destroy us.' She emphasizes the 'us' surprised by the power of this idea.

For the first time Bruno is aware of Amanda. She has been playing a steady insistent beat throughout, but it is only now that he really hears her, she sings with a plaintive, resonant voice,

> A kind of tenderness
>
> He destroys me
>
> With a kind of tenderness.

Bridget turns to Bruno and across the space, which seems, at this minute, vast to Bruno, she says:

'You couldn't hear me could you? When it was getting darker and colder, when you were so far away and it seemed so long until Christmas, you couldn't hear me. And now Dad, I don't know how to hear you.'

Bridget turns to Rona, the singing stops and there is silence. Bruno sees the tears on Rona's cheeks and realizes he is shivering.

Laura reaches into her pocket, finds a tissue and hands it to Rona,

'Well, Rona...'

Rona hated this bit; she always felt that she had to say something. She really wanted to let it settle, take it in, hold onto it and not share it with anyone else. The actors were looking at her expectantly.

'I don't know what to say,' she said wiping her eyes and blowing her nose. 'It was when Bridget said "a kind of tenderness"...that broke my heart. There is a tenderness there...but there's no...' She searched for the word. 'That's it...there's no robustness. I wish we could shout at each other a bit more...and Bruno, when you said, "smile, it may never happen" it was so like him!' Everyone laughed.

'I was worried I had gone over the top,' said Bridget, 'I just felt so angry when he said that bit about smiling, I want to hit him'...she growled and hit Bruno on the arm.

'Ow!' He cried, 'I just couldn't bear you to be worried...it was like I was talking to Sally...' he suddenly broke off and there was a pause.

'Of course! I hadn't thought of that... I knew I had to choose you to be my dad.'

'I knew you would,' Bruno smiled and Rona returned his smile.

Lawrence looked miserable. Laura asked, 'what's wrong, Lawrence?'

'I don't know, I feel so out of it...probably to do with not having a role.'

'Have you a story?'

'Yes,' said Lawrence.

Rona, Bruno, Bridget and Fran sat on the actors' chairs and Amanda returned to her music.

On 'the narrow ridge': the performers' response

A row of three to four actors are seated on the stage facing the audience, to their right a 'teller' recounts her story. Soon they will have to improvise that story for the teller and the audience. What is going on in the minds and bodies of the performers as they prepare for the enactment that will follow? What thoughts, impulses, images and ideas motivate the performers toward dramatic action? As they listen to the autobiographical narrative, what are they listening out for and what are the principles that inform their reception of the story? An investigation into the performers' response may provide insights into both the often hidden processes at work when we listen to autobiographical narratives *and* the strategies of representation used to dramatize them. It certainly will give some indication of what is happening in the minds and bodies of the performers as they begin the dramatization. Our response to a personal story is always more than a cognitive one. Emotion, image, memory and the body intervene to influence how we read and respond to the story.

This chapter will consider what is happening as the performers listen to the story. Analysis therefore will extend only to the point at which the actors begin to improvise together. Once the improvisation begins the complexity of the process increases exponentially. As one of the interviewees stated, 'This is where the fun begins' – when actors begin the complex negotiation and interaction that takes place in an improvisation. Up to this point, performers have developed, what one interviewee called, a 'template' for action which they will need to modify, assert or relinquish in the course of the interaction.

The following analysis will draw on a number of sources including personal experience and playback literature. However it will be structured around interviews conducted during the spring of 2005 with eight performing members of Playback Theatre York. These interviews took place either on the telephone or face-to-face; they were largely unstructured improvised conversations which began with my expression of interest: 'I am interested in what happens and what you are looking out for as you listen to the teller's story'. As the series of interviews progressed, the content of previous sessions sometimes prompted questions and opened up new areas of enquiry. Subsequently a number of themes have been developed, which although expressed differently by different performers, ran through all the interviews; these will help in structuring the chapter.

On the narrow ridge

In talking to actors, what is striking is the sense in which they seem to be working across a number of tensions; they seek to maintain a position between seeming opposites. Here are three examples of this as they have emerged through the interviews:

1. The actors need, in the words of one performer, to 'yield to the story' and allow themselves to be 'penetrated' by it, *while simultaneously* making use of their understanding of narrative structures and theatrical conventions to represent it.
2. They need to search in their memories for identification and empathy, *while at the same time* preserving some 'distance' to ensure the ethical and aesthetic representation of what they have heard.
3. They need to allow the enactment to emerge through improvisation with other performers, *while ensuring* that they continue to tell the story they have heard.

It may be that the capacity of the actors to maintain the tension between these apparent contradictions is a key constituent of 'open performing'. In other words, for a sense of ambiguity, indeterminacy and possibility to be maintained the performers need to stay on the 'narrow ridge' between attending to the self and telling the story; and between live performance on one hand and the representation of the story on the other. These tensions will emerge with more clarity through this and the subsequent chapter.

In order for this theoretical formulation to make sense, it is necessary to look in more detail at what performers experience as they listen to the story. Although, in this chapter, I have separated out some of the influences on the listening performers, it is important to appreciate these as intricately interactional and interleaved. Playback performing is a complex activity and one that is impossible to reduce into a closed, neatly articulated structure.

'The Story stuff'

It is striking that all of the interviewees began their answer to the question about what was going on as they listened to the story by saying that they attend first to what one interviewee called the 'story stuff'. Not surprisingly they all stressed the importance of remembering the sequence of events, the names of the main characters (especially that of the teller), and they looked out for 'crucial phrases' that they might subsequently use in the enactment. The performers attributed great importance to remembering these details accurately; this was not only because they would need to represent the story, but also because remembering the details was an indication of attentiveness, acknowledgement and care. As one performer put it, the story is 'precious cargo' that needs to be handled carefully. Although as many interviewees told me, stories have 'universal' and 'archetypal' elements it is their 'particularity' (names, places, particular expressions etc.) that makes them unique. To remember these details is to preserve the dignity of the individual story.

Remembering the chronology of events may also maintain the psychological safety of narrative order. Robert Musil expresses this clearly in *The Man Without Qualities*:

> [W]hen one is overburdened...the basic law of this life, the law one yearns for, is nothing other than that of narrative order... Terrible things may have happened to him, he may have writhed in pain, but as soon as he call tell what happened in chronological order, he feels contented as if the sun is warming his belly. (Cited in Abbott 2002, p.81)

It may be important for performers to remember events and details in their order to build the kind of trust between performers and audience members that is necessary for the handling of this precious cargo. As Musil's passage indicates, personal narratives – and perhaps a sense of identity – are held together by the 'cement' of chronology and factual detail.

In contrast to this, many of the performers also spoke about listening out for the 'sub-text' or for 'what the teller does not say' or 'what lies behind the story'. One person said about her particular response to a story that 'it was there hidden in the folds, in the gaps, of her story'. What can we make of this desire amongst performers to attend to the unsaid? Does this not raise ethical issues concerning the performers' right to reveal aspects of the story that had not consciously been intended? The danger of 'imposing' psychological interpretations is recognized by Jo Salas:

> Interpretation in the psychological sense means imposing one's therapeutic insight on the story; it is distinct from artistic interpretation, the filtering of the story through one's artistic sensibility, a process which is integral in playback. (Salas 1999, p.29)

Despite this necessary warning, narratives are, as Paul Cobley tells us, shot though with indeterminacies such that 'readings' will always involve imaginative speculations. When we listen to a story we add our own perspectives and colour it with our own experience. Wolfgang Iser expresses this succinctly in respect of the literary text: 'The stars in a literary text are fixed; the lines that join them are variable' (in Cobley 2001, p.137). As we shall see in the remainder of this chapter, there is no doubt that the performers while listening to the story are also starting to draw lines between the fixed 'stars' of the teller's account.

The self and the playback performer

> Perhaps the most demanding role of all is one that traditional actors are not usually called upon to master – being oneself. (Salas 1993, p.47)

> I want to yield to the teller's story. (A playback actor)

On the surface the positions represented by these two quotes seem contradictory. The first stresses the importance of the actor's self; the second emphasizes the desire to relinquish the self in order to yield to the story. There seems to be an apparent paradox with regards to the use of the self in the discourse of playback performing. On the one hand, practitioners will maintain that actors must be 'authentic' or be themselves. On the other hand, they will talk about 'letting go' of the self in order fully to play the teller's story. It seems that actors need to use the self and simultaneously relinquish the self.

What is important about these apparent paradoxes is that they make us re-examine our reasoning. The seemingly contradictory statements made regarding playback acting may offer us the opportunity to re-consider the self in performance. A consideration of each 'side' in this apparent contradiction will therefore be helpful.

Being oneself

In Chapter 5 I wrote of being moved by Viv's description of listening and empathizing with the teller's story. A description which I considered clearly demonstrated how playback can be an *encounter with one's own story* through the teller's. Performers inevitably filter the teller's story through their own experience. For example at one performance held soon after the death of my mother, a man told of the loss of his own mother and cast me to play him. It was inevitable that I would draw on my own experience to perform his story. There is no doubt that this enriched and energized the performance. But there is also no doubt that it endangered it, in the sense that it heightened the risk that my own experience would eclipse the teller's. These are discussions that I will consider in more detail in Chapter 9. For now I want to confine myself to exploring the self in performance.

The privileging of self-revelation of the actor is not new. Jacob Moreno requires that the protagonist/actor is

> asked to be himself on the stage, to portray his own private world. He is not an actor compelled to sacrifice his own private self to the role imposed upon him by the playwright. (Moreno 1987, p.140)

In a similar vein, the theatre director Constantine Stanislavski writes that the actor should not submit himself solely to the wishes of the director or the playwright but, in order to enter his role, 'he must use his own living desires, engendered and worked over by himself, and he must exercise his own will and not that of another' (Stanislavski 1995, p.254).

There has been a thread running through dramatic theory and practice, certainly since Stanislavski, which Richard Drain (1985), in his anthology of 20th century theatre theory, terms the 'Inner Dimension'. The demand for the revelation of the actor's self on stage can be seen in the work of Artaud, Grotowski, Copeau, Brook and Julian Beck for example. In different ways these practitioners and theorists have sought to establish theatre practice which is wholly or largely based on the self-exploration of the performers. They have often contrasted their work, as do Salas and Fox, with what they perceive to be a traditional or conventional theatre practice characterized by artifice, the subjection of the actor to the playwright or director, and the disappearance of the actor's self behind the role. Consider the words of Jerzy Grotowski, one of the most rigorous exponents of 'self revelation' in acting who writes:

> When I say that the action must engage the whole personality of the actor [...] it is a question of the very essence of the actor's calling, of a reaction on his part allowing him to reveal one after the other the different layers of his personality, from the biological-instinctive source via the channel of consciousness and thought, to that summit which is so difficult to define and in which all becomes unity. (Grotowski 1995, pp.279–80)

Grotowski seems to be saying that there is, at the 'summit', a unified foundational self – a 'soul', perhaps, that becomes a 'gift' and a 'provocation'. According to Philip Auslander, the problem with these ways of conceptualizing acting is that, without considerable nuance, they

> designate the actor's self as the *logos* of performance...and assume that the actor's self precedes and grounds her performance and that it is the presence of the self in performance that provides the audience with access to human truths. (Auslander 1995, p.60)

It presupposes in some way that the actor has a stable, authoritative reference point beyond mediation. It suggests that there can be a 'true' self beyond culture, language and context. Can we trust the 'self' as a source of 'truth' when playing the other? Does not the ineffable 'otherness of the other' always escape the inevitable limitations of the 'authentic actor'? It is the distrust of the self that gives currency to the seemingly contradictory position with regard to playback acting.

Yielding

Describing what she tries to do as she listens to the story, one playback actor told me that she wants to 'open up to the story'. The actor, she says, needs to 'yield' and be 'penetrated by the story'. Although not using this language, many of the performers speak of letting go of the self in order that they can 'hear the story deeply'. Phrases like 'making yourself defenceless' or 'letting go of the ego' were used to convey a particular attitude that is required for effective listening. The notion that the actor should in some way relinquish the self was regularly stated by playback actors.

It is possible to trace this desire to 'yield' to the other through a number of influential 20th century sources. The place to begin is, as Jonathan Fox does, with the theologian Martin Buber's analysis of the relationship between 'I' and 'Thou'. This has proved to be influential in conceptualizing an experiential and person-centred 'encounter' between the self and the other. He calls for a relationship characterized by the deep and present sensing of the other in which 'All real living is meeting [sometimes translated as encounter]' (Buber 1958, p.25). He goes on to write:

> The relation to the *Thou* is direct. No system of ideas, no foreknowledge, and no fancy intervene between *I* and *Thou*... No aim, no lust, and no anticipation intervene between *I* and *Thou*. Desire itself is transformed as it plunges out of its dream into appearance. Every means is an obstacle. Only when every means had collapsed does the meeting come about. (Buber 1958, p.25)

What Buber is calling for is a profound openness between 'I' and 'Thou' so they the other may be fully apprehended. This aspiration is recognizable in the psychotherapist Carl Rogers' notion of 'person-centeredness' which is characterized by qualities of unconditional positive regard, empathy and 'congruence' (genuineness and honesty). Inspired as he was by Buber, Rogers calls for a change in the therapeutic relationship which is neatly summarized by Peter Schmid as 'a shift of paradigms from the object to the person, from observation to encounter, and from interpretation to empathy' (Schmid 1998, p.50).

It seems that to 'yield' to the other is an act of empathy in which the self is suspended in order to 'walk in the shoes' of another. Perhaps it is Rowan and Jacob's notion of 'empathic resonance' that is most useful in helping to conceptualize the simultaneous desire of the playback performer to 'be oneself' and to 'yield' to the teller. These writers talk of acoustic resonance. They write:

> When two violins are located in the same room and a string is plucked on one, the string tuned to the same frequency on the other will also

> vibrate [...] This is not merely imagining, extrapolating or interpreting cues; the epistemic process is more direct. Subjectivity is suspended to attune to the other. (Rowan and Jacobs 2002, p.80)

Between being yourself and yielding

A closer examination of the responses of playback performers suggests that they are not wishing so much to relinquish the self as to open themselves up to 'deeper', somatic and subconscious promptings. For example Di said that she tries to, 'concentrate on listening, and let the story, my body, mind and heart go with it – then something will come.' Many of the interviewees mentioned that 'ego stuff' was a significant obstacle to listening: 'I try to let go of my ego stuff – my need to be seen as wonderful. If I am worried about how people see me I block myself.'

What is suggested here is not so much a relinquishing of self implied by the language of yielding and penetrating, but rather allowing the self to resonate with the other. Steve, one of the performers, uses this metaphor when he speaks of 'attuning to the emotional tone of the teller'. Sarah talks of 'drinking in the story' and in my own practice the idiosyncratic technique I employ is to 'breathe in' the story – as if 'inspiring' will lead me to inspiration.

This notion of 'yielding' raises significant issues that are not settled amongst playback performers. To what extent is it possible for them to relinquish their own subjectivity in this way? Is it not the case that as Josselson, with respect to writing ethnography, warns 'No matter how gentle and sensitive our touch, we still entangle ourselves in others' intricately woven tapestries' (Josselson 1996, p.70)? Furthermore if this yielding is possible is it desirable? As many of the performers pointed out to me, they need to listen beyond what the teller is saying. Claire, for example, drawing on her training with Jonathan Fox, talked of listening for three dimensions in the story:

- the personal: 'what does this story mean to me?'
- the communal: 'what is the story saying to the people in the audience?'
- the global: 'what implications does this story have beyond this performance?'

For her, the notion of 'yielding' is too passive and she preferred a more reciprocal relationship between listener and teller in which the former was more actively involved in making sense of the story. From this perspective, the risk is that ideas of 'yielding' deny the interpretive activity of the listener.

The notion of empathy has for some time been out of fashion – no doubt because of the radical recognition of difference called for in poststructuralist thought. From that standpoint the possibility of suspending subjectivity seems a fantasy and a pipedream; how can we ever apprehend the other free of culture and desire? But just because we recognize the inevitable dangers of empathizing with the other, there is no need to abandon it as a possibility and an aspiration. It may be that an aspiration to 'attune' ourselves to the other is crucial in a contemporary world in which the dangerous tendency to wilfully misunderstand others threatens civic life (Arnold 2005).

With respect to the use of the self in playback acting, it seems that performers need to maintain a tension between 'being oneself' and 'relinquishing' the self. To employ Buber's language, actors need to hold a position on 'the narrow ridge where *I* and *Thou* meet' – a place he terms the realm of 'between' (1949, p.32). They need to listen carefully to the self, but also to be very cautious of the self's desire. While recognizing that they will inevitably 'contaminate' the teller's story with their own subjectivity, they need to bring the self into 'acoustic resonance' with the teller – and later, of course, with the other performers.

'Whatever in me is jangling'

Describing what happens to her as she listens to the teller's story, Viv told me that she tries to notice 'whatever in me is jangling'. This metaphor suggests at least three areas for attentiveness on the part of the performer:

1. The first may be thought of as what 'rings a bell' for the actor – in other words, what personal memories are activated by the story. The performer is listening out for opportunities to identify with the teller's experience.
2. In some way, the story will 'jangle' in the performer's body and suggest possible directions for action and movement.
3. The jangling metaphor also suggests that there may be promptings on the part of the actor of which she is only vaguely aware – what may be called 'subconscious promptings' which suggest movement, dramatic action or narrative structuring.

I will consider these inter-related aspects of the actors' experience in turn.

Identification and the activation of personal memory

Personal memory can be a key source in response to the teller's story. Playback theatre can be an encounter with one's own story through the tellers. Consider this example which took place during a performance for people involved in a voluntary agency, which offered support to users of health services and professionals wanting to change the current provision. I was the actor in this example:

The teller described a period in his life in which he was 'desperate' and in a state of 'terror'. He chose me to play him. I stood up. He said that during his period of 'depression' his mother had died. It was a time in which he was overwhelmed and distressed by persecutory thoughts. He spent days in his room, afraid to come out. He described how, after his mother's death, he moved back to the North East and gradually began to improve with the help of family and friends. The conductor asked him for a title, he suggests 'Deliverance'.

I felt a strong identification with the teller – I recognized the obsession with persecutory thoughts, the wish to hide and I thought I knew what he meant by the word 'deliverance'. I was reminded of a period in my twenties when I had had similar experiences. I noticed my breathing was becoming heavier and there are 'churning' feelings in my stomach. I concentrated on these feelings, knowing that I could make use them in the enactment.

For Louise, the process of identification began at the beginning of the performance event and continued as the actor was chosen to be the protagonist.

In the pre-performance 'mingling', I was drawn to a group of young people sitting in the front row and talked to them about what had brought them to the performance. One of the young women, in particular, drew my attention. I had the experience of looking in the mirror and the face that looked back at me was one I know well. During the performance I found my eyes inadvertently meeting hers and a warm glance passed between us. This young woman came forward to tell the last story of the performance. I knew that she would probably choose me to be her and I was delighted when she did.

Their descriptions clearly exemplify the complex processes of identification at work as the actor listens to the story. This capacity for identification was stressed in different ways by all the performers I spoke to. As is evident in the example above, this can occur when the actor directly remembers an episode in their own life which is in some way analogous to that of the teller. It can also occur less consciously, as we shall see later, when the actor is aware of somatic and, what I will call, 'subconscious promptings'.

It is not necessarily the case however that the performers' personal identification derives from specific incidents in their life history. Consider this example provided by Di:

I remember a story in which the teller talked of 'the ghosts outside the window'. The image produced a strong reaction in me and it became the centre of my performance. It produced a physical spine-chilling sensation. I identified with it in some way – although now I have some idea what I was identifying with, at the time I didn't. I didn't try and analyze, I just went with it to see what would happen.

This search for identification with the teller is always risky. Marie, in common with many of those I spoke to, warned of the dangers of what she called over-identification: 'I used to identify too much – I don't do that as much now – it feels like it is robbing them a bit – like taking the story away from them'. This is a key point that will be considered more thoroughly in Chapter 9. For now however it is important to note the anxiety that actors have about identifying with the teller's story.

John Rowan conceptualizes identification along a continuum between over-identification in which the listener (in his case the therapist)'...becomes overly enmeshed' (Rowan and Jacobs 2002, p.52) and 'disidentification' where the listener fails to identify sufficiently. In playback theatre there is, as Marie and other interviewees told me, a risk of over-identification, in which the idiosyncrasy and ineffability of the other is erased by a naive assumption of 'sameness' between the listener's and the teller's experience. Disidentification may occur when the performer is anxious about self-performance and technique, or when external concerns are interrupting their capacity to empathize. In these cases the listener finds no connection to the teller's story. Both over-identification and disidentification are significant barriers to effective playback performing.

The useful body

> It is through my body that I understand other people. (Merleau-Ponty 1962, p.186)

Stanislavski writes the following:

> An actor on the stage need only sense the smallest modicum of organic physical truth in his action or general state and instantly his emotions will respond to his inner faith in the genuineness of what his body is doing. (Stanislavski 1983, p.150)

Most improvising performers must rely heavily on the body. With no written text to guide them they often find impetus through somatic impulses. An awareness of, and relinquishing to, the body seems to be important for the improvising performer (Marshall 2001; Pisk 1990; Zinder 2002). In a rather intimidating passage, for example, Lorna Marshall writes:

> you must be able to bring your body into free and easy contact with the emotions, other performers, the language of the text, style of presentation and, eventually, the audience. It must be fully alive, in dialogue with your inner life, and able to vividly express a chosen human reality. (Marshall 2001, p.9)

Her language, at this point, is full of imperatives, yet she does express what, in my experience of playback theatre, is relatively common: for the actor to make use of the physical experiences that occur both during the telling of the story and in the performance. It is clear from talking to playback performers that the process of identification engages at the somatic as well as at a cognitive/emotional level; autobiographical stories produce changes in the body of the listener.

For example, Sarah described a 'scream' that seemed to begin somewhere in her gut:

...I remember a scream coming from my gut. In the deepest part I was listening from there was a scream. It was like a dark cavern. I couldn't put words to it – an ache in me. The scream started as I listened to the story – I felt it in the pauses – it was not something that was said exactly, but it was there hidden in the folds in the gaps of her story. It started in my body. I don't know – it touched an old, pre-verbal, place of knowing. I felt connected to this, to her, and – in that moment – imagined I felt all our connection to it: her, me, the company , the audience, our collective humanity; where the edges of our unconscious selves touched hands and made a whole.

Another performer summarized her thoughts about the use of the body in playback acting by saying: 'I am trying to notice what parts of the body I am feeling the story in'. This use of somatic response amongst playback actors seems to be common. They are not alone in this: Robert Shaw remarks on the increasing importance given by therapists to their own somatic responses to the client. He writes:

> By being aware of what our bodies are saying to us while working therapeutically, and with the ability to use this information in an overt manner, it is possible to contribute to the intersubjective nature of therapy. Our embodied sense is a means of contributing to a therapeutic story that is co-constructed by client and therapist. (Shaw 2003, p.156)

There are two warnings that need to be made here. First, it is risky to regard the body as a primary and unproblematic source of 'truth'. The 'arrival' of these bodily sensations does not come, as it were, 'out of the blue'; they are located in an immanent network of associations triggered by the teller's story and the style of its telling. Sensations that are present in the actor's body are always mediated through its representations. The body cannot simply be conceived of as an originary source; the body is ideological. As Bordo writes: 'The body...is a medium of culture' (Forte 1999, p.249) and as some feminist scholars (Bordo 1998; Forte 1999) have indicated, the presumption of an authoritative, corporeal source for the performer's inspiration denies the cultural representations of the body, which will inflect the direction of any enactment. To maintain the body as an arbiter of truth in theatrical exchange is, as Auslander proposes, to hold 'a metaphysical even mystical concept; it is asocial, undifferentiated, raceless, genderless and therefore neutralized and quietist' (Auslander 1992, p.92).

Second, the listening performer needs to be aware that even though the performer may have a somatic experience of the other, it does not follow, as Zahavi notes, 'that I can experience the other in the same way as she herself does, nor that the other's consciousness is accessible to me in the same way as my own is' (cited in Shaw 2003, p.46). In relation to this point and to the dangers of identification, it would be well to bear in mind the French philosopher, Emmanuel Lévinas' stress on maintaining the 'unknowable' and ungraspable nature of the other (see Erikson 1999). He suggests that this ineffability calls us to responsibility toward the other.

Despite the problems of considering the body as a primary, unmediated source of action for the performer, somatic material remains key in providing direction to playback enactments. Indeed, I would argue that the 'receptor task', in which 'we must be in the moment, animal-like' (Fox 1994, p.101) is crucial to successful playback. The performer engages in a somatic encounter with the teller's narrative – the body serves as both source and as a key means of representation.

Subconscious promptings

> It is a remarkable thing that the unconscious of one human being can react upon that of another, without passing through the conscious. (Freud cited in Field 1989, p.512).

In the responses of playback performers there seems to a fairly consistent reference to what I will loosely call 'subconscious promptings'. By subconscious I mean here those psychophysical phenomena existing in the mind that are not immediately available to consciousness and which exist just below the threshold of consciousness.

In their descriptions of listening to the story, performers often refer to some sort of 'unconscious' or 'non-cognitive' apperceptions that can significantly guide their work. Indeed, for one performer, Sarah, this is the kind of listening which requires more courage and is likely to lead to a 'deeper' reception of the story: 'I struggle between latching on to some idea and having ambition for that and emptying myself, drinking in the story. The latter takes more courage. [In this state of mind] images will fleet in and out...'

Whilst recognizing her uncertainty with 'the technical use of the term', she calls this listening from 'an id place'. She contrasts this with an 'ego' place, which she conceives of as more cognitive, problem-solving and self-conscious. She told me:

I mean by 'drinking in the story' a more 'id' place (if that is the right word) than an 'ego' one. For me the 'id' place is an unconscious, deeper place where I am not making cognitive connections, but am letting the story emerge by itself. It's a place where I let go of my need to know what I'm doing. The images that come out are more spontaneous – me, the teller and the story all combine in this place. I yield to its formation, letting it create itself beyond my conscious capacity to control it. I am just a piece in its co-creation along with all the other parts – the actors, the musician, the way a piece of cloth might land upon the stage, the free-floating ideas that interlock with another one to form a third. As an actor in this place I feel vulnerable; not fully formed. I have lost myself a little to something greater than myself. But out of this nothingness, if I can be courageous enough to stay there long enough, I believe the best and most beautiful work emerges. We obviously have to hang it on the form we're doing, which keeps it anchored in the story; grounded in reality. It means that we can drape our unconscious co-creations upon a frame that we know will support them. And that this will give them enough shape and structure to give back to the teller in *their* service.

Nevertheless, for me it's always an act of great courage to surrender completely to not-knowing what will happen in each next second of an entire performance, and to take my place in that. Every step outwards into the enactment is a reminder to myself that I am stepping into this unformed void – into the trust that something truthful will emerge. Sometimes I feel more willing to do this than others.

While many of the performers choose the unconscious as the site from which such inchoate promptings emerge, one interviewee, Susanna, thought it may involve the performer paying attention to the 'ancient part of the brain – the amygdala'. The amygdala which lies in the temporal lobe of the brain is generally thought to have a role in the experience of emotion, particularly in the 'neurobiology of anxiety and fear' (Bear, Connors *et al.* 2002, p.597). What is of interest is its use as a kind of metaphor by the performer to convey a kind of pre-cognitive, emotional and ancient human response that she wishes to draw on in her work. In that respect it operates in the roughly the same way as the reference to the 'id' above. Both performers are trying to conceptualize non-cognitive, perhaps ancient, psychophysical processes that are at work as they listen to the story. There is some support for this notion in the psychoanalytic tradition. For example Nathan Field writes in arguing that therapists should pay attention to what he calls 'embodied counter-transference':

> it may well be that where very primitive emotions need to be communicated decent human rapport will not serve. Some states of fear, rage, longing and hunger may date back to a time when no words were available and psychic trauma could not be distinguished from physical injury. In these cases bodily symptoms in the therapist may provide the first clue to understanding. (Field 1989, p.519)

The theatre director Constantine Stanislavski talks about an unconscious objective 'which immediately, emotionally, takes possession of an actor's feeling and carries him intuitively along...' (cited in Drain 1995, p.255). The Polish director Jerzy Grotowski urges actors to 'reveal one after the other the different layers of his personality, from the biological-instinctive source via the channel of consciousness and thought, to that summit which is so difficult to define and in which all becomes unity.' (Grotowski 1995, pp.279–80).

Both theatre practitioners in their different ways have encouraged their actors to utilize what we have loosely called here 'subconscious promptings', however, it would be wise to sound a notion of caution from two different directions. First, as Sarah points out above, these apperceptions needed to be 'grounded and anchored' – there is the always the possibility that they will bear no relation to the experience of the teller and are merely the singular responses of the performer; an observation that raises significant ethical considerations for the listener. Second, we should be cautious of claiming authority for such self-promptings. As Judith Butler might say, we should be careful of an 'epistemological paradigm that presumes the priority of the doer to the deed' (Butler 1990, p.148) – one that presumes a self which exists prior to, and stands behind discourse (Butler 1993, p.70). Despite these warnings, however, it seems that performers value these kind of experiences as being potentially indicative of the teller's experience.

In relation to this is seems important to mention 'trance' at this juncture. Sarah speaks of a 'trance-like' state as a relatively common feature and describes it thus: 'The rest of the world falls away. You forget you are in the theatre. Like crossing the liminal threshold... Duende.'

While Marie recognizes the danger of 'trancing': 'I have trouble with trancing, it feels like springing off a diving board, diving into the water, swimming deeply, coming out of the water, shaking my hair and saying "What happened?"'

Trance acting, as Richard Schechner points out, is very widespread across cultures and contexts and involves the performer enacting actions 'not of their own devising' (Schechner 2002, pp.163–4) and, as is suggested by Marie's comments and by the striking difficulty performers often have in remembering, 'after the trance is over, an actor may or may not remember what she said and did' (Schechner 2002, p.164). It seems that performers can enter a state in some ways like trance as they listen to the teller. Perhaps however, as Claire, another performer, suggests, a better word for this may be a state of 'heightened concentration'. She told me that actors need to 'step into the world of the story – leave the world behind and *lose yourself* in embodying the story' [my emphasis].

Re-thinking the 'self'

How can we conceptualize the self of the performer in playback theatre? This is an important question because performers often call on the self as inspiration for their performances. What is inspiring them? The problems of regarding the self as autonomous and a stable source of 'truth' for the performer have already been noted. The self is always in flux; it is inflected by culture, context and desire. There is no point beyond contingency that can provide an authoritative source of truth for the performer.

Perhaps we need to see the self not as an irreducible entity, capable of self-knowledge and autonomy, but as a 'a flux of contextualized identities' (Hutcheon 1989, p.59). Or, as Lyotard puts it, a site or a 'post through which various kinds of messages pass' (Lyotard 1984, p.15).

In terms of performance, the self, as Auslander has maintained '...is produced by the performance it supposedly grounds' (Auslander 1995, p.60). In other words, selves are made and improvised within performance – rather like the protoselves created through autobiographical remembering (see Chapter 4 and Barclay 1994). Butler writes of the paradigmatic 'presentist' conceit that there is an 'I' that arrives in the world of discourse without a history.

> there is no 'I' that stands *behind* discourse and executes its volition or will *through* discourse. On the contrary, the only 'I' comes into being through being called, named, interpellated, to use the Althusserian term, and this discursive constitution takes place prior to the 'I'; it is the transitive invocation of the 'I'. (Butler 1993, p.70)

In light of the deconstruction of the 'presentist' self, we might instead regard the actor as a kind of '*intertext*' situated in a network of influences or impulses, which cannot be seen as separate from the context in which they arise. However, the choice of the trope 'intertext' limits the performative nature of the process. What is more correct perhaps is that the self is being created in performance. Duranti and Burrell suggest that jazz musicians are on 'a quest that is not only aesthetic but also existential' (Duranti and Burrell 2004, p.92).

In searching for a metaphor to conceptualize the self of the actor in relation to the story the Japanese playback practitioner, Makoto Tange's conception of a 'tube' may help: 'The actor is simply a tube on stage. His Ego, intention, personality can all vanish – a totally 'selfless' being. The lines of the play just pass through his/her body' (Tange 2002, p.12). The use of 'tube' was a translation from the Japanese and a 'conduit' may be preferable. However, the notion of effacing the self is a problematic one, as Benjamin noted in relation to storytelling: 'traces of the storyteller cling to the story the way that handprints of the potter cling to the clay vessel' (Benjamin 1970, p.92). Nevertheless, the sense of the transitive that is suggested by a 'tube' renders it preferable to 'being oneself' as a trope for the playback actor. It may be worth considering other possible metaphors for the playback performer (see Box 6.1).

This exercise is useful; however it is likely that the complexity of playback performing will make the search for a suitable metaphor a futile one. Each metaphor provides an insight into the process but none fully encapsulate it.

Box 6.1 Possible metaphors for the playback performer

A sponge: but a sponge that alters the water that is absorbed by it – too passive.

The performer breathes in and then exhales the story: in doing so, through complex chemical reactions, she changes it. This seems to lack a sense of agency; it seems too automatic.

A music producer at a mixing desk who blends the sound 'channels' together into a desired effect: useful for conveying the multiple 'channels', but misleading since it suggests a director capable of controlling the precise configuration of the piece. Performers do not have that level of control.

An alchemist: gives a sense of 'transformation' but seems too much of a mystical fantasy.

A resonating violin: this is a hopeful possibility since it enables us to appreciate the processes of 'attunement, decentring [...] and introspection' that Arnold (2005, p.23) believes constitutes empathic intelligence. However it does not allow for the imaginative and conjectural aspect.

Concluding reflections

One of my interviewees talked of the particular listening she aspires to: 'I am entering this other world half-way between self and character – a no-man's land, a half-way place'. In this liminal place, moment-by-moment, the performers' attention focuses and shifts: personal, representational, mnemonic, somatic, affective and imagistic perspectives collide, cohere and interact to inform the performer. In order to perform effectively they need to attend to these perspectives and resist what Abbott calls the desire for 'interpretive closure' (Abbott 2002, p.81) – the 'channels' need to remain open as the performers move toward dramatizing the complexity of their response to the teller's narrative. It is a state of mind which bears resemblance to Freud's free-floating attention or to what Balint called a 'harmonious, interpenetrating mix-up' (cited in Rowan and Jacobs 2002, p.52).

To return to Buber's notion of the 'the narrow ridge between *I* and *Thou*', there is a paradox in the listener's aspiration: as they allow this interpersonal merger to occur they must also be careful not to dissolve the tension between self and other – to do so would risk erasing the 'otherness of the other'. The performers wish to enter into the story with a receptive body and mind while maintaining their separateness – both empathy and distance need to be simultaneously at work as the actors listen to the story. In the next chapter I will be looking further at improvisation and importance of the performer holding a place on this narrow ridge.

Chapter 7

The Exploration of Occasion: Improvisation and Playback Theatre

Performing Michael's Story

This episode took place within a playback theatre performance at a community mental health venue.

Michael [pseudonym] comes forward onto the stage in response to a general invitation to audience members to tell their story. His story is set in Australia about ten years previously. He had been travelling through the continent on what he thought of as a 'voyage of discovery'. The excitement, sense of achievement and adventure made him feel happy and 'good about myself for the first time'. He told us that he felt that he had 'found his feet' and they were 'firmly planted on the ground' and he felt 'rooted' for the first time. As the only male actor, I thought it likely that he would choose me to play him. I hoped he would do so, as I was drawn to him and was beginning to get an idea of how to play the part. He told us that, as he reached the heart of the Australian continent and was visiting Ayers Rock, he began to lose his 'footing'. He began to 'over-reach' himself. He said,

'I began to believe unrealistic things about myself. I began to believe that I could be a model or an actor, that I could do anything I wanted.'

These feelings grew in intensity and became what he later (after psychiatric intervention) called 'manic'. The feelings gradually gave way to depression and he was hospitalized and eventually flown home to be re-united with his worried and concerned family. At home, surrounded by his friends and family he began to improve and he told us:

'What I have learned is that I need people around me to help me feel grounded.'

As Michael told his story the actors listened. They took the story into their bodies, through the half-forgotten passages of their memory; they let the story float through their minds searching for some image with which to express it. They hoped that maybe a metaphor or another cultural narrative would enable them to represent this story. They looked at the stage floor, the coloured fabric, the chairs, the other actors, hoping that they might find some resonance with the story there. They noticed how their bodies were responding to the story. But still, as is often the case, as they entered the stage they had very little idea of what to do – maybe just a movement or a word that has come to their minds, or maybe nothing. It is now that the other performers can help; perhaps one has an idea that they can all pick up, or perhaps through their interaction a direction will emerge. The important thing is that they *listen and respond* to the teller, to their own promptings, and to each other. Once they stop doing that the performance is lost; actors start talking over each other, they lose sensitivity to the aesthetics of space, they lose contact with the teller's story and they try to save themselves from the humiliation and shame of a poor performance.

Surprise and danger

If the actor is spontaneous a 'miracle can take place'. If she is uninhibited by the blocks of anxiety and self-consciousness 'the actor can intuit untold parts of the teller's story; use the cloth in such a way as to create a deep metaphor for the story's meanings; move the body in a way more expressive than words; or be still' (Fox 1994, p.84). For Jonathan Fox, spontaneity is 'juicy' and 'hot'; it loosens 'the grip of rationality' (pp.86–7); it is 'a kind of ecstasy, an attunement which encapsulates thought' (p.81). He is clear that spontaneity and improvisation of the teller's story add something extra – something that may not be so readily available to the performers if the enactment was planned beforehand. He would perhaps agree with Susan Leigh Foster when she speaks of 'the suspense-filled plenitude of the not-quite-known' that gives improvised performance its 'special brilliance' (Foster 2003, p.4).

There is something Dionysian about improvisation. It can unsettle accepted forms and bring an earthly vitality to the theatre. It can enliven the rehearsal process and the quality of scripted work. I have heard that in Mike Leigh's film *Vera Drake* for example, in order to maximize the shock of Vera's arrest for carrying out illegal abortions, Leigh kept the actors in the dark until the moment the truth was revealed to them on the set. He was looking to capture their immediate responses on film. Playback theatre looks for a similar kind of immediate reaction from the performers; it brings the immediate physical and emotional responses of the actors to the story. Improvisation takes us by surprise and so can offer new perspectives. Improvisation can revitalize the story. It can bring the past into the present moment. The emergence and vitality of the enactment through improvisation can bring the *then and there* of the story (told by the teller) into the *here and now* of the performance (explored by the performers). Rather like the notion of therapeutic 'transference', in which the patient's past is revivified in the here-and-now relationship with the therapist, improvisation in playback can 'loosen the grip' of the story, take the teller, audience and performers by surprise and provide an opportunity for them to see the teller's narrative in a different way.

Spontaneity is however a dangerous horse to ride: improvisers work on the edge of 'success' and 'failure'; cliché and stereotype are only a breath away. In a second the 'flow' that all improvisers experience can slip into actions that seem contrived and forced. One minute actors are responding to each other as if they were one mind and body; the next they are clumsily getting into each other's way. Roddy Maude-Roxby is right when he says that 'the most important moment in improvisation is when you don't know what will happen next' (cited in Frost and Yarrow 1990, p.55), but those moments can be the most terrifying and disturbing – the possibility for performers to feel ashamed and humiliated by their failure 'to come up with something' is always there. In playback theatre there is always the risk that the performers will get lost and, leaving the teller's story far behind, abandon themselves to improvisation's intoxicating play. There is always the danger that actors will be carried away by their improvisational skills and the enactment will become a vehicle for their flair – the integrity of the story lost to spectacle and ostentation. Improvisation and spontaneity are full of potential and surprise; they also hold risk for performers.

In between

Perhaps it is this fragility of improvisation that is behind one of the most striking features of the literature on the subject: the references many of the writers make to contradictions (Zapora 1995), polarities (Fox 1994) or 'tacking between' opposites (Foster 2003). There is a sense in much of the literature that the improviser is working *within and across* tensions and that success lies in maintaining the tension between positions along a continuum or across polarities. Susan Leigh Foster (2003) talks of the dancer tacking between the known and the unknown. Tufnell and Crickmay speak of a 'dialogue' between 'wildness and order' (1990) while Fox, in a similar kind of way, speaks of the actor oscillating between 'structure and freedom' (1994, p.94). Duranti and Burrell speak of an 'aesthetics of tension' present in jazz improvisation. They could as well be talking about playback theatre:

> the tension between what is known and what is unknown, what is possible and what is impossible, what is acceptable and what is

> unacceptable, what is expected and what is unexpected, what is right and what is wrong. (Duranti and Burrell 2004, p.85)

These references suggest a 'balancing act' in improvisation between the familiar and the new, between abandonment and control, and between freedom and structure. They indicate the delicacy of improvisation and the constant need for reflexive awareness on the part of the performer: awareness significantly heightened in playback theatre because the form deals in autobiographical narratives. The performers need to maintain deep respect and care for the story they have heard while at the same time expanding on its possibilities and associations. Rather like the 'narrow ridge' of the last chapter, improvisers find themselves *in between*. In this chapter I want to look at the quality of this position of 'in-betweenness' that seems so characteristic of the descriptions of improvisation.

It is perhaps inevitable that when speaking of such a fleeting and intangible process there is a need to draw on metaphor and allusion. Such ephemeral phenomena as dramatic and musical improvisation are difficult to convey through literal and linear language. Let's begin then with the metaphor of the threshold (the boundary *between* two spaces) implied by the term liminality.

Performers at the threshold...

> Liminal entities are neither here nor there; they are betwixt and between the positions assigned and arrayed by law, custom, convention, and the ceremonial... (Turner 1969, p.95)

No one has been cast; no one yet knows who will play whom. Everyone has heard the story but the direction the performers will take is as yet unknown. In *Performing Michael's Story*, which opens this chapter, the performers have only hazy ideas of what will happen next. This is a moment before the characters are created, the signs developed and the meanings read. There is potential and energy here – it has intensity and it is often one of the times of greatest uncertainty in a performance. This moment is a kind of 'primordial soup' full of affect, memory, signifiers and images.

> We improvise the moment we cease to know what is going to happen.
> Setting the mind loose from the ongoingness of everyday life
> To find what lies at the edge,
> Behind our thinking, seeing. (Tufnell and Crickmay 1990, p.46)

This 'at the edge', 'threshold moment' is one of the most fragile ones for the performers – it is now that they are often most vulnerable. It is important that this moment of uncertainty is maintained and so the performers must, to some extent, resist 'easy' resolution of the problems that face them. They need to allow the enactment to emerge through the dynamic tension between the task of representing the teller's story and their encounter with each other in the here-and-now: a task which requires risk and trust on the part of the performers. This uncertainty increases the level of vulnerability and the sense of exposure for the performers. The need for them to maintain a high level of awareness of the moment potentially increases their self-consciousness and may heighten their feelings of vulnerability and exposure. At the threshold of performance the players need to remain open and ready to respond to each other and to the emerging enactment.

Maria Elena Garavelli, the Argentinean psychodramatist and playback practitioner, puts the notion of being at a threshold in the following way. She terms playback theatre '*teatro espontaneo*':

> 'teatro espontaneo' is an archipelago with bridges and crossings where boundaries are erased.
> Between narrative and theatre
> Between the private and public
> Between the artistic and the therapeutic
> Between the personal and the social
> Between the spontaneous and the theatrical. (Garavelli 2003, p.127)

At this threshold, where Bachelard tells us the 'poet speaks' (1994, p.xvi), the performer and the teller's narrative are potentially at a place of *openness*: of offering new perspectives on the story. I qualify my statement by using the word 'potentially', because the level of risk for the performers and, to a certain extent, the teller continually acts as a counterweight to the freedom to explore the occasion. Indeed, Jonathan Fox writes that playback actors often fail because they fear 'liminality' (Fox 1994, p.101). At the threshold – at the 'entrance' where we may perhaps be 'entranced' – there is certainly possibility, uncertainty and unpredictability. There is a sense of the 'provisionality' to which Schechner (1993) refers in relation to playing – there is 'unsteadiness, slipperiness, porosity, unreliability, and ontological riskiness' (Schechner 1993, p.39).

Of course it is evident from the last paragraph that as I write I find myself wanting to say two incommensurable things simultaneously. The actor is free to improvise at the threshold but yet she is not. She is constrained by the other performers, playback's dramatic conventions, the task of representation and her own state of mind in the moment. There is a paradox here. The paradox is that she is both constrained and liberated. Those things that constrain – the context; the ensemble; the 'rules and conventions' of playback; the presence of the teller – are also those things that animate.

Being in the moment

Fox asks playback performers to 'be brave enough to enter the moment with a mind free from all protective considerations' (Fox 1994, p.171). Of course, the extent to which the 'mind' can ever be free from *all protective considerations* is debatable. The notion of the spontaneous 'happening', unfettered by psychological, social and historical constraints, is always a rhetorical one. It is the rhetoric of a particular type of ideological yearning. It is a yearning for the live and the unmediated – for 'actuals' as Schechner terms it (1988, p.51). Despite the careful caveats we must place on the notion of entering the moment, playback theatre is nevertheless an improvised form – one that requires a heightened awareness of, and openness to, the moment.

The paradox of Zeno's arrow points to the impossibility of conceiving of the present moment, since the arrow, in motion, can never be said to be in the present since that moment is infinitesimally small. Nevertheless, most writers on improvisation regard being present in the moment as crucial, for example, Johnstone (1999, p.171) encourages his students to keep their attention on 'what actually is happening'. Spolin maintains that 'the intuitive can only respond in immediacy – right now' (1999, p.26) and David Warrilow tells us, 'Improvisation only means that which is not foreseen, that which appears in the moment. Something is always appearing in the moment. The point is how much attention you pay to it' (cited in Lassiter 1995, p.317).

This absorption in the moment, characterized by Csikszentmihalyi (1988) as 'flow', or by the playback trainer, Deborah Pearson, as 'allowing the story to emerge' is one which seems crucial to effective improvisational acting, as indeed it is in the psychodramatic tradition. The emphasis on here-and-now awareness is clear, for example, in the work of Jacob Moreno. He writes that his first conflict with the work of Freud concerned the 'dynamics of the moment':

> The experiences which take place continuously in the context of the Here and Now have been overlooked, distorted or entirely forgotten [in Freudian theory]. Therefore, early in my writings…I began to emphasize the moment, the dynamics of the moment, the warming up to the moment, the dynamics of the present, the Here and Now, and all its immediate personal, social and cultural implications. (Moreno 1987, p.4)

He goes on to say that he is not writing from a purely philosophical perspective but from a therapeutic one. He draws attention to the here-and-now reciprocal 'encounter' (Moreno 1987, p.4) between participants in the therapy group. Moreno's emphasis points toward an intense awareness of others in encounter. It bears similarity to Buber's 'narrow ridge' and points to the central importance of the ensemble in playback theatre: a subject I will address in the next chapter.

In a section reminiscent of Moreno, Fox clearly expresses the importance of spontaneity in playback theatre:

> spontaneity first requires that the senses be open to information from the environment. To accomplish this receptor task, we must be *in* the moment, animal-like. Second, we must be able to stand *outside* the moment to make sense of what is occurring. We can then take action – that is, perform a conscious act – which is no small achievement. This action will in turn create a new environmental condition. Thus spontaneity is the ability to maintain a free-flowing constantly self-adjusting cycle of sensory input, evaluation and action. (Fox 1994, p.101)

Fox gives a vivid picture here of the task of the performer seeking to find a place between absorption inside the enactment and the cooler detachment that is needed to ensure that the teller's story is represented effectively. It is a tension between the performative and representative which I will consider in the next section.

Before continuing, it is important to sound a note of warning. Despite this emphasis on the awareness of the moment in playback performing, performers cannot achieve a state of ahistorical awareness of the present. We must be careful of fetishizing the present moment in a desire to recover the real from the 'mediatized' (Auslander 1999) and conclude that it is possible to obtain ahistorical contact with the moment. I agree with Auslander when he writes:

> It is not realistic to propose that live performance can remain ontologically pristine or that it operates in a cultural economy separate from that of the mass media. (Auslander 1999, p.40)

Performers are deeply influenced by memories and past performances that intervene in the phenomenologically experienced moment. If we cannot speak of being 'in the moment' directly without, in some way, fetishizing or reifying it, then we can only point to what may be the signs that an actor is 'in the moment'. These seem to be characterized by flexibility, responsiveness and openness. I present my own list drawn from experience and discussion with other playback performers:

- Flexibility to the changing circumstances on stage.
- A high level of physical and verbal responsiveness to the other performers.

- An ability to relinquish a planned direction in response to changing circumstances.
- Openness to personal memory, identification, emotion, physicality and sensation.

Karin Gisler, a Swiss playback practitioner, has summarized the characteristics of effective playback improvisers. Her list bears much similarity to my own:

> the ability to translate thoughts into physical shapes and images quickly and clearly; to say yes to what develops during a scene; to support your partner; to move the story forward; to be sensitive to the unfolding meaning of a story and to carry it further. (Gisler 2002, p.7)

Playback acting requires that performers allow the enactment to unfold or emerge. To do this they need to be open to the moment-by-moment changes onstage. In order to understand this more fully I want to return now to the notion of performers working within – or between – energizing tensions. In the following section I will consider three sources of tension: between the referential and the performative; between the known and the unknown; and between empathy and distance.

Tensions and the playback performer

Between reference and performance

In defining improvisation as 'the exploration of occasion', the poet Peter Riley (cited in Dean 1989) neatly conveys the quality of here-and-now encounter that is characteristic of improvisational acting in general, and playback acting in particular. The performers are exploring the occasion of the enactment – the moment-by-moment interaction with each other and with the environment. This is a key element of playback; it brings life to the enactment. By itself however it is not enough. The playback performers are not only 'exploring the occasion': they are also responding to the teller's narrative. We could say that playback enactments develop out of a tension between *an encounter with here-and-now circumstances on stage and the task of representing the teller's story*. To put this differently, I am referring to a tension between the *referential* and the *performative* functions of theatre (Fischer-Lichte 1997) or the 'performance structure and processual flow' (Lassiter 1995). Or, to use Parker and Sedgewick's colourful language, I am referring to 'the torsion, the mutual perversion, as one might say, of reference and performativity' (1995, p.3). In playback theatre the performers need to maintain the tension between representing the teller's story and exploring the occasion of the performance: if they represent the story without the vivacity of improvisation the piece will lack interest and life; if they lose contact with the story in their improvisations it will be, at best, self-indulgent and, at worse, unethical and exploitative.

This tension between the referential and the performative is most clearly evident in those remarkable moments during improvisation when what happens in the live encounter onstage corresponds, seemingly accidentally, to the story being enacted. When, by some wonderful synchronicity, what happens between the performers tells the story. Consider this example taken from a Playback Theatre York performance to gay and lesbian young people. It was the first 'full story' to be told in the performance. The teller had recently broken up with her female partner after the partner had been persuaded by her family to end the relationship. She felt angry and hurt. At one point she said 'I can't be who she wants me to be – I can't be a man'. This account is written from the point of view of the teller's actor.

THE PERFORMER

Across the space facing me stand three actors in a line; they are my lover's family. With words and gesture they beckon my lover toward them. She and I are connected by a thin piece of white elastic, which stretches across the stage as she moves away from me toward her family. I feel the increasing tension in my hands as she does so. The elastic is doubled up so that I hold two pieces. By the time she reaches her family it is fully stretched and I wonder what will happen if I let go...

I let go of one of the connections. There is a rapid succession of snapping, cracking sounds that shock me. The elastic is releasing its energy, unpredictably striking the performers as it does so. I say, 'I have to let go – I can't be what you want me to be'.

I still hold on to one piece of elastic. I am not sure whether to release it. The teller had said that she was still in love with her partner and so maybe I should hold on. But I do let go – perhaps because I want to repeat the shock that it produces, or perhaps because I want to say that this relationship is over.

I am left standing alone across the stage from my lover and her family. I look outwards towards the audience – not towards my lover and her family – and as clearly and assertively as I can say:

'I can only be who I am'.

I repeat it – perhaps they didn't hear it clearly and anyway, I can't think of anything else to say.

I bow my head; a trumpet plays mournfully.

The performers improvise with the elastic: with its physical, symbolic and referential qualities. Its properties – explored through moments of, what

Smith and Dean (1997) call 'non-referent' improvisation – inform the 'referent' improvisation. In what is a 'happy accident' (and these often occur in playback improvisations) the snapping elastic stands in for the snapping relationship. Of course, crucially, the performers are able to exploit these moments because the story has already been told. The suspense for the spectators lies not in the development of the plot since they already know the outcome of the story; it lies in what the performers do with it. The actor can therefore, 'play' with the echoes and resonances that exist between the story requiring representation and the embodied discoveries that emerge in the encounter. The tension that is felt in the elastic and the shock of its release across the stage is, in itself, both phenomenologically engaging and capable of representing the separation contained in the story. If the elastic is a metaphor, then the actors give space for it to 'live' so that they may explore its own properties, while still being aware of its referential function.

The surprise is important for both the audience and the tellers. The shock of the released elastic surprises the actors. They respond to the surprise of the snapping elastic while simultaneously maintaining awareness of established performance sequences (the use of elastic as a figurative device to explore relationship is familiar to the York Company) and of their representational 'responsibility'.

I would propose that explorations of the phenomenologically experienced moment such as this provide opportunities to, as Viola Spolin claims for improvisation, topple 'old frames of reference' (1999, p.24). This opens up a space for play on the meanings that may be attributed to the teller's narrative. For these brief moments the performers are led, not so much by the characters they are playing, nor by the narrative they are representing, but by the actions they are performing/experiencing.

In these moments there is a temporary disjuncture or rupture in the fabric of the narrative. The 'major building blocks of the apparatus of Western theatrical representation' (Lampe 1995, p.297) – 'acting', 'character' and 'narrative' – are disrupted. This allows new 'takes' on the teller's story; ones that are not totally circumscribed by the limitations of an autonomous controlling ego or the demands of narrative. It may be that these moments in playback undermine the limiting determinism of character and narrative and thus present the teller's experience in a Brechtian sense as 'not just taken for granted, not just natural' (Brecht 1964, p.47). In so doing they have the potential to expose the processes of narrative structuring and unsettle the teller's story because they dislodge it from the structures of psychologism and narrative construction.

The tension between the performative and the referential is a key one in playback theatre. My argument suggests that a seed of change is made possible in the heightened awareness of here and now. If personal, stable, fixed meanings are reinforced over time, in, what we might call, the 'executive boardrooms of the ego', then it is possible that the playback enactment unsettles these and exposes them to the effects of the performative. This can only happen when, to some extent, the performers can remain 'betwixt and between' the referential and the performative.

Between the known and the unknown

In her wonderful essay on improvisation Susan Leigh Foster proposes that the 'improvising dancer tacks back and forth between the *known* and the *unknown*, between the familiar/reliable and the unanticipated/unpredictable' (Foster 2003, p.3). For her there is a paradox here: the improviser can never accomplish an 'encounter with the unknown without engaging the known' (p.4). The etymological root of improvisation is from the Latin *improvisus*, which may be translated as 'unforeseen' (Montuori 2003, p.239), yet, as Foster argues, in order to reach the unpredictable, the unusual and the unforeseen, improvisers need to work with what is familiar. Improvisation is not the generation of the completely unpredictable, but rather may better be understood as the working and re-working of the familiar – a process of defamiliarization.

Specifically in playback theatre the performers are working with a tension between that which is already known and that which is unknown or is unforeseen. Indeed the effectiveness of playback enactments derives partly from the degree to which the performers exploit the *tension between the unforeseen and the familiar*. There is much that performers do that is already familiar. Their work does not escape the complex process of intertextuality as explained by Roland Barthes: 'Any text is a new tissue of past citations. Bits of code, formulae, rhythmic models, fragments of social language' (2000, p.183). In rehearsal and in previous performances it is likely that they will have enacted stories that bear similarity to the one they are currently performing. They will have developed sequences that can be adapted for certain types of stories and their personal and cultural histories will provide familiar points from which to work with the story. Improvisations are not brand new creations free from history or culture – they are also deeply influenced by what has already been and this is especially the case in relation to previous performance sequences.

Perhaps because the performers are under pressure to respond quickly, there are gestural patterns or 'past performance sequences' that are fairly regularly employed by the York Company for example. These are not consciously codified and discussed but they certainly are present in the company's repertoire. One may draw a parallel here with the practice of *commedia dell'arte*. In commedia improvisations the '*lazzo*' and 'burle' were tried and tested sequences which actors would introduce when they considered it fitting. David Griffiths writes:

> The main aspect of these lazzis and burles is that they would be most thoroughly prepared and rehearsed and honed, so that in performance they could almost certainly guarantee a favourable response from the audience. Such a 'stockpile' would take years to learn and assemble, and would most certainly be jealously guarded from plagiarist rivals. (Griffiths 1998, p.19)

The role of what Keith Sawyer calls these 'ready-mades' (2000) is well recognized in jazz improvisation. Charlie Parker, for example, is said to have made use of a personal repertoire of 100 motifs, each of them between four and ten notes in length (Sawyer 2000). Playback improvisers are no different. Playback performers also have these ready-mades. These are not playback 'forms': they are not explicitly codified, named or rehearsed by the performers like lazzo, but rather constitute part of the implicit 'language' of the company. The use of space to explore distance and intimacy in relationships is one example of these 'ready-mades'. As in the *love rejected* example above, once the actors are in relationship across space they have created a structure within which they can work. There no detailed plans for what will happen next, but performers may well feel more confident now that, to use a musical analogy, they are playing in the same key.

Like lazzo, these sequences are often used and adapted; they suggest the risk of over-simplification and caricature. Under the pressure of the improvisation there is always the danger that the performers will draw on tired and oft-used ideas and not permit the fearfulness of the unknown to enter their performance. Maintaining a state of not-knowing is a key ingredient of effective playback performing, yet often it is the most terrifying experience for the performers. Not knowing what will happen next and stifling the desire to just 'do something' while being watched by an audience is one of the most difficult aspects of improvisation. Additionally the pressure on the performers is heightened by the presence of the teller to whom they have responsibility.

Between empathy and distance

I do not intend to go over the points made in the previous chapter with regard to the use of empathy, personal memory, the self and the body in performance. It was clear from the performers' reports that they are aware of the dangers of over-identification. They recognize the distortion possible when a performer assumes that their own experience bears close similarity to that of another. Effective playback requires that the performers maintain a tension between 'using the self' to inform the enactment and employing enough detachment to recognize the limitations of identification and empathy. This is a crucial element of effective and *ethical* performance and will be discussed in more detail in Chapter 9.

A paradox on the threshold: being alive in the moment requires an acceptance of death

There is, it seems to me, an intimate relationship between improvisation and death. The improvised disappears as soon as it is created; indeed its creation partly depends on relinquishing the self. Ruth Quinn (2003) argues that the improvising, 'performative self' is released from the deadly hand of self-judgement and self-aggrandizement by 'an old close friend with archetypal significance. This is Death'. She goes on to argue that:

> A strong umbilical attachment to death means that we can move forwards into a new 'awake self', an alive self who is prepared to work with the unknown and court true spontaneity and improvisation. (Quinn 2003, p.18)

Victor Turner recognized that 'liminality is frequently likened to death' (Turner 1969, p.95) and, in the literature of improvisation, there certainly seems to be a sense of transience. For example, to Johnstone, 'Theatresports is disposable theatre' (1999, p.63); or to Dario Fo, the aim is to create 'a throwaway theatre, a theatre which won't go down in bourgeois history, but which is useful, like a newspaper article, a debate or a political action' (cited in Frost and Yarrow 1990, p.74). As Read tells us 'theatre is the transient art *par excellence*' (Read 1993, p.12); improvised theatre dies as soon as it is born. Memory of it fades quickly – in my experience more quickly than other kinds of experiences. Unless the enactment is regularly recalled or recorded in some way, it is lost. As Phelan writes: 'it may be that theatre and performance respond to a psychic need to rehearse for loss, and especially for death' (Phelan 1997, p.3). Sometimes I find this painful. For someone brought up to over-value recognition and who secretly – and not so secretly – harbours the need for accolades, the transience of playback can be a frustration. Perhaps this is why I write this book. It is a kind of monument.

There is paradox in Quinn's proposal: to live in the moment means to acknowledge and embrace death. This is what Fred Harris is referring to when he writes to fellow playback practitioners:

> the more we face the limitations that constrain us in life, the more fully we experience the courage to live. I refer to this state into which classical tragedy wakes us as 'mortal awareness' because it is about being mindfully mortal: vulnerable to fate and destined to die, yet committed to life and its strivings. (Harris 2002, p.8)

Benjamin (1970) believed that oral storytelling was dying out because our sense of the 'epic side of truth, wisdom' (1970, p.87) was being lost, presumably through the reductionism of science and the privileging of 'information'. He goes on to say that the loss of this wisdom leads to a weakening of our idea of eternity and, by implication, death. The storyteller he writes: 'is the man (sic) who could let the wick of his life be consumed completely by the gentle flame of his story' (Benjamin 1970, p.108).

Perhaps that partly explains our fear of 'entering the moment' and the 'fear of liminality'. Perhaps that is one reason why audiences often seem a little frightened by the storytelling and enactments in playback performances. Perhaps we know that it will play with and disrupt our own monuments against death – our autobiographical narratives. For whatever reason to remain 'in the moment' – to 'explore the occasion' – can produce a sense of vulnerability in the performers and in the audience. This idea that a sense of mortality is crucial to the improvising performer will be picked up later in Chapter 9 when the characteristics of ethical performance are considered.

Concluding comments

Despite the risks of caricature, formulaic acting or over-identification, the improvisation of the teller's story is central to playback's approach. Although rehearsal and preparation of the enactment may lead to a more carefully crafted and thought-through response, playback's founders and practitioners have preferred the immediacy of improvisation. The reason for this may be that improvisation can challenge predictable and settled versions of personal and cultural narratives; it loosens established cognitive schemas. Of course it can also confirm stereotypes and repeat tired and worn formulations, however I would support the claim of Viola Spolin that, in improvisation the

> combination of individuals mutually focusing and mutually involved creates a true relation, a sharing of fresh experience. Here *old frames of reference topple over as the new structure pushes its way upwards,* allowing freedom of individual response and contribution. (Spolin 1999, p.24) [my emphasis]

Improvised works allow new structures to emerge not only because of their unpredictability but also because, Barron claims, they unsettle the 'the rule of law and regularity in the mind' (Barron 1990, p.249). It may be playback enactments are improvised in order to maximize the possibility of this destabilizing dynamic – and so create *openness.* The tensions within which performers work are crucial in unsettling the story while at the same time maintaining its integrity. Playback actors have a great deal of freedom to play with the story, but to do so ethically and responsibly they need ongoing awareness of when the integrity of the story is sacrificed to the spectacle of the enactment, or the familiar (is sacrificed) to the exotic. They need to be hyperaware of how immediate action can affect the overall shape of the piece and of when the familiar slips into cliché. It is a state of mind and body that Foster calls 'vigilant porousness' (2003, p.7). As we have seen, it is a risky position to take and the ensemble has a crucial role in both safeguarding the performer and maintaining the necessary vulnerability and exposure.

Chapter 8

The Ensemble

The days following the death of my mother were a kind of 'confinement'. Removed from the everyday demands of my work I took time, as an Australian playback friend had advised me, to 'let it in'. Rather like the arrival of a baby in the household, the curtains were metaphorically drawn; the usual circadian rhythms of day and night were disrupted. The house was decorated with cards of condolence and people took the opportunity to write or say words of tenderness and intimacy that were both welcome and out of the ordinary. It was a time of separation... Some – mainly those at the edges of my social network, but not exclusively – were fearful of me, as if I was dangerous or fragile and likely to shatter if they spoke a clumsy word.

I had lost both parents. I was now, as some friends told me, an orphan. In the middle of the night as I made my way to the toilet, I would become aware of a silence. It was as if the sound of my parents had been extinguished. Paradoxically I was aware of their presence by their complete irrevocable absence.

It seemed to me, as it had done when my father had died three years previously, that those characteristics of the lost parent that, in some way, I acknowledged as my own, came to the fore. The death of my mother provoked feelings that seemed to lie beyond words – in the pre-verbal pre-cognitive world of the small infant.

I found myself wanting to reach for the ineffable – the fall of light on a leaf – I wanted to meditate, pray, reach for the spiritual. Early in the morning following her death, unable to sleep, I walked into York and took photographs of the Minster (the cathedral).

I had to return to the 'world'. One way in which that return was marked was the first playback rehearsal. As I left the house for the rehearsal on a Sunday morning following her death in late January, I could faintly smell the spring. I recalled the feelings of freedom that always accompanied going away with the company – like the trip to Poland in 1997. These feelings were tantalizing; they disappeared almost as soon as I became aware of them.

I knew what story I wanted to tell at the rehearsal – it was about the silence in the middle of the night. When I had the opportunity I told it. The conductor asked me what the voices of my parents sounded like. Later she told me she had wanted to hear their voices and then to have them silenced. I found it very difficult to answer the question. I said 'Loving and mildly critical,' but I wasn't very happy with that.

As the enactment began I found myself longing for silence. I wanted the actors to listen to the silence. All I wanted was that they would hear the silence with me – perhaps in respect of my mum and dad, but more profoundly, in solidarity with me. What I wanted was a kind of ritual – like those two minute silences 'for the dead of both wars' – in which I could 'mark' their absence together with the company.

When the enactment finished I told everyone about my wish for silence and we discussed the problems of conveying the quality of silence through theatre. What I did not say – perhaps because it seemed mawkish or too indulgent – was that what I wanted was simply to be silent with them – together to mark the absence and my loss.

> There is something special about a company. It is something I can feel in the air the minute I walk in the room. There's an energy, an urgency to make the most out of the moment. (Fox 1994, p.160)

Most playback theatre performances are staged by a company of players who have worked together for a significant length of time (in some cases over 20 years) and who meet regularly to rehearse. Each company is different in the way it balances performance and rehearsal, in its styles of conducting and performing, in its decision-making processes, and in the way it marks its separate identity; nevertheless there are significant similarities amongst them all. They all work within the recognizable structures of playback theatre and all tell their own personal stories during rehearsals. The fact that companies base their rehearsals around their own stories means that a significant amount of trust and intimacy is possible within the companies; it is often the case that company members will have told stories in rehearsal of many of the personal and professional triumphs and disasters that mark adult life. These are not therapy groups yet in some ways they do function as such – providing support and validation for their members. For example, my accounts of the death of both my father and mother were told to the company and these episodes have made their mark in the course of my grieving. For many playback practitioners, the intimacy and familiarity of 'company life' is an important factor in their continuing involvement in playback theatre – for many it is as important as performance.

It is my proposal that the ensemble is essential to both effective *and* ethical playback theatre and that a company that work together regularly and have reasonably honest and open relationships with each other are more likely to provide the necessary conditions for risk-taking and openness in performance. I will also propose that because they have worked regularly with each other's stories, they are more likely to have the necessary sensitivity to 'play the other'. I will conclude by considering the role the ensemble has to play in the providing the conditions for 'collaborative emergence', a key feature of effective playback.

Protecting the performers: providing psychic safety

Playback performing can be disorientating and stressful; without planning or preparation players step forward onto the stage to enact a story that they have just heard. They do not know what the other actors will do, they often don't know what they will do; they are always at risk of exposure and humiliation. Performers need to rely on each other during these moments of uncertainty. They need to trust the others sufficiently to be able to take risks, make 'offers' and wait for the enactment to develop. This can be vertiginous and psychologically disorientating. Ensemble, with its disciplines, may engender the conditions for openness of performance, but may also operate to contain and support its more disruptive and disturbing aspects.

Later in this chapter I propose that 'not-knowing' is an important quality in the playback performer. It is often the case that 'not knowing what to do' or what exactly is happening onstage can produce more lively and truthful performances. For that to be psychically possible the performer must be able to trust the others and know that if they are lost others will step in to support them. In my experience this is often the problem with working with impromptu companies that are, for example, formed at conferences; performers tend to force the direction of an enactment and avoid a state of 'not-knowing' because they do not have the trust or knowledge of each other's work and fear that they will be left exposed. Consequently the performance can lack the vivacity of working in the present moment.

It would be wise to avoid an over-simplistic formulation here however; the connection between the quality of relationships within an ensemble and the quality of their performances is a complex one. There is no guarantee that a company of players who get on well with each other will produce quality theatre. It is perfectly possible that a close company will be complacent, inward-looking, and self-congratulatory, 'shutting out' the audience from the dialogue between stage and auditorium that is crucial to playback's success. As Schechner writes:

> There is, unfortunately, no easy relationship between the quality of life in the group and the quality of the group's work… At some level the life of the group determines the life of the work. But it is necessary to be delicate and discriminating before announcing what the relationship is between group life and work life. (Schnechner 1994, pp.271–2)

There is always the possibility that groups will 'turn inward' and pay more attention to their internal life than to the requirements of performance. Yet if 'close companies' do not necessarily lead to good quality work, the reverse is perhaps more likely to be true: that good quality playback theatre is not possible without relatively clear and honest communication between the performers. Performers need to respond quickly to each other on stage, they need to take risks and trust that other actors will support them; they need to maintain a high level of here-and-now awareness, and they need to relinquish their own ideas and quickly assume those of another performer without too much resentment. These are requirements best fulfilled in an ensemble that, over time, has built up fairly robust relationships with each other.

Protecting the tellers

The relative safety of rehearsal can provide the opportunity for performers to develop the necessary sensitivity to each other and to each other's stories. Being able to 'practise' with each other's stories is crucial in this respect. It sensitizes performers to the impact dramatizing personal stories can have, it gives the actors the opportunity to find the 'narrow ridge' between self and other. Being able to enact the stories of others in the rehearsal room gives the actors the chance to take risks and explore the limits of their risk-taking.

Of course there is no guarantee that an established company will necessarily provide ethical protection for tellers. Over-confidence, over-zealousness, discord or an imbalance of power-relations in the group can blind the company to the sensitivities of tellers. In performance actors and musicians have a great deal of power. To paraphrase Marx, in their hands they have the means of representation and interpretation. The openness and playfulness of effective playback performing can lead performers to be exhilarated by this power and so be at risk of abusing the teller's trust. The ensemble, in rehearsal and in performance, can steady the performer and obviate some of the risks of playing the other.

The ensemble acts as a brake on the performers' 'exhibitionism' *and* it can encourage actors to be less timid and tentative. The rehearsal room is often the place where performers take responsibility for their work and where they discover the limitations of their emotional and theatrical range. In performances it is rare for tellers to directly challenge the work of an actor – in rehearsals it is not. For this reason the work of a company in rehearsal is essential for both the aesthetic and the ethical quality of playback theatre.

Collaborative emergence

Usually improvisation emerges out of the interaction of the players; no one performer provides the dominant voice or can impose the direction of an enactment. Not even the teller's actor is given authoritative control of the direction of the piece. To use Keith Sawyer's phrase, the enactment develops through a process of 'collaborative emergence'. Although Sawyer's analysis relates to children's play, a brief adapted survey of his work will support my point. Collaborative emergence is characterized by the following qualities: it is unpredictable and contingent; 'it emerges from the successive actions of all the participants' (Sawyer 2002, p.340), and so is not the conscious creation of any one person, and, crucially,

> the emergent narrative cannot be analyzed solely in terms of the child's [actor's] goal in an individual turn, because in many cases a child [actor] does not know the meaning of her own turn until the other children [performers] have responded. (Sawyer 2002, p.340–1) [my additions in square brackets]

Narrative and meaning are created not through the authoritative control of one perspective or voice, but through the multiple consciousnesses of the performers. Meaning is not so much immanent but is emergent, discovered through the response of others, and, one might add, by the interpretive work of the audience.

Consider this example of a Playback Theatre York performance which took place in a town in Northern England near Christmas time. It was to an audience of users of mental health services and the professionals who work with them. In providing this vignette I am trying to convey how the enactment emerges through the collaboration of the performers. No one quite knows how it will develop – they are taking cues from each other as the piece unfolds. It is also evidence of the complex processes of identification between the teller and the actor that shape the work. The actor describes his experience thus:

Early in the performance a man in his mid-forties referred to a story I had told at the outset of the performance concerning the illness of my mother. He spoke about this with some emotion. He glanced at me a few times as he spoke and I was aware of him nodding in recognition as he did so.

He comes onto the stage to tell his story. I know he will choose me. He tells us about the death of his own mother 11 years previously. He had been in hospital for depression and he tells us that his mother had visited him regularly. When he was discharged he received a phone call to say that she was very ill and he should visit her soon. He describes being in two minds. It was his 'pay day' and he had to collect his money. However he decided to visit his mother. This was the last time he saw her, she died a short time after his visit.

He chooses me to play him and Greta to be his mother.

I stand waiting for the others. Remembering my own mother, I am trembling and feel close to tears. When the music stops I walk out to stage right and face the audience. I see Greta/Mother to my right. She is smiling. I cannot look at her.

I say, 'It is December 1999 and it is very close to Christmas. Now I want to remember my mother and to tell you about her'.

Voices from uncast actors behind whisper 'She's here to see you, look at her'. I don't know what to say, my mind is blank, Greta/Mother is smiling, I walk toward her dazed. The voices behind me call out 'She has a gift'.

She is holding a yellow cloth. Everything seems very slow, very deliberate. I worry that everyone will know that I don't know what to do. I feel foolish. I look into her eyes. I still can't think of much to say except 'I'm glad I have seen you'.

Greta/Mother says 'Here, son,' and hands me the yellow fabric. I hear my own mother's voice in hers.

The other actors move in front of her. They draw her away stage left. She is disappearing. I plead, 'Mum, Mum! Please don't go. I've got more I want to say to you'.

I am left on my own. I have closed my eyes. It is silent. I am holding this piece of yellow cloth. The music plays, it sounds plaintive. I open my eyes, it feels different – more definite somehow. The other actors have draped Mother in a purple cloth. They surround her. I try to approach, but they hold up their hands to indicate that I should come no closer.

I look at the yellow fabric in my hands and caress it. Voices from the other actors call out, 'Remember her,' and 'Tell us'. They repeat this. Finally, after what seems like a long time, I look to the audience and say 'It is now a long time since my mother died. I still remember her. I will not forget her'. Indicating the yellow fabric, I say 'I still have this. She gave it to me. I will always have it. There are still things I want to say to her. I want to say thank you to her. I want to tell her that I love her'.

We all turn to the teller.

As I face the teller I am aware of a deep sense of connection and recognition between us. He stumbles to thank me.

I hope the reader can get a sense of the actor stumbling through this piece. He has very little idea what to say or to do next, and it seems he is being moved forward by two related impulses: his identification with a dying mother and by what the company are doing around him. It appears that the actor does not know what to do from moment to moment and is dependent on the other performers for the development of the piece. From after the moment that the actor spoke those brief opening words about remembering his mother he is led forward through interaction with the other performers – who themselves have very little idea of how the enactment will progress. Everyone is in the dark; no one really knows what will happen next. The not-knowing is crucial to playback's effectiveness. It is crucial because allowing the enactment to emerge – or 'to become' – through the interaction of multiple 'voices' opens up the possibility for what Mikhail Bakhtin calls 'event potential'. Bakhtin proposes that:

> It is quite possible to imagine and postulate a unified truth that requires a plurality of consciousnesses, one that in principle cannot be fitted within the bounds of a single consciousness, one that is, so to speak, by its very nature *full of event potential* and is born at a point of contact among various consciousnesses. (Bakhtin 1984, p.81)

I am using Bakhtin here to suggest that in course of a playback improvisation, 'truths' will emerge through the contact of 'various consciousnesses' – truths that possess the vivacity of 'event potential'. Bakhtin searches for a 'dialogic sense of truth' that does not transcribe away the 'eventness of the event' and does not exclude the particular, the unfinalizable and the unforeseen. Morson and Emerson explain:

> The dialogic sense of truth manifests unfinalizability by existing on the 'threshold' (porog) of several interacting consciousnesses, a 'plurality' of 'unmerged' voices. Crucial here is the modifier unmerged. These voices cannot be contained within a single consciousness, as in monologism; rather their separateness is essential to the dialogue. Even when they agree, as they may, they do so from different perspectives and different senses of the world. (Morson and Emerson 1990, pp.236–7)

Bakhtin was describing the novel, not the theatre. In fact he argues that drama is 'a monolithic genre' in which the focus on the character, the authority of the director, and the drive toward the final resolution of differences in classic tragedy, reduce the possibilities of polyphony (Carlson 1999, p.314). Despite this Carlson proposes that because of the 'multiple voices of enactment', Bakhtin's notion of dialogism and polyphony 'should provide a rich area for the study of the creation of meaning and of psychic relationships' (Carlson 1999, p.322).

It is the potential for capturing the complexity of reflexive voices in playback enactments and the stress Bakhtin places on the threshold event that makes his ideas so fruitful for conceptualizing playback theatre. The actor, moved by memories of the death of his own mother, enters the enactment. There he reacts to, and interacts with, what is happening on the stage. He does not know what will develop and so he depends upon the other performers to provide him with ideas and with something to respond to. In these circumstances what can develop is work enlivened by freshness and *surprise.* In some ways like the shaman, the actor enters into or relives the teller's experience. The performer, with memories of his own loss in mind and body, responds to what is happening before him in order to represent the teller; to do this he is, in many cases, reliant upon what the other actors and musicians offer. The requirement on Greta and me to represent the teller's story and to play their parts never disappears, but rather is inflected, moment-by-moment, by phenomenological experience. I would suggest that it is the task of the ensemble to create the conditions where moments of collaborative emergence can be shaped into theatre capable of responding to the teller's narrative.

My reference to the shaman may ring alarm bells in the reader. I am cautious of drawing parallels to practices such as shamanism which are deeply embedded in their own culture. The tendency to borrow from other cultures in this way is fraught with danger: the indiscriminate use of 'ritual' in playback discourse for example tends to mask the cultural contingency of ritual practices. Despite this warning, as we have seen in Chapter 6, there often is a desire amongst playback actors to enter into, or allow themselves to be penetrated by, the teller's story; in that sense, like the shaman, the actor performs the person's 'affliction'. But, as Dwight Conquergood points out in his essay on the Hmong shamans, such 'intimacy leads to vulnerability on the part of the shaman as much as the patient' (Conquergood 1999, p.45). In playback theatre performers often become vulnerable as they emotionally and somatically identify with the teller's story; it is the presence of the ensemble that allows them to take that risk. As importantly for an ethical performance, the ensemble provides a brake to over-identification and its attendant risks.

Concluding remarks

I have argued in this chapter that ensemble work is crucial for both effective and ethical playback theatre. The rehearsal constrains *and* liberates playback performers; it also provides some protection for its tellers. Allowing the enactment to emerge through the collaboration of the performers has its risks, but it is, nevertheless, the means by which the story can be opened up and new, surprising and fresh perspectives introduced.

Chapter 9

The Ethical Limitations of Playback Performing

In Barry Unsworth's novel *Morality Play*, a group of medieval travelling players arrive in a small town in Northern England to perform their *Play of Adam and Eve*. Finding that the townspeople are more concerned with the recent murder of a young boy, one of the players proposes to the troupe that they 'play the murder' instead. Initially shocked by the proposal, it prompts the company to debate the ethical and epistemological questions raised by the suggestion. Is it morally acceptable to play someone who is still alive? What authority do they have to represent events that have recently taken place? Their discussion has direct relevance to playback theatre:

> 'Play the murder?' he said. On his face was an expression of bewilderment. 'What do you mean? Do you mean the murder of the boy? Who plays things that are done in the world?'
>
> 'It was finished when it was done,' Straw said. He paused for a moment or two, glancing round into the barn with his prominent and excitable eyes. 'It is madness,' he said. 'How can men play a thing that is done only once? Where are the words for it?' And he raised both hands and fluttered his fingers in chaos.
>
> 'The woman who did it [the murder] is still living,' Margaret said. 'If she is still living, she is in the part herself, it is hers, no one else can have it.' (Unsworth 1996, pp.63–4)

To these medieval performers, the idea of playing something that has only been done once and for which there is no authoritative words seemed strange and somehow blasphemous. What 'authority' did they have to enact and interpret real events? Surely, they argued, it is only God who can give things meaning. As one actor remarks, 'Players are like other men, they must use God's meanings, they cannot make meanings of their own, that is heresy' (Unsworth 1996, p.64).

There is, as Margaret makes clear, one further anxiety for the actors which goes to the heart of my concerns in this chapter: how can they play someone who is 'still living'? Surely 'she is in the part herself, it is hers, no one else can have it.' Margaret's concerns are ontological ones (how is it possible to take a part of another when they already have it?) rather than ethical ones; nevertheless she does raise the crucial question for those involved in the dramatization of autobiographical narratives: how can we presume to take on (or 'take over' perhaps) the persona of another? For these actors, playing the murder involves two transgressions from their understanding of what can properly be played: they become involved in making meaning, which they consider a divine task and they presume to take on another's identity – a seemingly impossible one.

They do go on to 'play the murder' and, like the players in *Hamlet*, expose the real culprit through their dramatic exploration. What are of interest for the purpose of this book are the ethical issues these passages raise for playback theatre. Performers risk 'heresy' by making 'meanings of their own' from the real events of people's lives and they presume to take on the identity of another. Is this ethically acceptable and, if it is, what are the principles that should guide the performers? This chapter will debate these issues.

Before getting into the substantive arguments however, a consideration of some questions I have asked myself as 'a white, heterosexual, English, middle-class, male performer' will locate the issues raised by Unsworth's book within contemporary playback theatre practice:

> I have asked myself what I would do if, as a white, heterosexual, English, middle-class man, I was cast as the teller's actor when the teller was, say, a black New York rapper, or a man into and identified with the London gay scene, or for that matter a woman who is openly expressive around sexuality. Would it be possible for me to do justice to their stories? Of course it is immediately obvious that my choice of tellers exposes my cultural limitations, assumptions and even 'hang-ups'. Why did I choose those tellers in particular? I am sure that my choices tell you far more about me that they do about them. Nevertheless my dilemma does raise some issues that are critical for me as a playback actor.
>
> If cast in these roles how should I react? I could, of course, refuse saying that I am unable to play such a role convincingly...

In this chapter I will attempt to address my dilemma. The questions raised go to the heart of the playback and bring into question the ethical responsibilities of the performer: what are the limitations of the playback actor? Can we play a teller no matter how culturally unfamiliar to us? If we accept that our performances are always influenced by our culture and ideology then is it ethically acceptable to represent another? Can the performer ethically assume the power of interpretation over another's story? We should not kid ourselves here, the mediaeval players were correct; playback enactments are always adding meaning to the teller's story. If all of this is ethically acceptable, then what might be some of the principles that would guide performances?

These issues and questions are not new to the playback community. The March 1996 issue of *Interplay* (the newsletter of the International Playback Theatre Network) was a key one in marking a significant change in the development of playback with respect to issues of cultural diversity. With the subtitle 'What special education will white companies and actors need?' the movement seemed to formally recognize for the first time the cultural limitations of the performer. More specifically Johnson asks, 'where will white conductors get training in decoding the African-American schema and story so that actors can playback these stories with integrity?' (Johnson 1996, p.4).

It appears that, at least in this publication, the playback community was, for the first time, confronting the cultural limitations of the playback movement. The notion of the 'authentic' actor able to respond to any story, no matter how culturally 'strange' was being brought into question. This is an important moment in the development of playback theatre. For the first time they were asking: what are the limitations of playback acting? Can we assume that with good will and 'authenticity' an actor can take on any role no matter how culturally unfamiliar? Can there ever be such a thing as the 'universal performer'?

In order to get this question into focus, it will be helpful to look at opposite sides of the debate. This will enable a clear view of the arguments for and against what we might call the possibility of the 'universal performer'. The debate might be said to lie between the 'organic approach' to acting on one side and, what I will call the 'radical difference approach' on the other. In other words, between those who consider that the performer can discover organic truths through her authentic encounter onstage, and those who would argue that whatever is produced by the actor is always inflected by culture and ideology. Although to create this oppositional binary may prove a useful strategy, it has its dangers. Few would take up a trenchant position on either side of this debate; most would respond by saying, 'It depends' – on the context of the performance, the nature of the audience, the experience and cultural sensitivity of the performers and so on.

The 'organic approach'

I have already considered this approach under the heading of 'being oneself' in Chapter 6, and so will not rehearse the arguments at length here. Briefly, it is an approach to acting which would hold that if the actor is *authentic* and fully reveals herself on the stage then she can transcend difference and find *universal truths.* It is an attitude to performing which emphasizes the power of *empathy* to close the difference between self and other. It stresses the truthfulness of the performer's *identification* with the teller.

As an apologist and enthusiast of playback theatre, this concept of authenticity is one for which I have a great deal of sympathy. I am aware of many times in which I have felt that I have revealed something of myself in portraying the teller's story. Or at least, I have made use, for example, of my own experiences of depression, neurotic anxiety, loss or the joys of parenthood. I find myself in an uncomfortable position, since questioning these ideas of authenticity and self-revelation expose me to the risk of 'losing my footing' as a playback performer. I confess to a fear that such an examination may lead me to destroy the beliefs that sustain me as an actor and make playback theatre such an important part of my personal and professional life.

Nevertheless the question remains: can we trust the actor's self to that degree, especially when it comes to playing another who is significantly different? Can we trust in the performers' authenticity? Or do we conclude that to do so is to rely on a true, universal self beyond culture and language, a position that is difficult to sustain given the impact of the post-structuralist rejection of single truth and stable meaning?

The 'radical difference approach'

This 'approach' comes from two main directions in order to critique the notion of the authentic actor who can depend on the 'truth' of the actors' experience. The first direction stresses the radical, idiosyncratic and ineffable difference of the 'other'. The second emphasizes the inevitable cultural and ideological influences on all acting; this may be especially the case for improvised acting where, under pressure to do 'something', the dangers of slipping into cliché and stereotype are so present. I will look at each in turn.

The first critique of the 'organic' approach focuses on *the risks of eradicating the other through representation.* The feminist Hélène Cixous warns of the delights and dangers of identification. Elin Diamond explains:

> Cixous is describing the mimetic pleasures of identification – becoming or inhabiting the other on the stage or in spectatorial fantasy; I stand in for her, act in his place. Such acts are distinctly imperialistic and narcissistic: I lose nothing – there is no loss of self –

> rather I appropriate you, amplifying my 'I' into an authoritative 'we'. (Diamond 1999, p.390)

Cixous's concern is that the consequences of identification are the denial of difference and distance. I force myself into the teller, engulfing the subtleties of his experience, erasing his identity and replacing it with my own. I possess him. My empathy precludes his otherness. Because the processes of identification are so intense in playback, this danger is always present. The presence of the teller and the need for the actor to improvise may potentially collapse the psychic distance between performer and character and between teller and actor. Far from offering a viewpoint on the idiosyncrasy of the other, empathy may occlude it. Differences of gender, ethnicity and sexuality may be erased in this process of identification.

Cixous is not alone in her concerns; the point is compellingly made by bel hooks in a passage which could be read as a forceful and rather sarcastic critique of playback.

> No need to hear your voice. Only tell me about your pain. I want to know your story. And then I will tell it back to you in a new way. Tell it back to you in such a way that it has become mine, my own. Rewriting you, I write myself anew. I am still author, authority. I am still the colonizer, the speaking subject, and you are now in the centre of my talk. (hooks 1990, p.152)

A recent playback performance to delegates at a conference exemplifies these concerns. During the enactment of a story concerning the problems encountered by a man travelling by train with a disabled friend, an actor represented the disabled man as passive, and suggested through his speech and movement that he may also have a learning disability. In his feedback the teller said, 'That was great, except my friend was much more capable than you portrayed; he was, in fact, a lawyer'. This was a gross example of the dangers of playing the other. It highlighted the risk that through stereotyping and presumption the idiosyncrasy of the other is appropriated and erased.

Second, the organic approach can be criticized for *ignoring culture and ideology*. If we cannot escape ideology and culture then we cannot rely on the personal experience of the actor as a source of incontestable 'truth' (Love puts it this way: 'representation is inextricably embedded in dominant ideology', 1995, p.276). She encourages actors to resist acting practices which trust in the 'truth of the actor's experience' – the most well-known of these being, of course, the 'Method' and asks the question: 'Whose experiences can reflect any truths other than those of the culture in which they were raised?' (Love 1995, p.277). From this position then, playback performers can do no other than reveal their cultural and ideological position in performances – the notion of the 'universal performer' is a fiction.

Brecht takes a slightly different tack and warns that identification will mask the socio-political circumstances of the drama. He writes:

> In order to produce A-effects, the actor has to discard whatever means he has learnt of getting the audience to identify itself with the characters which he plays. Aiming not to put his audience into a trance, he must not go into a trance himself... Even if he plays a man possessed he must not seem to be possessed himself, *for how is the spectator to discover what possessed him if he does?* (Brecht 1964, p.49) [my emphasis]

In this sense identification risks a mystifying 'naturalness' potentially suggesting that the circumstances of the protagonist could be no other, that they are immutable. As Brecht writes in his prologue to *The Exception and the Rule*, 'We ask you expressly to discover/That what happens all the time is not natural' (Brecht 1930, p.110). The processes of identification and empathy which are so revered in the 'organic approach' are rejected here because they either eradicate the idiosyncrasy of the other, or mask the socio-political forces at work in all identification.

Performance as a way of deeply sensing the other

Should these concerns leave us pessimistic about the possibilities of representing the other in playback? Must we see it always as a form of colonization or possession? These issues have been considered by Dwight Conquergood in relation to his practice as an ethnographer of performance – a researcher and performer of cultural practices. While recognizing that performances cannot take place in 'ideological innocence' (Conquergood 1985, p.2), he wonders if they have the epistemological potential of 'deeply sensing the other' (a hopeful possibility for playback practitioners). In the remainder of this chapter I want to introduce Conquergood's mapping of different 'performative stances toward the other' and propose some ethical strategies that may reduce the dangers and worst excesses of 'playing the other'.

Conquergood identifies four performative stances toward the other which he considers 'immoral' (it is important, I think, that Conquergood is not afraid to use the unfashionable language of ethics here).

1. *The custodian's rip-off.* This is characterized by detachment and the plundering the experience of the other. In playback terms it could be considered as treating the stories of the other as trinkets to be collected and taken home. For Conquergood the

immorality of such performances 'can be compared to theft and rape' (Conquergood 1985, p.6).

2. *The enthusiast's infatuation.* This leads to facile and over-eager identification with the other. It assumes that goodwill and enthusiasm are sufficient. Conquergood quotes Tzvetan Todorov to illustrate his point:

   > Can we really love someone if we know little or nothing of their identity, if we see, in place of that identity, a projection of ourselves or ideals. (cited in Conquergood 1985, p.6)

   The 'enthusiast' makes the assumption that their feelings of goodwill toward the other will overcome the problems of representing him. In playback terms it may be the belief that because I have experienced, say, bullying at school I can understand the systematic oppression of black people in the UK. As Walter Benjamin argues, if we do so we will fail 'to touch the strangeness and the resistance of a reality genuinely different from our own' (in Conquergood 1985, p.7). This position is, for Conquergood immoral because it trivializes the other.

3. *The curator's exhibitionism.* Here Conquergood identifies the danger of making the culturally different exotic – of romanticizing the other in order to astonish the audience. He writes that the 'manifest sin…is Sensationalism, and it is an immoral stance because it dehumanizes the other' (Conquergood 1985, p.7). In playback theatre the danger is that the performer will use the teller's story to shock, astonish or excite the audience.

4. *The sceptic's cop-out.* Finally, the sceptic concludes that the chasm between the self and the other is so deep that there is no possibility of closing it. To Conquergood this is a morally reprehensible position because it 'forecloses dialogue'. As I have argued throughout this book, in playback theatre the performers respond to the story out of their subjectivity, their sense of the theatrical, and in response to the rest of the ensemble. This is what playback can offer; the teller and the audience understand this and give the performers their permission to show their response. The 'sceptic' relinquishes this possibility and, in the face of the impossibility of fully playing the other, leaves the stage.

Towards and ethics of playback theatre

The teller is not asking that the actor get the story 'right', for this is impossible, and implicitly understood by the teller. Rather, they are asking that the actor meet the spirit with which they themselves told

> their story. '*The actor's attempt here is what is crucial – not the outcome.*' (Penny 2002, p.4) [my emphasis]

As an antidote to the pessimism of these 'immoral' performative stances, Dwight Conquergood writes the following:

> One path to genuine understanding of others, and out of this moral morass and ethical minefield of performative plunder, superficial silliness, curiosity-seeking and nihilism, is dialogical performance... [T]he aim of dialogical performance is to bring self and other together so that they can question, debate and challenge one another. (Conquergood 1985, p.9)

Never has a sense of the other seemed more crucial for our own humanity. When there seems so much wilful misunderstanding of the other, it may well be that playback theatre can offer a forum where the self and other can be brought together: a space as Jonathan Fox puts it for 'radical social encounter' (1995, p.4). In Conquergood's words it can 'bring self and other together so that they can question, debate and challenge one another.' There is no doubt in my mind that playback theatre can offer such an opportunity largely because audience members dare to tell their stories and actors dare to embody them.

However, as we have already seen, there is always a risk that we will eradicate the difference of the other in our performances – that well-intentioned empathy becomes oppressive colonization of the other. I would like to offer some suggestions toward an 'ethical disposition' in relation to the other that may work against this. I have deliberately chosen the word 'disposition' rather than 'principle' because it more accurately conveys the relational, active nature of the playback experience. I wholeheartedly support the words of John Caputo: 'On their best day principles are the faded copies of the singularity of concrete situations... Principles fall before the demands of concretely situated responsibility' (Caputo 2003, p.179). He then goes on to say that in real life situations, principles give way to:

> the insight, the acumen, the nimble skill, the adroit light-footedness, and the heartfelt love that holds sway in the multiple settings of ethical life, settings so diverse and unpredictable, too polymorphic and unprecedented, to be gathered up and codified. (Caputo 2003, p.179)

The vivacity of the living experience is lost in codes of conduct and so is the relational. I would support Richard Kearney when he proposes that the question of ethics concerns the face-to-face 'disposition' toward the other.

Ethics concerns how we are 'disposed' to the other, not a 'position' which is closed and non-relational.

> It is clear that this notion of the ethical subject as a dis-position before the face of the other is radically social and political in its implications. (cited in Read 1993, p.91)

As playback performers, we cannot escape from ideology or from our own partiality. However, in my view, this is morally acceptable as long as we don't claim to be doing more that is *humanly* possible and that we recognize our *agency* and *accountability*. Christian Penny's (2002) statement that it is the 'actor's attempt that is crucial – not the outcome' seems to express clearly the point I am making. As a rule of thumb perhaps we should accept Anna Livia's advice when it comes to playing the other: 'conjecture good, appropriation bad' (1996).

One might ask why we need an ethics of playback theatre. Maybe we should do what comes 'naturally' to us. Maybe as we have sometimes said in Playback Theatre York: we just need to 'be ourselves'. But, as we have seen, what is natural is always ideological and anyway, as Richard Kearney has pointed out, 'Ethics is against nature because it forbids the murderousness of my natural will to put my existence first' (cited in Read 1993, p.94). I would concur with Alan Read:

> An ethics of performance is an essential feature of any philosophy and practice of theatre. Without it a set of cultural practices which derive from a very specific arrangement of power relations between people are unhinged from responsibility to those people. (Read 1993, p.6)

What then might an ethical disposition toward playback performing look like? To consider this I would like to return the reader to the dilemma I posed at the opening of this chapter: am I able to play a teller whose cultural experience is significantly different from my own? My thinking continues in the following way:

If I was to improvise one of these tellers I would have little to go on except for cultural stereotypes which, given the tellers' social position, would most likely be oppressive and insulting. So what am I to do? Well, of course, the first thing is that I would avoid the immediately obvious characterizations – just as I hope an actor would if he were to play a middle-class Englishman. But then what?

There is no point in denying difference: being black, from New York and into rap music, or being into the London gay scene is part of personal identity and to deny its importance would surely be a renunciation of the person's identity.

My conclusion is that the answer to my dilemma must lie in two directions. First, I must acknowledge and, as best as I can, represent the experience of the teller. There will be much of his or her experience with which I will be able to identify. My own life experiences will to some extent be a guide. For the teller it will be important that I make an attempt and that I show him that I have listened to and understood his story.

But there will always be a gap – or perhaps a chasm – between my portrayal and his experience. So what I need to do, I think, is keep the gap between me as the 'actor' and me as the 'character' open and represented. In other words, I must allow the limitations of my acting to be visible.

My first recommendation for an ethical playing of the other could therefore be expressed as:

1. Make the process of representation visible

If we, as playback actors, dispense with the idea of authentic acting, then we need to make the gap between self and other visible onstage. Our responsibility is to convey that the enactment is not the authoritative version of the story – that it is work in progress, that it is one interpretation of many that are possible. We have a responsibility to expose the processes of representation at work in the performance. In other words we accept, along with Brecht and then Boal (Boal 1979), that the theatrical illusion must be punctured so that the spectators are aware of the provisional and mutable nature of reality.

To some extent I am arguing for the kind of acting that Brecht (1964) recommends in *The Street Scene*. The actor is not totally absorbed in empathic identification with the character but, to some extent, she is a 'demonstrator' who tells the story but maintains a visible gap between herself as performer and the character she is demonstrating. An example may illustrate the issues facing the performer in these circumstances:

I was asked to play an angry and disturbed 13-year-old boy. I am in my 50s. How can it be possible for me to play someone whose experience is to far from my own? Clearly the audience were aware and probably a little amused by the problem I faced. I did not want to pretend to be 13 – that might cause some laughter if I did it well, but would be disrespectful to the boy I had been chosen to play. It would only ever have been a caricature. So all I could think to begin with was a rather twisted posture, an arm covering my face (I had a vague image of Anthony Sher playing Richard III here) and the opening line: 'I am 13 and I don't want anyone to see me'. This piece of dialogue seemed more like reportage than the natural speech of a 13-year-old boy, and as such may have worked to represent the gap between performer and character.

I stayed with this twisted and closed posture throughout, occasionally jabbing at those who came too close while reaching out with my small finger feebly trying to make some contact. It was not a convincing performance – but perhaps it did offer the teller (the boy's sister) an image on stage with which to think and wonder.

What else could I have done? The following are some strategies that may help the performers 'enact' the inevitable gap between the actor and the character:

- Use, like Brecht, the narrator role and so comment on the action from a rather more distanced position.
- The teller's actor can *briefly* express – as a performer – the problems of representation she faces. I have seen this done occasionally by Playback Theatre York, it has the virtue of drawing attention to the gap between actor and character.
- The performers may choose to work with an extended metaphor which allows exploration of the story, but avoids the problems of naturalistic portrayal.
- The teller's actor is careful not to give herself up to strong emotional identification. The tension between the performative and the representational needs to be maintained.

However the teller's actor and the company do this, the key point is that the gap needs to be visible and represented. Of course a black teller who casts a white person from a very different cultural background to play him will be aware of the disparities and will make allowances for that. The spectator has a choice about how far they enter into the 'as if' of the theatre event; it would be a mistake to underestimate the active involvement of the audience member. Nevertheless the maintenance of the gap between the actor and the character is an acknowledgement on the part of the actor of the inevitable 'failure' of their work. It is an acceptance that their playing of the other will always be partial and 'inaccurate'. At a political level it is also a refusal of – or a resistance to – the idea that 'we are all the same really'. From the point of view of 'radical difference' the notion of universality always eradicates difference and usually replaces it with the images and discourse of the dominant ideology.

2. Vulnerability: body awareness and mortality

In the conversations of Playback Theatre York there is one piece of advice which, like the wisdom of the tribe, is regularly repeated. It is that when you are feeling vulnerable and uncertain of yourself you are most likely to give a good performance. The company recognizes, as I am sure many playback practitioners do, that the vulnerability of the performer is one of the factors that permit lively and committed work. Vulnerability can permit the performer to be open to the teller's story as well as to be closer to their own emotional world. It can of course work in the other direction: the performer, haunted by fearful vulnerability, can close off and be defensive. In that case their work is likely to be formulaic and lacking in responsiveness; nevertheless in order for the performer to work sensitively and, I would argue, ethically, he needs to remain vulnerable and a little uncertain. The proverb *pride comes before a fall* is never truer than in playback theatre where the risks of exhibitionism are so great. Without a certain level of vulnerability the performer is in danger of sacrificing the teller's story to their own desire to be seen.

How can we conceptualize this vulnerability without slipping into self-abnegation and self-serving, false humility? One answer I would suggest lies in the body. Accepting that we need to search for an ethics that is 'relational' and is based on our 'disposition' toward other, I am drawn to Terry Eagleton's work. He argues, in his search for what he calls a 'material morality', that it 'is the mortal, fragile, suffering, ecstatic, needy, dependent, desirous, compassionate body which furnishes the basis of all moral thought' (Eagleton 2003, p.155). For him it is in the vulnerability and exposure of the body that a relational ethics may lie. He argues for what he calls a 'materialist morality' located in the 'moral body' (2003, p.157). Taking Lear as his example, he writes:

> In the course of the drama, Lear will learn that it is preferable to be a modestly determinate 'something' than a vacuously global 'all'... [This is because] he is forced up against the brute recalcitrance of Nature, which reminds him pitilessly of what all absolute power is likely to forget, namely that he has a body. Nature terrorizes him into finally embracing his own finitude. (Eagleton 2003, p.182)

Relinquishing the 'fantasy of disembodiment', Lear finally comes to recognize that when his subjects told him, 'I was everything; 'tis a lie – I am not ague-proof' (Act 4, Scene 6). Eagleton goes on to argue that, not only does the recognition of mortality allow us 'fellow-feeling'; it also acts as a brake to power. Wonderfully pithily he writes: 'If power had a body, it would be forced to abdicate' (Eagleton 2003, p.183).

An ethics of playback developed out of being 'before the face of the other' may best be found in the body. It is the body that stands before the other. It is in the vulnerability and exposure of the body that a relational ethics lies. I am not suggesting here however that the body provides a final and authoritative source for an ethics of playback. It would be wise not to fall back into the trap of recreating an 'essential' body. However, the material, mortal body may be a useful trope to construct such an ethics.

Fred Harris, a playback practitioner from the United States, proposes in a similar vein to Eagleton that, what he calls 'mortal awareness', is a key characteristic of effective playback performing. For Harris it is about being 'mindfully mortal: vulnerable to fate and destined to die, yet committed to life and its strivings.' He suggests that a performer who possesses such awareness helps 'us remember that our lives are limited and final, the actor helps us feel a renewed connection to life energy' (Harris 2002). Readers may also be reminded of the links between improvisation and death I drew in Chapter 7.

3. Standing before the teller

The performer stands *in* for the teller; she also stands *before* the teller. The teller watching on stage is never more than a few feet away from the performer playing her. There is no opportunity for the teller to directly influence the enactment except by her presence. If audiences are called to suspend willingly disbelief in the theatre, then in playback theatre the teller is called to suspend willingly and temporarily control over how her personal story is represented. This is a tremendous gift on the part of the teller and a huge responsibility of the part of the performers. Jo Salas writes that the performer draws her work from 'an empathic sense of an actual, present human being' (1999, p.25). She contrasts this with what she calls 'traditional actors' whose technique may distance them from the teller. I am not sure I fully accept Salas' contrast; nevertheless her call for an acute awareness of the teller is surely important in maintaining ethical performance.

4. Sensitivity to and keen awareness of difference: the 'otherness of the other'

In searching for a contemporary ethics and politics of playback beyond 'the illusion of a universally binding ethic', Jutta Heppekausen writes:

> Playback theatre is one of those practices that enable the complex possibility of real contact, real meeting to take place between people. In this, it represents a form of moral learning… The meetings, which occur between people, happen *face to face*; there is an emotional relationship. (Heppekausen 2003, p.3) [my emphasis]

She finds an ethics of playback in the acceptance and recognition of difference; the 'opening of a dialogue' through the recognition of the 'other'; and the acceptance of ambiguity and uncertainty. Her approach to playback eschews organized or codified formulations of ethical positions, instead preferring to stress the ethics that are called for in relationships with others. This notion of the 'face-to-face' encounter as the ground of ethics is found in the work of the French philosopher, Emmanuel Lévinas (see Erickson 1999). Lévinas considered the other to be 'unknowable' and ungraspable. He suggests that this fact calls us to responsibility toward the other. Jon Erickson writes of Lévinas:

> Lévinas continually states the importance of the maintenance of separation between self and the Other as essential for maintaining the ethical relation; in particular he marks the separation that prevents one from seeking reciprocity with the Other, which could as some point easily dissolve into an illusion of a complete identification between the two parties. (Erickson 1999, p.10)

Over- and easy-identification with the other (Llewelyn 1995) is, as we have already seen, one of the dangers of representation in playback theatre. Lévinas calls for a sustained awareness of the irreducible *otherness of the other.* It is an attitude essential in playback performing.

5. The role of the 'citizen actor'

Most playback practitioners are not professionally employed in that role. Most are employed in other fields and only perform in their spare time. Jonathan Fox believes this to be one of its virtues. He asserts his belief in the 'citizen actor' who performs as needed and 'melts back into the social fabric', who 'voluntarily absorb[s] the pain and problems of others' and who offers 'Service without security, without fanfare, without adulation' (Fox 1994, p.214). This together with the disciplines of the ensemble discussed in the previous chapter may work as brakes on the worst excesses of playing the other.

6. Making the everyday extraordinary

Alan Read, in his consideration of the ethics of theatre, argues that theatre is 'a domain beyond everyday tyrannies to take better notice of the real pleasures of everyday life' (Read 1993, p.36). As Conquergood did, he warns of the dangers of sensationalizing the life and practices of the other. In an argument, which I think we can adopt for playback theatre, Read says, 'the critical task might not be to domesticate the exotic but to exoticise the domestic' (Read 1993, p.7). We should be wary of looking for the sensational in conducting and performing and celebrate the astonishing nature of the everyday.

Concluding remarks

The mediaeval actors in Unsworth's *Morality Play* were right to question the ethics of playing the lives of others. They recognized the responsibilities attendant to this act. Playback theatre is, from one viewpoint, an act of astonishing hubris. How can performers with no detailed understanding of the complexity of the life of the teller enact his story? Yet they do and often the tellers are very pleased that they have taken this risk. In this chapter I have tried to explore some of the questions their work raises and to suggest some recommendations that may allow ethical performing.

The worst temptation for the playback performer is to be intoxicated with his own skill – to believe that what he is doing is some sort of 'magic' and that it somehow affords special insight for the teller. Humility is always a problematic word – it so often seems to mean a kind of false self-abnegation; nevertheless humility is the performer's friend. It protects him and the teller from the dangers of being seduced by the spectacle; it provides a defence against the presumption and arrogance of psychological interpretation.

Chapter 10

Reflexivity and the Personal Story: Playback Theatre as Social Intervention

Oh wad some power the Giftie gie us
To see oursels as others see us!
It wad frae monie a blunder free us

Rober Burns, 'To a Louse', *The Poems of Robert Burns* (Oxford University Press, 1904), p.139

In January 2000, Playback Theatre York performed to a group of users and professionals of mental health services. In the course of the performance a man told of his first admission to an acute psychiatric ward. On his first evening there he told us how he watched the charge nurse punch another young man in the chest and force him to take medication. He described his fear and concluded by saying 'I have never really been able to trust a mental health professional since that night'.

After the enactment the 'conductor' invited comments from the audience. The teller's community psychiatric nurse raised her hand and talked about her reaction to his story. She said she felt very 'angry and ashamed' about what had happened to him. She went on to describe her feelings as she watched him tell. She wondered if she should have 'brought' him to the performance and worried that it might make him upset and 'ill'. She then recognized that she was being over-protective and he could make a decision about whether he attended or not. She concluded by saying that she was pleased she had heard his story. From his seat in the audience, the teller reassured her that he felt 'OK'. This was followed by a professional in adolescent psychiatry coming onstage to describe her feelings of 'inadequacy' when working with young people with acute mental health problems.

Jonathan Fox argues that playback 'has the capacity to broker between worlds' and goes on to say that the 'ultimate purpose of playback' is to promote a 'radical social encounter' (Fox 1995, p.4). The dialogue between the mental health user and the nurse in Dundee might be seen as such a 'radical social encounter'. It exposed the operation of power in psychiatry and enabled people with very different experiences of those power relations to speak to each other. The 'teller' recounted an episode of the gross misuse of power; he told a story that challenged and produced a response from mental health professionals who saw themselves, in some way, as complicit with this exercise of power. It is an indication that playback can allow a dialogue amongst groups with very different power and status relations.

In this chapter, I will analyze the claim that playback can be a tool of social intervention. This claim for playback is certainly present amongst its practitioners and it generally seems to take three interrelated forms: that playback theatre gives an opportunity for radical social encounter and for opposing voices to be heard, that it provides a space for building what Feldhendler calls 'a culture of remembrance' (2001, p.8) in which the political and collective importance of remembering is emphasized, and third, that playback theatre provides a forum for marginalized and oppressed groups to tell their story. In the course of this chapter and in order to consider these claims I will briefly look at work in Fiji, India, Argentina, Germany and Britain.

With respect to its role as a tool of social intervention, however, playback theatre has its critics. The form does not develop strategies to counter oppression in the manner of the theatre of the oppressed, nor does it usually explicitly dramatize the social and political forces acting upon the lives of individuals and communities. Indeed, attempts to dramatize the social and political circumstances of the teller have sometimes been criticized by members of the playback community as dismissing the teller's unique story. The criticism is that playback lacks the social and cultural perspectives that frame individual experience – it can be seen as being over-individualistic.

Additionally and somewhat paradoxically, however, playback has been criticized for not attempting to resolve personal issues invoked by the teller, as would be the case, for example, in the psychodramatic or dramatherapy process. Some feel that the telling of personal stories in public places over-exposes the teller while allowing him no real opportunity for resolution and closure. As we saw in Chapter 2, this has sometimes been the critique when York Playback Theatre Company has performed to groups of people with mental health problems.

The form, therefore, finds itself in a difficult position, vulnerable to critique from two different standpoints – from those (usually therapists) who would criticize it for opening up personal issues that cannot be resolved in a public arena, and from those who would argue that its concentration on the individual narrative may be a bourgeois indulgence which misses a political analysis. It may be that being neither in the 'individualistic' therapy camp, nor in the 'political theatre' camp has meant that playback has found it hard to be accepted in either world. Of course one needs to be careful of polarizing these 'camps' – in reality they are not tightly drawn – nevertheless there is a sense in which playback does not have a place within culturally accepted categories.

In this uncomfortable position, what claims can playback theatre make? In this chapter I will provide examples that support the claims of playback practitioners for its political and social efficacy. I will give examples of how playback can provide the opportunity for social and political encounter through recollection and storytelling. I will then go on to examine in some detail two challenges to playback theatre that come implicitly from the practice of psychodrama and the theatre of the oppressed. I will go on to address these challenges and, in doing so, establish one further proposal regarding playback's political and social purpose: that the form allows individual stories to be opened up to multiple perspectives that allows tellers, spectators and performers insight into the provisional – and thus changeable – ways in which we *'story' our experience.* To put this another way, it will be proposed that the multiple levels of reflexivity opened up by the playback process challenge what one might call *the tyranny of the closed, fixed viewpoint*; they present alternatives to the point-of-view that does not recognize the contingency of all points-of-view.

Building a culture of remembrance

Milan Kundera tells us out of his experience of Soviet-controlled Czechoslovakia that 'the struggle of man against power is the struggle of memory against forgetting' (1982, p.3). For him, remembering is an act of resistance. Richard Kearney makes the same point when he writes that 'the horror of moral evil must be retrieved from oblivion by means of narrative remembering' (Kearney 2002, p.48). It is memory – and particularly public remembering – that can provide a resistance to the powerful. I want to explore here the claim that playback provides a space for what Kearney calls the 'little narratives of the vanquished' (p.61), narratives he opposes to the 'Grand Narratives' of the victor.[1] Playback can, and often does, provide a forum for those who have been silent or silenced. As Fox writes:

1 Of course Kearney's binary is problematic; since it places both the 'oppressed' and the 'oppressor' in seemingly immutable positions in relation to each other, and, therefore, masks the nuances and subtleties of their circumstances (the 'victors' may also have 'little narratives' to tell).

> I believe that the forces for whitewashing history are very strong – often the rich and powerful write it to their advantage – and that therefore it is necessary to make a place for the 'unofficial history' of those who suffer or are not heard. (Fox and Dauber 1999, p.196)

Although certainly not exclusively, playback theatre has often been performed to audiences whose stories comprise 'unofficial history': children who suffered in the political violence in Fiji; lesbian, gay and transgender people in the United States; the relatives and friends of 'the disappeared ones' in Argentina; stories from Germany's Nazi past; refugees in France; playback in prisons and, of course, with users of mental health services in Britain.

The following account by Maria Elena Garavelli in *Interplay* in 2001 illustrates the point. She describes a performance that took place in La Plata, Argentina, in March 2000. Her playback theatre company, 'El Pasaje', was invited to perform at the first 'Conference on the Construction of Collective Memory'. The event was organized to acknowledge and record the experiences of the relatives of those who had 'disappeared' during the Argentinean dictatorship. The disturbing stories told at that performance convey the terror of the dictatorship and the inability and unwillingness of many to forget. Garavelli writes about the 'collective amnesia' that accompanied that period and the potential of playback theatre to aid in the process of 'the collective construction of memory':

> The silence and amnesia which veil the years of repression and the military dictatorship...create black holes produced by state terrorism among communities, and leave us alone and isolated – rendering us impotent against the unbridled power of those who thrive through the complicity of our skepticism, or our failure to take part in acts of solidarity.
>
> The Playback Theatre Company offers a space to patch up around these holes, to restore a fabric ravaged by hate, corruption, abuse and the merciless struggle for power. An empty stage to be filled with stories that people are ready to tell about their experiences, and which need to be passed on to the community – a space where trust allows these stories to be told; stories that bear witness to other truths about what is happening. [playback provides] *A space to build this alternative reality, to register opposing accounts, to look for the truth in other versions and voices...to make the truth apparent through the accounts of witnesses.* (Garavelli 2001, p.3) [my emphasis]

In this last sentence, Garavelli eloquently describes a vision of playback theatre to which most of its practitioners would subscribe. For example, the German playback practitioner, Daniel Feldhendler, in the same issue of

Interplay (perhaps significantly the first to appear after the September 11 attacks), develops this notion of the role of playback theatre in the 'collective construction of memory' in relation to the experience of the German people. He summarizes it as the 'culture of remembrance' in the following way: 'Playback theatre is an instrument of the culture of remembrance, where the personal stories of many people may come together, and where they can be connected to the wider history' (Feldhendler 2001, p.8).

Maria Elena Garavelli claims that playback theatre provides a space in which to bear witness; register opposing accounts; and look for the 'truth' in different voices (presumably those of tellers and performers). In my view these claims are borne out by the work done in many different places of conflict throughout the world. It would take too long to list them, however these examples will suffice: Aviva Apel-Rosenthal and Nurit Shoshan in Tel Aviv, who bring together Palestinians and Israelis for performances; or Cyril Alexander and his company Sterling Playback Theatre, based in Chennai, Southern India (Garavelli 2003, p.18) who work with audiences of different castes; or, by way of contrast, the Hudson River Playback Theatre Company in New York State who staged a series of performances before the 2004 Presidential election with the aim of encouraging reflection and to 'help bring back a meaningful democracy' (Salas 2004b, p.7).

There are many accounts in the playback theatre literature of personal and political oppression told in performances and it is clear that the telling and witnessing of such stories is considered by its practitioners to be one of the key reasons for the work. Sometimes, however, members of the audience do not welcome these stories. Peni Moore (2002) has written about playback theatre with children in Fiji who suffered in the recent coup d'etat. She recounts one story, told during a performance, of a young Muslim girl made to watch as the women in her family were forced by 'the rebels' to strip and cook their food. Later during a performance interval one of the teachers came up to Moore and angrily asked why the company 'brought up these sort of stories when we are all just trying to forget and carry on with our lives'. Moore replied that it was important that the story had been told and had been 'accepted so that she would be able to get on with her life'. She went on to observe that this 'attitude of hiding the truth and talk of forgetting' is very common amongst 'male members of the oppressed community' (Moore 2002, p .8).

Heather Robb (1995), a New Zealander practising playback in France, described a similar episode in which attempts were made to 'silence' the voices of children in a performance held within a UNESCO event entitled Charter for Children's Rights. Her company had worked with a group of 30 to 40 children to prepare them to tell their stories at a forthcoming performance. The children had told many stories of physical abuse. When it came to the main event at which in the audience, together with the children, there were 'municipal officials and other official people who had been invited to speak on a panel after the performance', the children continued to tell their stories of abuse. As the conductor, Heather Robb, wrote 'I couldn't get them off the subject':

> I now get to the point where something totally unexpected happened: some adults suddenly interrupted to say how 'shocked' they were to see what they considered to be an abuse of these children's rights to intimacy. And the 'shocked' adults turned out to be those invited on the panel to talk about children's rights. (Robb 1995, p.1)

Robb continues by questioning the way that she handled the performance and noted 'the tremendous political implications that playback can have' and that she enjoyed the 'role of a political stirrer up and provocateur'. It was in response to this performance that Fox commented on the 'ultimate purpose of playback' being to promote a 'radical social encounter' (Fox 1995, p.4).

Closer to my home, it has been the experience of Playback Theatre York that, during their performances to users of mental health services, professionals have occasionally criticized the company for opening up a 'can of worms' which, they claim, may exacerbate the problems of individual members of the audience. I have looked at some of the important criticisms some have made in Chapter 2. Not surprisingly where playback has provided a forum for opposing accounts to be heard or for 'unofficial histories' to be told, it has produced some controversy.

The claims for playback theatre as a form of social intervention need to be considered alongside the challenges to its practice that come implicitly from the practice of the theatre of the oppressed and psychodrama in particular and it is to this I now wish to turn.

Two challenges to playback theatre

Who speaks? Who listens? Who is silent? Who is making meaning? These questions are always political ones. They are of course highly relevant to playback theatre, but also to qualitative research where the writer needs to be explicit about how subjectivity and ideology may influence the production of their work. This attempt to be 'explicit' about the provenance of the writing is recognition of the power inherent in interpreting the world and so in making knowledge; it is an attempt to reveal the dynamics at work in the production of any research. Usually termed *reflexivity* this process, Helen Callaway suggests, opens 'the way to a more radical consciousness of self in facing the political dimensions of fieldwork and constructing knowledge' (cited in Hertz 1997, p.viii). It is an attempt to be more aware of how ideology, culture, and politics are at work in any interpretive process. In this chapter I will propose that playback can work reflexively by increasing awareness of the interpretive processes at work in creating autobiographical narrative. But initially I will also consider two key challenges to playback practice: first, that because the teller of the autobiographical narrative remains a witness – not an active contributor – to the production of the drama this limits the reflexive and mutative possibilities of playback. Second, I will consider the criticism that because there is no explicit attempt to reveal the subjectivity and ideology of the performers the reflexive potential of the form is limited; as spectators we can only guess on what grounds the performers make their interpretive decisions.

The position of the teller in playback theatre

In playback theatre the teller is not involved in the enactment, he remains a spectator – albeit a spectated upon one. From the tradition of psychodrama and the theatre of the oppressed, this constitutes a significant and problematic difference. In his analysis of the history of catharsis, the founder of psychodrama Jacob Moreno identifies two kinds of catharsis, one primary and active, the other secondary and passive. He proposes an 'avenue' which led, on the one hand, 'from Greek drama to the conventional drama of today' (Moreno 1987, p.49) in which 'the process of mental catharsis was conceived as being localized in the spectator – a passive catharsis' (p.49). On the other hand, he proposes another avenue, which emerged from the religions of the East and the Near East in which 'the process of realization took place in the subject – the living person who was seeking the catharsis' (p.49). Moreno goes on to argue that psychodrama has performed a synthesis of these two avenues, yet he is very clear that passive catharsis is 'secondary' (p.50) to what he calls 'active catharsis'. He argues for the 'central, axiomatic and universal' (p.12) importance of *embodiment* in psychodrama and believes in the mutative power that derives from the active protagonist, empowered by his or her embodiment upon the stage. He might then comment unfavourably on playback's practice in regard to the teller.

Augusto Boal's analysis of the importance of the active involvement of the spectator (or spect-actor) comes from a different source than Moreno's. Boal's inspiration is Marxist in the sense that one might say that he argues for the protagonist 'seizing the means of representation'; and Brechtian, in his rejection of Aristotelian catharsis (Boal 1979). For Boal the 'mainstream theatre juxtaposes two worlds, the world of the audience and that of the stage' (Boal 1995, p.41). What happens on stage is 'autonomous' in the sense that the audience do not have the opportunity to change what is happening. 'The conventional theatre ritual' he argues 'is conservative, *immobiliste*, opposed to progress' (p.41). Although he does not deny that such theatre can transmit ideas, which are 'mobilizing', nevertheless, for him 'the ritual remains immobilizing' (p.42). Boal argues that the theatre of the oppressed activates theatre, creating a 'totally transitive' relationship between the stage and the audience. In this transitive relationship (later to be termed 'transitive democracy' in legislative theatre in Boal 1998) the spectator becomes the artist creating a 'world of images of his own reality' (Boal 1995, p.44).

For Boal, the oppressed must 'create their own world of images of their own oppressions' (p.42). Instead of being 'penetrated by the emotions of others', the 'oppressed becomes the artist' (p.43). Moreno's assertions come from the liberation of the individual through spontaneity, embodiment and the re-enactment of the traumatic, whereas Boal's emerge out of a political analysis of power in the theatre. Nevertheless both, from their own positions, pose a serious challenge to the relative passivity of the teller in playback theatre practice. Denying the protagonist the opportunity to perform seems, from the standpoint of Boal and Moreno, to be disempowering and, perhaps, even elitist since it emphasizes the interpretive authority of the actor.

The power of the performer

Bertold Brecht was famously critical of bourgeois theatre for hiding the ideology of the performance behind the representative illusion. Spectators left the theatre politically unchanged, because the play did not reveal the processes at work in the act of representation. Swept away by the illusion the audience did not have the opportunity to analyze how it was created; in his theatre he wanted the process of representation to be visible.

In light of this should it be of concern to playback practitioners that audience members, having seen the form for the first time, often say that it seems like 'magic'? Are the performers concealing ideological, interpretive processes behind the spectacle of improvisation? Does the sometimes astonishing versatility of the improvising performers obscure their cultural and personal blind spots? This is a challenging and difficult question for playback theatre practice and it is not one that allows an easy rebuttal. Playback is set up in such a way that there is no systematic means by which the performers can reveal their *a priori* assumptions to the audience. The actor is in a powerful position, they have as Barthes puts it 'the ownership of the means of enunciation' (cited in Richardson 1994, p.27). They must therefore accept responsibility for their interpretative roles.

These are two significant critiques of playback theatre and in the remainder of this chapter I want to address these challenges to its practice. I fully accept the power of the critique and do not wish to offer an apologetic or shy away from that. While accepting their validity I will argue that the form can provide a particular kind of space for building 'a culture of remembrance'. I will argue that this space is characterized by:

1. The exposure of the teller's story to multiple levels of reflexivity.
2. The 'dramatization' of the often contested relationship between the personal and public. Playback theatre implicitly and explicitly always raises the politically loaded question: 'What personal stories can be revealed in a public place?'
3. The improvised and polyphonous response of the performers.
4. The importance of the visibility of a gap between the actor and character.

1. Multiple levels of reflexivity

Stories can, as Ben Okri writes, 'drive you mad' (Okri 1996, p.25). They can 'be either bacteria or light: they can infect a system, or illuminate a world' (p.33). Stories can imprison us as much as they can validate and provide the 'container' for inchoate experience. Although the stories we tell often seem to be immutable versions of the events that happen to us, they are always only partial (see Clifford 1986) in both senses of the word; they represent only 'part of' any experience and they are inevitably inflected by our 'preferred' perspectives on what has happened. It is my proposal that playback theatre provides a space in which the story can be 'loosened from its bindings' in order that the teller and the other spectators can see that what happened to the teller may be represented (re-presented) in other ways. To put this another way I am suggesting that playback opens the story up to multiple levels of *reflexivity*.

As we have seen, from the perspective of Moreno and Boal, the fact that the teller does not act in their own story presents a serious challenge to the credentials of playback theatre as a tool for social intervention. However I would argue that the non-involvement of the teller is not just a key difference; it is also a crucial constituent aspect of playback's dramaturgy – an aspect which builds complex levels of reflexive awareness into the performance. My argument goes like this: in full view of the audience, the teller recounts her story, casts the actors, as invited by the conductor, and, when the conductor says, 'Let's watch', turns to observe the ensuing enactment. She has become a spectator and, most importantly to my argument, a *spectated-upon spectator.* It is, I think, immediately clear that the spectatorship of the teller is very different from that of the audience member. She is, first, in view of the audience and, second, she is watching her own story being enacted – a fact that will profoundly effect the spectators' reception. Crucially, the fact that the audience are aware that they are watching the teller watching her own story will add a certain reflexive complexity to their viewing. Such complex viewing will surely bring a particular reflexive dynamic to the playback *mise-en-scène.* 'By most accounts', writes David MacBeth:

> reflexivity is a deconstructive exercise for locating the intersections of author, other, text, and world, and for penetrating the representation exercise itself. (MacBeth 2001, p.35)

The audience have, at least, two 'objects' in view: the teller-as-spectator and the performers' enactment. Moreover, the fact that the story has already been told in a playback performance may mean that the audience is more likely to pay greater attention to the means of representation employed by the performers. Through being a kind of 'exemplar of spectatorhood' the presence of the teller-as-spectator is likely to draw our attention to the 'representation exercise' and so remind the spectator of the contingency of what is taking place. The complex gaze of the spectator is likely to undermine the possibility of one, authoritative position from which to view, interpret or understand our personal experience. It may be that in this way playback expresses its 'political purpose': to reveal the processes through which humans make meaning out of their experience and so reveal these processes to be mutable and contingent: the 'cops in the head' (Boal 1995), those internalized figures of oppression, are divested of their totalizing authority.

2. Dramatizing the tension between the public and the personal: a border transgression?

Susan Bennett writes that theatre audiences' 'receptive processes are pre-activated by their anticipation of a particular kind of event' (Bennett 1997, p.112). For audience members unfamiliar with playback theatre, there may be some ambiguity in their anticipation. The practice invites spectators to share autobiographical material publicly in what resembles and is designated by the performers as a theatrical event. This expectation, conveyed by either pre-show publicity or by the performers, is likely to produce a degree of uncertainty since most theatre performances do not ask audience members to participate in this way. Since, as Bennett goes on to propose, a crucial determinant of audience involvement is 'the degree to which a performance is accessible through the codes audiences are accustomed to utililizing' (Bennett 1997, p.112), this uncertainty is likely to be an important factor in the decisions spectators make concerning the nature of the performance and therefore their involvement in it.

In what may be an unfamiliar event, spectators need to make decisions concerning their level of personal disclosure. Playback theatre, as some of its critics point out, does not offer the carefully constructed boundaries of the therapy space, yet it invites participants to tell personal experiences; this produces a tension in audiences that heightens awareness of what may or may not be revealed in particular types of public space.

Mary Douglas (1966), in her anthropological study of the categorization of the sacred and the profane, stresses the dangers cultures attribute to that which falls outside established categories. Perhaps that is the 'danger' that some critics detect in playback theatre – it is an event difficult to characterize: is it a 'performance' or a 'therapeutic' occasion of some kind? Playback theatre is haunted by this confusion. The fact that autobiographical experiences are called for and that the actors in their opening often tell personally revealing stories, together with the fact that a dialogue takes place between conductor and teller, suggests a therapeutic event of some kind. Yet the event is billed as 'theatre', actors perform, audiences applaud and laugh and the relationship between auditorium and stage suggests a relatively conventional theatre event. We might argue that playback theatre is, as Bill Nichols might put it, a 'deliberate border violation', which serves 'to announce a contestation of forms and purposes' (Nichols 1994, p.x). Violation is a strong word and I would prefer to use the phrase 'border transgression'. What is being contested or transgressed here? It is, among other things the relationship between the personal/private and the public. Playback invites and dramatizes this transgression.

It serves as a site for the negotiation and exploration of ethical concerns concerning the relationship between the personal and the public. Each time a teller steps forward to recount their own story they dramatize, in the decisions they make about what and how much to tell, that debate. Each time a spectator vicariously watches the telling and the enactment, questions are raised about what should and should not be told in public places. The telling of personal stories in public places seems to raise questions in the minds of the participants, not only about the specific issues that the stories evoke – the treatment of those with mental health problems or the 'disappearances' in Argentina, for example – but the telling also potentially invites a debate about speaking out or staying silent. This question is always a political one.

Consider this example taken from the experience of Playback Theatre York. During a performance to people with mental health problems, a woman came forward to tell of her suicidal thoughts. She described voices which called her to the sea to drown herself and the support friends gave her to resist their call. In the subsequent enactment some of the performers embodied those voices to present the terrifying sense of the story. It was performed, not as an 'illness story' but as an acknowledgment and validation of a distressing experience. However to some of the mental health professionals it was considered to be potentially disturbing for the teller and even, in some way, an exoneration of her 'illness behaviour'. It may be that this episode demonstrates, together with the incidents in Fiji and at the UNESCO event, that by inviting personal stories to be told in public places, playback theatre raises questions about the conditions necessary for the beneficial disclosure of autobiographical material. Implicit in the playback performance are the politically weighted questions: 'Is it acceptable to tell my story here?' or 'What status does my story have here?' and 'What effect will my story have?'

3. The improvised and polyphonous response of the performers

As discussed in Chapter 8, there is no authoritative playwright in playback theatre; the enactment develops out of the interplay of many 'voices'; each performer brings different perspectives to the enactment. There is no authoritative version of the story; it is brought together by the collaboration and interaction of multiple points of view: a process inherent in Sawyer's notion of 'collaborative emergence' . Although, as we have recognized, the interpretive power of the performer is relatively unchallenged by the audience in playback theatre – it certainly is challenged by the other performers.

The polyphony built into the design of playback theatre allows the teller's story to be opened up to many voices; no single person can control what will emerge during the performance; and in interacting with each other these voices 'discover' new perspectives on the story. Their interaction creates something new, and something that may challenge the unexamined and taken-for-granted. Of course the risk is that, under the pressure to 'produce' something, the performers may rely on stereotype, cliché and unconsidered assumption. The particularity of individual experience may be erased by the partiality (in both senses of the word) of the performers' response. This risk is always present, nevertheless the improvised nature of the form does allow the potential for registering multiple and reflexive voices.

4. Maintaining the gap

In Chapter 9 I stressed the importance of performers maintaining a gap between actor and character in order to reduce the risks of playing the other. I went on to suggest some ways in which that could be done. For the purposes of this discussion such strategies are equally important. The political and oppressive risk in playback theatre is that teller, performers and audience will be seduced by the spectacle and so lose their critical edge – that they will lose sight of the fact that any dramatization is an exercise in interpretation and meaning-making and thus always partial and contingent. Strategies which puncture the 'illusion' of the theatrical spectacle and maintain the gap between the teller's story and its representation will work to permit the kind of reflexivity that is necessary for playback to be effective.

Concluding remarks

> If theatre changes the world, nothing could be better, but also let us admit that it has not happened so far. It would be wiser (and less euphoric) if we accepted that it is possible to change our own lives through theatre. (Bharucha 1993, p.10)

Playback theatre, I have argued, does offer an opportunity for marginalized voices to be heard and acknowledged and for opposing accounts to be registered. That is certainly the claim of the playback community, and it is one that can be readily exemplified. However, what is perhaps more interesting about the form is the way in which it provides a space in which the processes of representing experience can be made visible and thus seen to be contingent and provisional. The multiple levels of reflexivity apparent in a playback theatre performance can reveal and question the assumptions we make as we construct the stories we tell of ourselves. It is in this way, I think, that playback theatre expresses its political purpose: by disclosing the mutability of 'storied' selves. To paraphrase what Mary Douglas says of the joke: an effective playback enactment 'is a play upon form that affords an opportunity for realizing that an accepted pattern has no necessity' (1975, p.96).

Chapter 11

Concluding Thoughts

Throughout this book I have suggested ways in which players can avoid the worst dangers of playing the other. It has been proposed that working within an ensemble; allowing the limitations of the actors work to be visible; keeping a sense of vulnerability in the face of the teller and the audience; maintaining a keen awareness of difference; being cautious of presuming a 'sameness' between our experience and that of the teller; and seeking to preserve a position *in between* exploration in the performance and the representation of the teller's story, are all important in reducing the risks of improvising personal stories. In the discussion on an ethics of playback I have largely avoided the call for 'authenticity' in the performer largely because such a term is so difficult to define, is easily misunderstood and can, if misused, conceal the motivations and limitations of the performer. As this book draws to a close I want to reclaim this term. Doing so will enable me to draw together some of the lines of argument that have been developed.

Authenticity reconsidered

'I have always taken the tips of my fingers for the beginning of her hair' writes Jarbés (in Hughes and Brecht, 1978). In this book I have pointed to the complex slippage of identities, the projections and identifications that are inevitable in the improvisation of personal stories. It is not surprising, therefore, given the ethical sensitivity of playing the other's story that the playback community have sought to find solid ground for their work through the notion of authenticity. In this book I have questioned the notion of 'authentic acting' by arguing that the complexity of influence and impulse at work within and between the performers and their audience make the idea of authentically 'being yourself' as an actor a highly problematic one. The desire for the solid ground of a trustworthy authentic self on which the ethics of playing the other can lie is understandable but unsustainable. Despite this critique however the concept of authenticity is far too important to be abandoned all together. In this section I want to reconsider it and retrieve it.

For Adorno the 'jargon of authenticity' forestalled critical thought and provided a smokescreen for intolerance. This jargon, he wrote, ascends 'beyond the realm of the actual, conditioned, and contestable' (Adorno 2003, p.7). He is not alone in a concern about contemporary perspectives on authenticity. The philosopher Charles Taylor laments what he calls the 'degraded, absurd or trivialized forms' (1991, p.29) of authenticity which have come to dominate contemporary thought. These emphasize the individual search for self-knowledge and self-discovery, without recourse to the social and cultural influences on identity. They use such phrases as 'find the real self within' or 'discover who you really are' without recognizing the crucial role played by culture and relationship. In fact these approaches often distrust society and culture as forces that deflect and seduce the individual on his or her path to self-discovery. Taylor (1991, p.25) suggests that this modern take on authenticity is 'a child of the Romantic period' which lamented the loss of the individual to the forces of industrialization.

Charles Guignon (2004) in his valuable overview of the history of the authenticity also writes of this contemporary view of authenticity which emphasizes the inner personal journey to find the true self within. Guignon writes that from this distinctively modern outlook:

> the self is experienced as a nuclear self, something self-defining and self-contained, rather than as the extended self of earlier times. Understood as a knowing subject, the self is a centre of experience, with no definite relations to anything outside itself'. (Guignon 2004, p.43)

To be authentic in the contemporary formulation is to be *autonomous.* The aim is to discover the self; there is no need necessarily to look beyond the self to do that. The social is to be distrusted as a force which will delude the true self into serving inauthentic ends.

Both Taylor and Guignon are critical of this search for authenticity, which they suggest fails to recognize an individual's dependency on others. They are concerned about the loss of social solidarity that results from this desire for self-discovery. In their different ways they argue for a view of authenticity which is 'a *social* virtue' (Guignon 2004, p.161) rather than a personal one. Taylor writes that we can only define our identity 'against the background of things that matter' and that to 'bracket out history, nature, society, the demands of solidarity' would be to eliminate all those things that could matter to us. Authenticity, he proposes 'is not the enemy of demands that emanate from beyond the self; it supposes such demands' (Taylor 1991, p.41). In other words, our identity is found in *relation* to others, not through an isolating internal search. Guignon puts this nicely when he calls for a stance on authenticity that 'is motivated less by a concern with making than with finding, less by calling forth than being called' (Guignon 2004, p.167).

What implications do these arguments have for the practice of playback theatre? As we have already noted, there are significant ethical demands on performers because of the immediacy and intimacy of the dramatization of personal stories in public places. It may be that a reworking of the notion of authenticity along the lines suggested by Taylor and Guignon will provide a more robust concept in developing an ethics of playback theatre. Along with them I want to argue for a social and *relational* notion of authenticity. That if it is possible to talk of authenticity at all then we look to authenticity *in and through relationships with tellers, spectators, and performers.*

In this book, I have stressed the importance of the ensemble as providing the necessary conditions for risk-taking and openness in performance and that a company who have worked together regularly are more likely to have the necessary sensitivity to 'play the other'. The ensemble is both the defender and protector of the teller and of the performer. I have stressed the relational nature of playback performing through such concepts as 'empathic resonance', 'collaborative emergence', 'dialogic truth', and the vulnerability of the performer in the face of the audience.

To be more specific, we might identify the following characteristics of relational authenticity in respect to the playback performer:

1. *Openness*: particularly the characteristics of the open performer stressed in Chapter 2. The open performer allows the action to emerge or be discovered through the act of performing; the performers work closely together; there is a sense of risk on the part of the actors and musicians which is 'held' by the ensemble; and the performers leave interpretive space for the teller and the audience to attribute their own meanings.
2. A willingness, as a performer, to *stay in a place of uncertainty* between awareness of the self and awareness of the other. Guignon (2004) talks of two basic life-orientations: the first, 'enownment' refers to our desire and ability to know the self, to be self-reflective and to be aware of the impact one is having on others. The second he terms 'releasement', here he refers to our capacity for giving ourselves over to the flow of events, of suspending the ego in order to contribute to whatever is emerging. He argues that both capacities are necessary for the 'good life'. As we have seen, they are both recognized as important in playback. Self-knowledge and reflection are important to ethical performance since an actor who does not know the impact of his work, or the personal 'ghosts' that may haunt it, takes risks with others' stories. But the performer must also have the capacity to give way to others, to allow himself

to 'yield' and be 'penetrated', and to allow enactments to emerge. As I stressed in Chapter 6 ethical performers are on a 'narrow ridge' between these two orientations.

3. The *sensitivity* of the performer to the impact they are having in the audience. I am referring to the performers taking responsibility for their interpretations and the meanings they inevitably create. I have stressed the dangers of over-identification and caricature. Under the pressure to 'do something', or in a desire to create a spectacle for the audience, there is always the risk that actors will lose their sense of the teller's narrative and the effect their work is having on the audience. The sensitivity of the performer is a mark of relational authenticity in playback performing.
4. The *vulnerability* of the performer. In Chapter 9 I stressed the importance of the actor maintaining a sense of vulnerability in their work. I suggested that it can produce lively and committed work and permit the performer to be open to the teller's story as well as be closer to their own emotional world.
5. A *commitment to the ensemble.* As I have stressed in Chapter 8 the company can both support and protect. It supports actors to take risks and, through work in rehearsal, protects tellers from the worst dangers of playing the other.

I am proposing these criteria as characteristic of relational authenticity in playback performing. They are proposals which point to our ethical disposition as playback performers and so can be read alongside the suggestions made in Chapter 9 for an ethical playing of the other.

Playback theatre has its critics. It is always in a difficult position, lying as it does between the theatrical and the therapeutic. It rarely satisfies those dedicated to the craft of theatre or to the carefully contained work of group and individual therapy. It can be criticized by those who feel it over-emphasizes the individual story and misses a political analysis and by those who consider that the telling of personal stories in public places is potentially risky and exploitative. These criticisms have weight and should not be dismissed lightly. As I have argued in Chapter 10, playback theatre expresses its political purpose by first providing a space for the stories of those who have been silenced or marginalized and, second, by introducing a complex level of reflexivity to the telling and dramatization of personal stories in order that tellers and spectators are aware of the provisional and mutative nature of those stories. In this final chapter I wish to turn again to the criticism that playback lacks the boundaries necessary to protect tellers.

Readers will recall the criticisms made in this regard in Chapter 2. Playback's critics had two main concerns: the first that a public performance is an inappropriate place to ask for personal stories to be told, and the second that the tellers are being manipulated for entertainment and spectacle. It is clear that these critics felt that they had attended an event that did not possess the 'boundaries' they believed to be important when personal stories are told, more than that they felt that the tellers, at best, were not fully informed about the nature of the event and, at worse, manipulated into providing personal stories for 'entertainment'.

In dramatherapy, psychodrama, psychotherapy and counselling, boundaries mark out a space. They are considered to provide defence and protection for those inside, defining what lies within and what is excluded (Clarkson 1995, p.48). In these disciplines the notion of the boundary seems to be employed both literally and metaphorically. Literally, it denotes the physical space within which the consultation occurs. Don Feasey, for example, stresses that attending to the place where the therapy occurs helps to create a therapeutic relationship. He writes 'It is the secret and confidential world in which the therapist and the client can come together' (Feasey 2000, p.13). Boundaries are also used metaphorically to suggest the delineation of a period within which certain relationships and levels of exposure are possible. It is common for therapists to have very clearly defined sessions – the 50-minute hour, for example.

Boundaries are also employed to establish the relationship between therapist and client. They are maintained in order to suggest the level of possible personal intimacy, to mark the limits of any personal disclosure by the therapist, and to control communication outside the sessions. A practice in which personal exposure is desirable and in which complex transferential relationships take place, requires robust attention to its boundaries. The process of transference, for example, involves the loosening of the boundaries between self and other as the client (or therapist) symbolically recreates in the therapist (or client) qualities that are repressed or that belong to a significant other (Brooks 1994; Clarkson 1995). It is a process which involves a certain 'slippage' of identity. Clarkson defines it thus: 'The transferential/countertransferential relationship is the experience of unconscious wishes and fears transferred on to or into the therapeutic partnership' (Clarkson 1995, p.62).

It is axiomatic of psychotherapeutic practice that, in order for that 'slippage' of identities across the 'therapeutic partnership' to take place, it is necessary to create and maintain well-defined outer 'frames' (Clarkson 1995; Langs 1976). Critics see, in terms of what the teller is being asked to do, similar processes to the therapeutic encounter. The teller is encouraged to reveal personal experience within a space that is unprotected by the usual therapeutic protocols, within relationships that have not been clearly defined, and witness an enactment in which it is likely that processes of identification and transference will occur. It is not surprising that some find this disturbing.

In the light of this how can playback practitioners respond? I want to offer two responses here, mindful of the fact that these will be coloured by my enthusiasm for, and support of, playback practice. The first response to the risk of telling personal stories in public places is to argue that there are protective boundaries in playback; the second is that the 'confusion' of categories between theatre and therapy is an important and definitive feature of the practice.

First response: there *are* 'boundaries' in playback practice

In her introduction to dramatherapy, Sue Jennings writes of the 'distancing mechanisms' of theatre, which 'paradoxically...serve to bring us closer to ourselves' (Jennings 1998, p.36). For her, and for many theorists in dramatherapy (Jones 1996; Landy 1993), theatrical conventions which clearly define the fictional and dramatic from the everyday, such as clearly defined stage areas or the use of costume, provide psychic distance from the events onstage at the same time as paradoxically allowing intense identification with them. This theory has proved important in countering the arguments of those concerned with the danger of introducing drama to vulnerable client groups and has proved useful in shaping therapeutic decisions concerning the level of engagement. Phil Jones (1996, p.104), for example, shows how, according to the client's needs, the therapist can devise dramatic structures in order to promote close empathic identification with the material or allow distance and perspective upon it. In dramatherapy the 'dramatic paradox' (Landy 1993, p.15) – we come closer to ourselves through the distance that theatre provides – has proved a key concept in establishing and understanding the therapeutic possibilities of drama.

The boundary between the telling and the enactment is clearly drawn in playback theatre. For example, clear 'rules' exist concerning the relationship between the actors and the teller. The actors are discouraged from talking to the teller during the telling; at this stage their role is confined to listening. The actors will stand when cast by the teller, but will only move into enactment when the conductor calls 'Let's watch' and the musician begins to play. These 'rules' are designed to give the performers the necessary 'permission' to improvise; they clarify the boundary between the telling and the enactment for tellers, spectators and actors.

The playback form is a relatively simple and stable one and, by and large, performing companies do not veer too far from the standard playback conventions. For Fox these conventions constitute rules, which invest playback with a ritual quality:

> The teller must come to the chair; the teller must stay in the chair during the enactment; the teller must tell a personal story. The actors stand when picked for a role; the actors do not talk during the interview. The conductor does not interrupt the enactment; the conductor checks in with the teller after the enactment; the conductor dismisses the teller from the chair. These are *some* of them. Without the clear framework provided by the rules, spontaneity can quickly turn into chaos, creativity to confusion. With it, the members of the audience feel safe enough to let themselves go into trance, allowing unforeseen breakthroughs. (Fox and Dauber 1999, p.128)

Throughout his essay, entitled 'A Ritual for our Time', Fox is making the point that what he calls the 'ritual' elements of playback hold (p.124) or contain the vulnerabilities of both the performers and the audience. In this book I prefer not to use the term ritual,[1] preferring to think of playback's formal conventions.

Playback theatre practitioners often do seem to attend carefully to boundaries. There is, in the practice of Playback Theatre York for example, an at times obsessional attention to 'edges' or to the 'margins'. The company will spend considerable time in pre-performance rehearsals working out the precise order of the opening sequence or they will rehearse and re-rehearse the conventions used at the beginning of each enactment. Members of the company will enjoin others to turn to the teller at the conclusion of each dramatization or remind each other to stay still until the teller has finished speaking and only then 'tidy up' the stage. Of course, this may be due to a certain performance anxiety; after all in improvisation there is little one can control except these conventions. However, its purpose is almost certainly also related to a recognition of the importance of attending to the edges that create boundaries between the 'telling' and the 'enactment'.

Schechner's 'axiom of frames' may be important here. He proposes 'an axiom of frames which generally applies in the theatre: the looser an outer frame, the tighter the inner, and conversely, the looser the inner, the more important the outer' (1988, p.14). The attention to the rules and boundaries in playback theatre may well be an attempt to tighten the outer frame so that the inner one can be loose enough for improvisation and openness of telling and performing.

1 It seems to be that ritual is not, by virtue of its cultural contingency, easily transferable across cultures. Rituals carry canonical messages that are embedded in their practice and culture. Playback does not, or should not, carry canonical messages. The danger of conceiving of playback as ritual lies in the implicit assumption that it, therefore, carries some sort of truth, or ideology or system of belief. Once we conceive of a playback performance as a kind of ritual, we seem to implicate the spectator in an event that they most likely did not sign up for. The individual member of the audience becomes an unknowing celebrant. Rappaport, R. (1999) *Ritual and Religion in the Making of Humanity*. Cambridge: Cambridge University Press.

Second response: the blurring of categories is a key characteristic of playback theatre

In Chapter 10 I considered the anomalous nature of the playback event and the fact that, for some, it sets up a confusion of categories. The event is billed as 'theatre', actors perform, audiences applaud and laugh and the relationship between auditorium and stage suggests a relatively conventional theatre event. Yet personal stories are invited in an atmosphere that, for some, can seem like therapy. This 'confusion' is a definitive feature of playback and a characteristic that challenges and brings into question the proper and appropriate conditions for the telling of personal stories in public places.

The *sine qua non* of therapy is privacy. The client rightly expects that the consultation will be confidential and the therapist is bound to accept the ethical principles concerning the privacy of the patient (Rowson 2001). By inviting personal stories to be told in public places, however, playback queries assumptions about the conditions necessary for the beneficial disclosure of autobiographical material. As 'apologists' for the form, Steve Nash and I wrote the following in response to the criticism that playback was an 'up-market *Oprah Winfrey Show*':

> It is our contention that playback theatre challenges the 'privatization of the personal' – a characteristic of modern Western European culture. Ours is a culture in which stories of personal distress have been increasingly colonized by the expert, the counsellor and the therapist. The experience of distress is thus not only segregated from the everyday, but it is also separated from the collective by the overwhelming emphasis on the necessity for individual personal growth. Together with the privatization of the railways has arrived the privatization of personal pain and distress. (Nash and Rowe 2000/2001, p.17)

The 'apologist' for playback may go on to argue that the desire to expose more of the personal and autobiographical through such programmes as, for example, *The Jerry Springer Show* and *Big Brother* does not contradict the argument but rather reinforces it. As Laura Mulvey (1975) writes scopophilia – the pleasure that derives from looking – turns the other into an object for sexual gratification. The desire to expose and be exposed in contemporary culture may be a sign of repression, a sign that 'real' contact is denied. Nash and Rowe continue:

> are these [reality TV programmes] not the signs of the very privatization that we are suggesting? Are they not the visible signs of repression? The personal has become pornographic precisely because it has gone underground. Are we not titillated by TV's seedy revelations

> because we no longer have the real thing? The sentimental and the voyeuristic are replacing emotion and intimacy and in their place we have an ersatz experience. (Nash and Rowe 2000/2001, p.17)

Despite the problems of arguing that playback might offer a return to the 'real thing', it does raise questions about the proper place of the personal within the public domain and thus poses, albeit implicitly, a challenge to therapy. If playback is a 'border transgression' then it presents a challenge to the individualized, privatized and de-politicized nature of therapy. Playback is not alone in doing so. What is loosely called the 'anti-psychiatry movement' also challenges the privatization – and therefore the apparent apolitical nature – of therapy (Masson 1990; Spinelli 1994; Tottin 2000). Critics have noted the sequestration of personal distress by the therapy services, the mystification of the means of offering help and, in Masson's (1990) view, its conspiratorial professionalization. The sternest critics of therapy have aimed their fire at its inability to engage with issues of social justice. Jeffrey Masson, for example, writes that every therapy he has examined 'displays a lack of interest in social injustice... Each shows an implicit acceptance of the status quo. In brief, almost every therapy shows a certain lack of interest in the world' (Masson 1990, p.283).

The confusion of categories that characterizes playback unsettles cultural conventions concerning the telling of personal stories in public places and thus poses a challenge to therapeutic orthodoxy. The question: 'Can I tell my story in this place and in front of these people?' is, in part, always a political one. Playback theatre always raises this and other questions; in doing so challenges the status quo that exists around the telling of personal stories in public places.

The risks of playback are many: the performers can become dazzled by their desire to create a spectacle; they can use the freedom they have to show off their skills to the expense of the teller's story. The performers can be so convinced that their own experience matches the tellers that they become lost in self-delusion. They can eradicate the difference and individuality of the teller's story by assuming too much correspondence with their own. They can over-interpret and impose meanings that are a step to far.

But there are also opposite kinds of risks too. Out of their desire to be 'loyal to the teller' the performers can play it too safe and not engage in the exploration with their fellow players that, as I have proposed in this book, gives playback its energy. Viola Spolin is right when she maintains that improvisation can 'topple old frames of reference'; playback performers need to be prepared to risk adding something new to the story as it was told. Otherwise the endeavour becomes a rather stale and uninteresting exercise.

Final comments

The following words from Georges Bataille capture my desire to rethink playback theatre in such a way that its humanness comes into the foreground. He writes: 'My wish is that in any love of the unknown...we can, by ousting transcendence, attain such great simplicity as to relate that love to an earthly love, echoing it to infinity' (1997, p.97). In this book I have proposed that playback performers offer a *response*: one that is never more than fully human, always partial and inevitably shot through with subjectivity and omission. Playback theatre can be tender, sad, exquisitely funny, enlightening, and terrifying. It can also be crude, over-psychological and poorly performed; with improvised theatre failure and caricature is only ever a breath away. In whatever way playback is performed, its humanness is its greatest strength and its greatest weakness. In this book I have tried to bring this humanness to the fore and to explore the opportunities and risks when performers play the other and tellers recount personal stories in public places.

Jonathan Fox finishes *Acts of Service* with the following words: 'For me, what is most important is to create a theatre that is neither sentimental nor demonic, hermetic not confrontational, but ultimately a theatre of love' (1994, p.216). In light of my reconsideration of authenticity, 'love' needs to be characterized as a consciousness of contingency – a realization of our vulnerability and finitude. In this book I have sought to find ways of conceptualizing playback theatre that recognize the inevitably incomplete, fallible and vulnerable nature of the performer's response to the teller's story, in doing so I have questioned some of the current discourse that has developed to explain the practice.

In Bataille's words, I have been keen to 'oust transcendence' and reject suggestions that some sort of magic is taking place (Bataille 1997). That is never the case; to conceive of playback as some sort of 'magic' is always dangerous because it suggests a process that detaches the teller and the audience from the performers. It gives the performers some sort of power and supposed privileged insight that they do not in reality possess. For me the most effective playback takes place when everyone knows that they are taking part in a theatrical event in which the performers are given the space and opportunity to respond, through their skill, experience and personal history, to the story of the teller. For tellers, spectators and performers alike this can become a fascinating process which exposes the ways in which personal stories can be represented and potentially opens up new perspectives for tellers and spectators. This takes place when there is the quality of what I have called 'openness' in telling and performing.

As I write this at the end of eight years of researching and practising playback theatre, I am drawn to some lines taken from a poem entitled

Happiness by Jane Hirschfield: 'for what else might happiness be/than to be porous, opened, rinsed through/by the beings and things?' (Hirschfield 2005). Her lines convey, for me, the openness that I have referred to throughout this book. At its best the playback event can permit this kind of porousness and opening up. Tellers have the courage to tell their personal stories in public places and to give room for the performers to explore their story; the performers for their part respond to this out of their skills, desires and histories. They try to find a way to match the gift of the teller's story. In effective playback the story becomes 'porous, opened, rinsed through' as it is exposed to the improvising performers in relation with each other and with the audience. For me, the most interesting playback is that which is a little irreverent, which plays, sometimes almost parodies, the meanings that may be attributed to the teller's story. It is axiomatic of the current interest in 'narrative therapy' that we can be trapped, as well as validated, by our own stories. Effective playback, through the processes of openness, loosens the 'ties' of the story, opens up other possible interpretations and reveals the means through which we make sense of our experience.

Appendix 1

Playback Theatre: A Short Story

Below is the full text, and background to Rona's story, which is discussed in Chapters 1 and 6.

Rona had arrived half an hour early to put the heater on, but still the room felt cold. It was the kind of damp cold you get in English church halls in November. The heater only served to create the promise of warmth, a promise which Rona knew would never be realized before the others arrived. She sighed and began to fill the hot water boiler.

'I'm going to make sure I tell a story tonight,' she thought to herself as she gathered the chipped and stained coffee mugs together.

She began to wonder what story she would tell. It was never easy to decide. There was the one about Helen, her work colleague, who had argued with her over the meaning of the word 'spirituality', the row had been a flaming one, and in retrospect, Rona was sure that it was about something far more important than they were acknowledging. Perhaps the company would help her to work it out.

Or perhaps she should tell the one about her father phoning earlier in the week. He never phoned, well only for discussions about money or travel direction, so when Rona heard him say, 'Hello love, it's Dad,' she was both surprised and a little anxious.

'I thought I'd phone for a chat. Your mother is out and there's nothing on the TV, so I thought why not phone my daughter. How are things?'

'Fine,' replied Rona and began to tell him about the changes in work that had been concerning her so much recently. This was the usual pattern of their conversations, Rona would talk of her work and he would interject with stories from his own working life which were intended as advice, but which only irritated Rona. As she launched into a detailed explanation of management reorganizations, Rona was aware that something was different, usually her father would have interrupted by now, usually he would have begun one of his stories intended as an illustration of what she was saying. But today there was a silence. A demanding, blackening silence was expanding into the space between them. Rona's monologue was beginning to lose its energy and purpose, as this silence sucked the strength from her. She stopped abruptly. There was a silence, then her father said: 'I've been to the hospital today.'

'Yes, I could tell that story' she thought as she sat by the heater trying to gather the warmth into her thin body. Usually Rona was pleased with her body.

She had been something of a dancer in her twenties and still, in her mid-forties, and after two children, she had a poise and a freedom of movement which marked her out. But at this moment, sitting in front of a single heater in a damp English church hall in November, she did not feel pleased with her body at all.

Rona's thoughts were interrupted by the sound of the outside door being opened, and as she rose to her feet, Bruno entered opening his arms to invite Rona into one of his big warm embraces. Rona and Bruno had known each other for nearly five years, and over that time, through all the rehearsals and performances, a physical easiness had grown between them. As Bruno drew her to him, she enjoyed the soft roundness of his body and exhilarating smell of the outside world he had brought with him.

'How's your daughter?' asked Rona. Bruno's 14-year-old daughter had been seriously ill recently and this had put enormous stress on the whole family. As Bruno said at the last rehearsal, 'Her illness has made us all question what we are doing together...we don't use the word family any more.'

'She's much better,' said Bruno, and he went on to tell her of the endless visits to hospital and the sleepless nights they had spent sitting by her bedside. As Bruno spoke Rona's mind drifted to her father's phone call...

'Yes, I must tell a story tonight,' she thought to herself.

Rona squeezed Bruno's hand.

By now other members of the company had arrived. Bridget, Laura, Amanda, Fran and Lawrence were standing in a circle laughing about something.

As Rona caught sight of the gathering company, she felt a small knot of dread that usually accompanied her on these occasions. There was little real sense to it; she'd known these people for years and they were, she knew, glad to see her. Every group of people finds its own way of handling those difficult moments of meeting. The tricky questions about whether to hug, kiss, shake hands or merely nod to each other, are answered, or at least eased by establishing patterns of behaviour that suit the group and its aims. This group had evolved a style of meeting which comprised of hugging and kissing accompanied by shouting, screaming and laughing. It was a very noisy affair which, to the outsider, would confirm whatever prejudices they had about 'theatre' people as being rather insincere and over-demonstrative.

It was not so much the hugging which caused Rona that small sense of dread, but the moments in between. Having hugged and exchanged greetings with Bridget and established that they were both 'Fine', she found herself, for a moment, alone. It was this she found so difficult. Watching uncertainly as others greeted each other with far more fulsomeness than she felt she could muster, it seemed to her that they were far more at ease than she was, far more able to receive warmth from each other. In her worst moments these thoughts would burrow into her, subtly affecting all her relations with others in the company.

But there was another feeling that always seemed to be present during the only moments of each rehearsal. This was a kind of excitement and anticipation, which could not quite find an object and so was always accompanied by mild disappointment. It reminded her of when she was a child and her father, returning home from work, would play with her for a few minutes before turning his attention to the newspaper or a discussion with her mother and she was left stranded with feelings of that had no outlet.

By now Bridget, Amanda and Lawrence had got their coffees and formed a smoking group outside in the cold November air. Rona joined them.

'Can I scrounge a cigarette off someone?'

'I thought you'd given up,' said Amanda as she passed a packet of cigarettes to Rona.

'I have. It's great to be a non-smoker!' She said that as she watched the blue smoke swirling in the night air. Everyone laughed and joined in one of the greatest pleasures of smokers: its delicious conspiracy.

'Let's get started!' shouted Laura from inside and the smokers took their last drags and made their way into the hall.

A group of seven people stood in a circle. Rona began her customary series of stretches which were so familiar they required no thought. Bruno slapped his belly letting out deep roaring sounds. Amanda and Lawrence leant against each other back to back, while Bridget sang, trying to match the rhythm of Bruno's belly slapping. It was the usual beginning for this group.

'Let's do some warming up,' said Laura. 'Does anyone want to lead us in something?'

Amanda suggested this game in which each person close their eyes and tried to find their partner by calling out a pre-agreed signal, and the rehearsal began.

* * *

'I've got a story!' shouted Rona as she moved toward the storyteller's chair. She had to move quickly, otherwise someone would get there before her. She was determined to tell a story this week since, over the last few rehearsals, she had missed out. Either she did not think of one, or one of the others got there before her, but tonight she was going to make sure. She landed on the chair, skidding as she did so from the speed of arrival, and waited for one of the company to sit on the chair next to her.

Laura joined her and said, 'So what your story, Rona?'

The truth was that Rona had been in such a rush to get to the chair that she hadn't totally decided. She hoped that when she got there it would be clear what she wanted to say, and now, with Laura and the whole group waiting, she experienced a moment of panic. 'I'm wasting people's time' she thought to herself.

'It's about my father,' she said finally.

'OK,' said Laura. 'Choose someone to be you.'

Rona looked at the line of four actors sitting on chairs in front of a rack of coloured cloth. Who would she choose to play her? As her eyes moved along the group she was drawn to Bridget. It was something about the way she was sitting in the chair, slightly slumped as if pressed down by some force, a tension in her face and, unlike some of the others, not looking at Rona. It was likely, Rona thought, that Bridget did not want to be chosen, but there was something about her vulnerability, her reluctance, that drew Rona to say 'Bridget'. Bridget stood up.

'OK, so tell me about your story,' said Laura putting her hand on Rona's knee. Rona spoke of the phone call from her father telling her that he was going into hospital. She spoke of the darkening silence that had seemed to push out everything between them, filling the space with its demanding presence.

'It made me feel cold,' said Rona, suddenly feeling cold herself. 'I can feel it now.'

'Describe it to us,' said Laura.

'It's kind of bleak and very, very empty...well, empty yes, but also lonely, bereft, like...' Rona paused for a minute. 'It's like Sunday evenings at boarding school, in November, it's getting darker and colder and there are weeks and weeks before Christmas. Dark, cold, Victorian, cheerless buildings. That's what it was like.'

Rona hadn't expected to say the last bit, but having done so she felt a little leap of excitement, an almost sexual excitement.

'OK,' said Laura. 'So what happened next?'

'My father said that he had been to the hospital and he'd had some tests and was waiting for the results – something to do with pains in his stomach. He'd never told me about that before.'

'Choose someone to be your father,' said Laura.

Again Rona looked at the actors. This time she had no doubt. 'Bruno,' she said, and Bruno sprang to his feet as if he had always known he would be chosen.

'Give Bruno some words to describe your father in this story.'

'Oh, I don't know, I think he was a little nervous, a little irritated by me going on about work...it was so strange for him to phone and he seemed ill at ease.'

Laura patted Rona's hand as she said, looking toward the actors, 'This is Rona's story of a phone call with her father. Let's watch.'

* * *

Bruno felt he was bursting. His heart was thumping hard and he had a sick feeling. He knew Rona would choose him and he knew what he would do. Well no, that wasn't quite true. It would be more accurate to say that he had no worries about what he would do. An insistent energy would carry him. Amanda's music was feeding that energy, viscerally changing Bruno, and he used it to find his place on the stage. He dragged one of the chairs into the centre of the stage, and drawing himself in as tightly as he could manage, he sat on the chair and waited. He knew that the other actors would be forming a tableau around him but he couldn't see anything; they must all be behind him. He could hear, but not see, movement. It went silent and, it seemed to Bruno, rather dark. They too were waiting, he guessed.

There is a directional instruction that the company had often spoken about. It was that if, as an actor, you do not know what to say it is often effective to say how you are feeling at that moment because it is probably related to the character you are playing. Remembering this, Bruno said,

'I can't see you, it's dark here. Where are you?'

Enclosed tightly, as he was by his arms and by the hardness of the chair, Bruno waited. It seemed to him that his words were spreading a cold darkness across the stage and, he guessed, were freezing the actors. He felt a moment of panic. 'They don't know what to do with this,' he thought.

However, he was determined to stay with it, to wait. He could hear movement in the darkness, a quick movement across the stage to somewhere in front and to the left of him. There was silence and then a sound, he wasn't sure, but it was as if someone's lips were moving, mouthing sounds with no words. There was something terrible about this sound and, in the darkness, he felt, for a fleeting moment, a terrible emptiness. The sound had a nightmarish quality, like a child calling for help through sheets of impenetrable glass. He could hear some movement too and he imagined grotesque, spastic movements.

He called out, 'I can hear you! Do you need help?' The sound continued, oblivious to his call. He repeated, 'I can hear you! Do you need help?' There was no response.

A voice whispered in his ear, 'Can you not hear her? She needs your help.' Bruno experienced a shock; he had been so caught up in that sound in the darkness that he had totally forgotten about the other actors.

'Open your eyes, look at her,' continued the voice.

Bruno couldn't open his eyes. If he did everyone would see him, and he couldn't bear the thought of that.

'I can't, she'll see me,' he found himself saying.

'What will she see?' asked the voice which he now identified as Lawrence. Bruno didn't know, or at least, he couldn't find the words for it. He felt exposed and suddenly aware of Rona and Laura watching him. He felt he was holding things up, he worried he was boring everyone. It seemed, all of a sudden, rather boring, self-indulgent and not very good theatre. He had forgotten Rona's story and was now somehow playing out his own. Almost unbearably the face of his daughter formed in his mind – that terrible look of accusing pain that she had given him when she first went into hospital.

With a massive effort of will Bruno said, 'I've been to the hospital today, I've had some tests.'

He opened his eyes. What surprised him first was the light. The harsh light of the church hall seemed so merciless, so terribly everyday. It hid nothing and so showed nothing. He then saw the source of those strange mouthing sounds: it was Bridget. Of course, he knew it would be her, but nevertheless he was surprised. He was surprised by the presence of her – a vulnerable presence, looking at him, present, sensual, alert.

'Why didn't you tell me before, Dad?' said Bridget.

'I didn't want to worry you, it may be nothing – and there's no point worrying about things that may never happen,' and warming to a theme which suddenly occurred to him and struck him as characteristic of Rona's father, he continued:

'Don't worry! Smile, it may never happen! You've got to keep going, no point in worrying, you'll make yourself ill.'

For the first time Bruno was aware of Rona. He heard a sound like a sigh or a stifled laugh. He then realized that Bridget was angry with him.

'Smile…that's what you always do…so much talking and smiling, you never listen, do you? You never listen…'

'Whoa, hold your horses. Wait one doggone minute.' Where this came from Bruno had no idea, clichés were piling up, one upon the other, and Bruno seemed to have no control over them. He was still in the chair but was now leaning forward, his hand reaching out towards Bridget to silence her. He wondered if he should go over to her but he rejected the idea. There had to be that space between them. It was filled with tension, longing and fear.

Then Bridget turned toward the audience.

'He always does this, he silences me, not by force but by a kind of tenderness…' She searches for the words. 'Everything is so fragile…the fear that if I speak I will break him, destroy him – destroy us.' She emphasizes the 'us' surprised by the power of this idea.

For the first time Bruno is aware of Amanda. She has been playing a steady insistent beat throughout, but it is only now that he really hears her, she sings with a plaintive, resonant voice,

A kind of tenderness
He destroys me
With a kind of tenderness.

Bridget turns to Bruno and across the space, which seems, at this minute, vast to Bruno, she says, 'You couldn't hear me could you? When it was getting darker and colder, When you were so far away and it seemed so long until Christmas, you couldn't hear me. And now Dad, I don't know how to hear you.'

Bridget turns to Rona, the singing stops and there is silence. Bruno sees the tears on Rona's cheeks and realizes he is shivering.

Laura reaches into her pocket, finds a tissue and hands it to Rona,

'Well, Rona…'

Rona hated this bit; she always felt that she had to say something. She really wanted to let it settle, take it in, hold onto it and not share it with anyone else. The actors were looking at her expectantly.

'I don't know what to say,' she said wiping her eyes and blowing her nose. 'It was when Bridget said 'a kind of tenderness'...that broke my heart. There is a tenderness there...but there's no...' She searched for the word. 'That's it...there's no robustness. I wish we could shout at each other a bit more...and Bruno, when you said, "smile, it may never happen" it was so like him!' Everyone laughed.

'I was worried I had gone over the top,' said Bridget, 'I just felt so angry when he said that bit about smiling, I want to hit him'...she growled and hit Bruno on the arm.

'Ow!' He cried, 'I couldn't just bear you to be worried...it was like I was talking to Sally...' he suddenly broke off and there was a pause.

'Of course! I hadn't thought of that... I knew I had to choose you to be my dad.'

'I knew you would,' Bruno smiled and Rona returned his smile.

Lawrence looked miserable. Laura asked, 'What's wrong Lawrence?'

'I don't know I feel so out of it...probably to do with not having a role.'

'Have you a story?'

'Yes,' said Lawrence.

Rona, Bruno, Bridget and Fran sat on the actors' chairs and Amanda returned to her music.

* * *

Appendix 2
'Short Forms' Used in Playback Theatre

The opening contributions – 'moments' in the York Company – are usually enacted through *'the short forms'*. Although 'fluid sculpts or sculptures' and 'pairs' or 'conflicts' seem to be common throughout, these short forms do vary a little from company to company. Although short forms provide a structure for the action, it is not uncommon for performers to 'break the rules' if they feel it will benefit the enactment.

The choice of which short form to use is made by the conductor, she will say something like 'Let's see this in a fluid sculpt'. Playback Theatre York have developed, as far as I can tell, an unusually large number of these short forms. These are set out below. It is important to stress that this is not an exhaustive list, and no doubt other practitioners will be able to add others developed in their own companies.

Short forms used by Playback Theatre York

1. Fluid sculpt

Upon hearing a moment or a short story, any one of the actors moves forward and produces a movement with sound or words. They do this as, one by one, other actors join the developing sculpt. The piece concludes when the first actor freezes. Usually actors maintain their movement and sound throughout the piece, however, occasionally they will change in response to what the other actors are doing.

2. Three Solos (Soli)

Three actors move forward and form a line. Beginning stage-right, Actor 1 begins and moves with sounds and or words perhaps playing off Actors 2 and 3 (who do not generally respond). At some point and in any position, Actor 1 freezes and this is the cue for Actor 2 to begin. The general idea is that the three actors will show different and contrasting aspects of the story. The piece finishes with Actor 3.

3. Three voices

In this 'short form' the idea is to build up a melody (or cacophony) of sounds that represent the teller's story. As in 'Three Solos', three actors move forward into a line. This form has three stages:

- Actor 1 gives a voice and sound without movement or significant expression. When this actor concludes she is followed by Actor 2 and when she is finished by Actor 3.
- All three actors then make their sounds simultaneously.
- The three actors now vary their own sound, respond to each other and pick up and repeat the sounds of others. They improvise together around the sounds that have been developed.

4. Three stops

As many actors as wish to, come forward; the story is then played in three short scenes, each concluded by a freeze in the action. This is used only rarely by Playback Theatre York because, I think, of the difficulties of finding the freeze points together.

5. Free impro

All actors step forward into the space and an improvisation commences.

6. Poetry and music

One of the actors volunteers to be the 'poet'. The 'poet' sits on a chair centre stage and a musician sits either on the floor or in a chair next to him. The poet creates a poem in response to the teller's story and the musician accompanies or takes the lead accordingly. This form is occasionally used in performance but regularly used in rehearsal.

7. Pairs

This short form is used to work with conflicting emotions, wishes or motivations. The actors are in pairs; one actor stands behind the other. Having heard the conflict, the partners take on the two 'sides'. Then, either back to back and revolving, or facing the front, they play out the two sides of the stated conflict. There are three variations to pairs in the York Company:

- B quickly tells A which side of the conflict they are going to be playing, and whether it will be played back to back or facing the front. This is now no longer used. Members of the Company prefer the next variation.
- No discussion takes place and the first partner to start defines the action.
- If we are working with an odd number of actors, then one may embody both sides of the conflict.

8. Chorus

In 'chorus' the actors work together, usually in close physical proximity and with few words. Generally the aim is to produce synchronized sounds and movements. This is also incorporated in the 'full story' when, usually uncast, actors form a chorus to comment on or add to the enactment.

9. Tableau

This form is usually used when the conductor or the teller feels that the actors have missed an element from the enactment or when the conductor wishes to quickly summarize a moment, story or a feeling in the audience. The actors simply form a tableau and hold it for a short time.

10. Chorus 'interruptus'

This form was developed with the Amsterdam Playback Theatre Company. A chorus begins and, at a point of their choosing, the musicians 'interrupt' it with music. When they do, the actors freeze into a tableau. The actors choose when to interrupt the musicians with movement and sound.

Short forms used by other companies

Other forms used by other companies of which I am aware are:

11. Transformations

This is used when the story involves a clear transformation from one state to another. The actors usually work together as in a chorus and move from one state to another, charting the passage through the 'transformation'.

12. The wise being

In this form, usually used at the end of a performance, a teller is told that the actors will answer any question put to them by the audience through a choric enactment. The audience is directed to non-prophetic, quasi-philosophical questions. I have seen this form performed only once by an all-male company – Playback Jack based in Perth, Australia. I asked the 'wise being' 'What is the spirit of Australia?' having newly arrived in the continent. It is not a form used by Playback Theatre York. We experimented with the form some time ago (in Autumn 1999) but found it difficult to do without giggling or lapsing into oracular declamation.

13. Tableau stories

The Melbourne Company developed this short form. The conductor divides a story into a series of titles and as he or she calls them out, the actors form a still tableau to portray each title.

14. Action Haiku

This short form is described by Jo Salas (1993, p.41) as a form suitable for use at the conclusion of a performance. The audience call out themes that they are aware of from the performance. One actor stands centre stage and makes a statement derived from one of those themes. For example 'There is a gaping hole inside me,' might be a statement derived from the theme of 'Loss'. Another actor then sculpts that actor's body in a way that is expressive of loss. This continues with other statements.

References

Abbott, N. (2002) *The Cambridge Introduction to Narrative.* Cambridge: Cambridge University Press.

Adorno, T. (2003) *The Jargon of Authenticity.* London: Routledge.

Alexander, C. (2003) 'Diversity and Difference: Playback in Chennai, India.' *Interplay 8,* 2, 5–7.

Arnold, R. (2005) *Empathic Intelligence: Teaching, Learning, Relating.* Sydney: University of New South Wales.

Artaud, A. (1998) 'The Theatre of Cruelty'. In G. Brandt (ed.) *Modern Theories of Drama.* Oxford: Oxford University Press.

Aston, E. and Savona, G. (1991) *Theatre as Sign-system: A Semiotics of Text and Performance.* London: Routledge.

Auslander, P. (1992) *Presence and Resistance: Postmodernism and Cultural Politics in Contemporary American Performance.* Michigan: Ann Arbor University of Michigan Press.

Auslander, P. (1995) 'Just Be Your Self'. In P. Zarrilla (ed.) *Acting (Re)Considered.* London and New York: Routledge.

Auslander, P. (1999) *Liveness: Performance in a Mediatized Culture.* London and New York: Routledge.

Bachelard, G. (1994) *The Poetics of Space.* Boston, MA: Beacon.

Bakhtin, M. (1981) *The Dialogic Imagination: Four Essays.* Austin: University of Texas Press.

Bakhtin, M. (1984) *Problems of Dostoevsky's Poetics.* Minneapolis: University of Minneapolis Press.

Bakhtin, M. (ed.) (1994) *The Bakhtin Reader.* London: Edward Arnold.

Barclay, C. (1994) 'Composing Protoselves through Improvisation'. In U. Neisser and R. Fivush (eds) *The Remembering Self: Construction and Accuracy in the Self-narrative.* New York: Cambridge University Press.

Barron, F. (1990) *Creativity and Psychological Health.* Buffalo: Creative Education Foundation.

Barthes, R. (1967) *Image Music and Text.* London: Fontana Press.

Barthes, R. (1979) 'From Work to Text'. In J.V. Harrari (ed.) *Textual Strategies: Perspectives in Post Structuralist Criticism.* London: Methuen.

Barthes, R. (1989) 'The Death of the Author'. In P. Rice and P. Waugh (eds) *Modern Literary Theory: A Reader.* London: Arnold.

Barthes, R. (2000) 'Intertextuality'. In J. Hawthorn (ed.) *A Glossary of Contemporary Literary Theory.* London: Arnold.

Bataille, G. (1997) *The Bataille Reader.* Oxford: Blackwell.

Baudrillard, J. (1983) *Simulations.* New York: Semiotext(e).

Bear, M., Connors, B., *et al.* (2002) *Neuroscience: Exploring the Brain.* Baltimore: Williams and Wilkins.

Benjamin, W. (1970) 'The Storyteller: Reflections on the Works of Nikolai Leskov'. In W. Benjamin (ed.) *Illuminations.* London: Collins/Fontana.

Bennett, S. (1997) *Theatre Audiences: A Theory of Production and Reception.* London: Routledge.

Berliner, L. and Briere, J. (1999) 'Trauma, Memory and Clinical Practice.' In L. Williams and V. Banyard (eds) *Trauma and Memory.* Thousand Oaks: Sage.

Bharucha, R. (1993) *Theatre and the World.* London: Routledge.

Blanchot, M. (1986) *The Writing of the Disaster.* Trans. Ann Smock. Lincoln: University of Nebraska Press.

Boal, A. (1979) *The Theatre of the Oppressed.* London: Pluto Press.

Boal, A. (1995) *The Rainbow of Desire: The Boal Method of Theatre and Therapy.* London: Routledge.

Boal, A. (1998) *Legislative Theatre: Using Performance to Make Politics.* London: Routledge.

Bollas, C. (1995) *Cracking Up.* New York: Hill and Wang.

Bordo, S. (1998) 'Bringing Body to Theory'. In D. Welton (ed.) *Body and Flesh: A Philosophical Reader.* Oxford: Blackwell.

Brecht, B. (1930) 'Prologue to The Exception and the Rule'. In R. Drain (ed.) *Twentieth Century Theatre.* London: Routledge.

Brecht, B. (1964) 'The Street Scene'. In C. Cousell and L. Wolf (eds) *Performance Analysis.* London: Routledge.

Brooks, P. (1994) *Psychoanalysis and Storytelling.* Oxford: Blackwell.

Brownstein, O. and Daubert, D. (1981) *Analytical Sourcebook of Concepts in Dramatic Theory.* Westport and London: Greenwood Press.

Bruner, J. (1990) *Acts of Meaning.* Cambridge, Mass.: Cambridge University Press.

Buber, M. (1949) *Paths to Utopia.* London: Routledge.

Buber, M. (1958) *I and Thou.* London: T and T Clark.

Burns, R. (1904) *The Poems of Robert Burns.* Oxford: Oxford University Press.

Butler, J. (1990) *Gender Trouble: Feminism and the Subversion of Identity.* London: Routledge.

Butler, J. (1993) *Bodies That Matter: On the Discursive Limits of 'Sex'.* New York: Routledge.

Cancalon, E.D. and Spacagna, A. (eds) (1994) *Intertextuality in Literature and Film.* Gainesville: University of Florida Press.

Caputo, J. (2003) 'Against Principles'. In E. Wyschogrod and G. McKenny (eds) *The Ethical.* Oxford: Blackwell.

Carlson, M. (1996) *Performance: A Critical Introduction.* London and New York: Routledge.

Carlson, M. (1999) 'Theatre and Dialogism'. In J. Reinelt and J. Roach (eds) *Critical Theory and Performance.* Michigan: University of Michigan Press.

Clark, K. and Holquist, M. (1984) *Mikhail Bakhtin.* Cambridge, Mass.: The Belknap Press of Harvard University Press.

Clarkson, P. (1995) *The Therapeutic Relationship.* London: Whurr Publishers.

Clifford, J. (1986) 'Introduction: Partial Truths'. In J. Clifford and G. Marcus (eds) *Writing Culture: The Poetics and Politics of Ethnography.* Berkeley and Los Angeles: University of California Press.

Cobley, P. (2001) *Narrative.* London: Routledge.

Conquergood, D. (1985) 'Performing as a Moral Act: Ethical Dimensions of the Ethnography of Performance.' *Literature in Performance 9* (April).

Conquergood, D. (1999) 'Performance Theory, Hmong Shamans, Cultural Politics.' In J. Reinelt and J. Roach (eds) *Critical Theory and Performance.* Michigan: Ann Arbor University of Michigan Press.

Cox, M. (1978) *Coding the Therapeutic Process.* Oxford: Blackwell.

Cox, M. and Theilgaard, A. (1987) *Mutative Metaphors in Psychotherapy: The Aeolian Mode.* London: Jessica Kingsley Publishers.

Csikszentmihalyi, M. and Csikszentmihalyi, S. (eds) (1988) *Optimal Experience: Psychological Studies of Flow in Consciousness.* Cambridge: Cambridge University Press.

Dean, R. (1989) *Creative Improvisation: Jazz, Contemporary Music and Beyond.* Milton Keynes: Open University Press.

Diamond, E. (1999) 'The Violence of "We": Politicizing Identification'. In J. Reinelt and J. Roach (eds) *Critical Theory and Performance.* Michigan: Ann Arbor University of Michigan Press.

Dickinson, E. (1970) '1129'. In Johnson (ed.) *The Complete Poems.* London: Faber and Faber.

Dor, J. (1997) *Introduction to the Reading of Lacan: The Unconscious Structured Like a Language.* Northvale New Jersey: Jason Aronson.

Douglas, M. (1966) *Purity and Danger.* London: Routledge and Kegan Paul.

Douglas, M. (1975) *Implicit Meanings. Essays in Anthropology.* London: Routledge.

Drain, R. (ed.) (1995) *Twentieth Century Theatre: A Sourcebook.* London: Routledge.

Duranti, A. and Burrell, K. (2004) 'Jazz Improvisation: A Search for Hidden Harmonies and a Unique Self.' *Ricerche di Psicologia 27*, 3, 71–102.

Eagleton, T. (2003) *After Theory.* London: Allen Lane.

Eco, U. (1984) *Semiotics and the Philosophy of Language.* Basingstoke: Macmillan.

Eco, U. (1989) *The Open Work.* Cambridge, Mass.: Harvard University Press.

El Guindi, F. (1999) *Veil: Modesty, Privacy and Resistance.* Oxford: Berg.

Erickson, J. (1999) 'The Face and the Possiblity of an Ethics of Performance.' *Journal of Dramatic Theory and Criticism 13*, 2, 5.

Evans, S. and Layman, W. (2001) 'A Playback Debriefing... Some Lessons.' *Interplay 7*, 2: This can also be found at: http://www.playbacknet.org/interplay/Previousissues/Dec01/Lessons.htm

Feasey, D. (2000) *Good Practice in Psychotherapy and Counselling*. London and Philadelphia: Whurr Publishers.

Feldhendler, D. (2001) 'A Culture of Remembrance.' *Interplay 7*, 2.

Field, N. (1989) 'Listening with the Body.' *British Journal of Psychotherapy 5*, 4, 512–22.

Fischer-Lichte, E. (1997) *The Show and the Gaze of Theatre: A European Perspective*. Iowa City: University of Iowa Press.

Forte, J. (1999) 'Focus on the Body: Pain, Praxis, and Pleasure in Feminist Performance.' In J. Reinelt and J. Roach (eds) *Critical Theory and Performance*. Michigan: University of Michigan Press.

Foster, S. (2003) 'Taken by Surprise: Improvisation in Dance and Mind'. In A. Albright and D. Gere (eds) *Taken by Surprise*. Middleton, CT: Wesleyan University Press.

Foucault, M. (ed.) (2002) *The Archeology of Knowledge*. Performance Studies: An Introduction. London and New York: Routledge.

Fox, H. (2000) 'The Beginnings: Reflecting on 25 Years of Playback Theatre.' *Interplay 6*, 2, 7–9.

Fox, J. (1994) *Acts of Service: Spontaneity, Commitment, Tradition in the Nonscripted Theatre*. New Paltz: Tulsitala Publishing.

Fox, J. (1995) 'Jonathan's Reply.' *Interplay 6*, 1, 2–3.

Fox, J. and Dauber, H. (eds) (1999) *Gathering Voices: Essays in Playback Theatre*. New Paltz, New York: Tusitala Publishing.

Freeman, M. (1993) *Rewriting the Self*. London: Routledge.

Freud, S. (1995) 'The Interpretation of Dreams'. In A. Brill (ed.) *The Basic Writings of Sigmund Freud*. New York: The Modern Library.

Frost, A. and Yarrow, R. (1990) *Improvisation in Drama*. Basingstoke: Macmillan.

Garavelli, M. (2001) 'Tales Rescued from Oblivion.' *Interplay 7*, 2, 4–8.

Garavelli, M. (2003) *Odisea en la Escena*. Cordoba, Argentina: Editorial Brujas.

Gergen, K. (1993) *Refiguring Self and Psychology*. Aldershot: Dartmouth.

Gilmore, L. (2001) *The Limits of Autobiography: Trauma and Testimony*. Ithaca and London: Cornell University Press.

Gisler, K. (2002) 'The Seven Virtues of Good Playback Acting. What Makes a Performer a "Good" Playback Actor?' *Interplay 7*, 3, 1–2.

Greimas, A. (1991) 'Debate with Paul Ricoeur'. In M. Valdes (ed.) *Reflection and Imagination: A Ricoeur Reader*. London: Harvester Wheatsheaf.

Griffiths, D. (1998) *The Italian Commedia and Please be Gentle*. Amsterdam: Harwood.

Grotowski, J. (1995). 'Methodological Exploration'. In R. Drain (ed.) *Twentieth Century Theatre*. London: Routledge.

Guignon, C. (2004) *Being Authentic*. London: Routledge.

Harris, F. (2002) 'Tragedy, Mortal Awareness and the Art of Playback.' *Interplay 7*, 3, 7–9. This may also be found at: http://www.playbacknet.org/interplay/Previousissues/March02/tragedy.htm

Heppekausen, J. (2003) 'The Politics of Playback Theatre.' *Interplay 8*, 2. This may be found at: http://www.playbacknet.org/interplay/Previousissues/December02/juttaenglish.htm

Hermans, H. and Hermans-Jansen, E. (1995) *Self Narratives*. New York: Guildford Press.

Hertz, R. (ed.) (1997) *Reflexivity and Voice*. London: Sage.

Hillman, J. and Ventura, M. (1993) *We've Had a Hundred Years of Psychotherapy and the World's Getting Worse*. San Francisco: Harpur.

Hirschfield, J. (2005) 'Happiness'. In *Each Happiness Ringed by Lions: Selected Poems*. Tarset, Northumberland: Bloodaxe Books.

Holstein, J. and Gubrium, J. (2002) *The Self We Live By: Narrative Identity in a Postmodern World*. Oxford: Oxford University Press.

hooks, b. (1990) *Yearning: Race, Gender and Cultural Politics.* Boston, MA: South End Press.

Hughes, P. and Brecht, G. (eds) (1978) *Vicious Circles and Infinity: An Anthology of Paradoxes.* London: Penguin.

Hutcheon, L. (1989) *The Politics of Postmodernism.* London: Routledge.

The Improbable Theatre Company (ITC) (1998) *Lifegame: Programme Notes.* Leeds: Leeds Playhouse.

Jennings, S. (1998) *Introduction to Dramatherapy: Theatre and Healing.* London and Philadelphia: Jessica Kingsley Publishers.

Johnson, J. (1996) 'Reaching for Diversity: Inclusion, Multiculturalism in Playback Theatre.' *Interplay 6,* 3, 3–4.

Johnstone, K. (1981) *Impro: Improvisation and the Theatre.* London: Methuen.

Johnstone, K. (1999) *Impro for Storytellers: Theatresports and the Art of Making Things Happen.* London: Faber and Faber.

Jones, P. (1996) *Drama as Therapy: Theatre as Living.* London: Routledge.

Josselson, R. (1996) 'Ethics and Process'. In R. Josselson (ed.) *The Narrative Study of Lives.* London: Sage.

Kearney, R. (2002) *On Stories.* London and New York: Routledge.

Kitzinger, C. and Wilkinson, S. (1996) *Representing the Other: A Feminism and Psychology Reader.* London: Sage.

Kristeva, J. (1980) *Desire in Language: A Semiotic Approach to Literature and Art.* Oxford: Blackwell.

Kuhn, A. (1995) *Family Secrets: Acts of Memory and Imagination.* London and New York: Verso.

Kundera, M. (1982) *The Book of Laughter and Forgetting.* London: Faber and Faber.

Lacan, J. (1988) 'The Purloined Letter'. In J. Lacan (ed.) *The Seminars of Jacques Lacan, Book II.* Cambridge: Cambridge University Press.

Lampe, E. (1995) 'Rachel Rosenthal Creating Her Selves'. In P. Zarrilla (ed.) *Acting (Re)considered.* London and New York: Routledge.

Landy, R. (1993) *Persona and Performance: The Meaning of Role in Drama, Therapy, and Everyday Life.* London: Jessica Kingsley Publishers.

Langs, R. (1976) *The Bipersonal Field.* New York: Jason Aronson.

Lassiter, L. (1995) 'David Warrilow, Symbol and Cypher'. In P. Zarrilla (ed.) *Acting (Re)considered.* London: Routledge.

Lefebvre, H. (1991) *The Production of Space.* Oxford: Blackwell.

Livia, A. (1996) 'Daring to Presume.' In C. Kitzinger and S. Wilkinson (eds) *Representing the Other: A Feminism and Psychology Reader.* London: Sage.

Llewelyn, J. (1995) *Emmanuel Lévinas: The Genealogy of Ethics.* London and New York: Routledge.

Love, L. (1995) 'Resisting the Organic'. In P. Zarrilla (ed.) *Acting (Re)considered.* London and New York: Routledge.

Lyotard, J.F. (1984) *The Postmodern Condition: A Report on Knowledge.* Minneapolis: University of Minnesota Press.

MacBeth, D. (2001) 'On Reflexivity in Qualitative Research.' *Qualitative Inquiry 7,* 1, 35–68.

MacIntyre, A. (1985) *After Virtue: A Study in Moral Theory.* London: Duckworth.

Marshall, L. (2001) *The Body Speaks: Performance and Expression.* London: Methuen.

Massey, D. (2005) *For Space.* London: Sage.

Masson, J. (1990) *Against Therapy.* London: Fontana Harper Collins.

McConkey, J. (ed.) (1996) *The Anatomy of Memory: An Anthology.* Oxford: Oxford University Press.

McLeod, J. (1997) *Narrative and Psychotherapy.* London: Sage.

Merleau-Ponty, M. (1962) *Phenomenology of Perception.* London: Routledge and Kegan Paul.

Mollon, P. (1998) *Remembering Trauma: The Psychotherapist's Guide to Memory and Illusion.* London and Philadelphia: Whurr Publishers.

Montuori, A. (2003) 'The complexity of improvisation and the improvisation of complexity: Social science, art and creativity.' *Human Relations 95,* 2, 237–260.

Moore, P. (2002) 'Playback in Fiji.' *Interplay 8,* 1, 9–11.

Moreno, J. (1987) *The Essential Moreno: Writings on Psychodrama, Group Method and Spontaneity.* J. Fox (ed.). New York: Springer.

Morson, G. and Emerson, C. (1990) *Mikhail Bakhtin: Creation of a Prosaics.* Stanford: Stanford University Press.

Mulvey, L. (1975) 'Visual Pleasure and Narrative Cinema'. In C. Cousell and L. Wolf (eds) *Performance Analysis.* London: Routledge.

Nash, S. and Rowe, N. (2000/2001) 'Safety and Danger in Playback Theatre.' *Dramatherapy 22,* 3, 14–15.

Nichols, B. (1994) *Blurred Boundaries: Questions of Meaning in Contemporary Culture.* Bloomington and Indianapolis: Indiana University Press.

Okri, B. (1996) *Birds of Heaven.* London: Phoenix Paperbacks.

Parker, A. and Sedgewick, E. (eds) (1995) *Performativity and Performance.* London: Routledge.

Pearson, D. (1998) *An Interview Concerning Conducting in Playback Theatre.* Rowe, N. Perth, Australia.

Penny, C. (2002) 'Acting in Playback Theatre. Walking on Stage with a Teller's Heart.' *Interplay 8,* 1. This can also be found at: http://www.playbacknet.org/interplay/Previousissues/September02/penny.htm

Phelan, P. (1997) *Mourning Sex: Performing Public Memories.* London: Routledge.

Phillips, A. (2002) 'On Translating a Person'. In A. Phillips (ed.) *Promises, Promises: Essays on Literature and Psychoanalysis.* London: Faber and Faber.

Pisk, L. (1990) *The Actor and His Body.* London: Methuen.

Playback TheatreYork (2002) *Playback Theatre: Company Brochure.* York: Playback Theatre York.

Polkinghorne, D. (1988) *Narrative Knowing and the Human Sciences.* New York: New York University Press.

Quinn, R. (2003) 'The Performative Self: Improvisation for Self and Other.' *New Theatre Quarterly 19,* 1, 18–22.

Rappaport, R. (1999) *Ritual and Religion in the Making of Humanity.* Cambridge: Cambridge University Press.

Read, A. (1993) *Theatre and Everyday Life.* London: Routledge.

Richardson, L. (1994) 'Writing: a method of enquiry'. In N. Denzin and Y. Lincoln (eds) *Handbook of Qualitative Research.* Thousand Oaks: Sage.

Robb, H. (1995) 'Heather's Story.' *Interplay 6,* 1, 2.

Roine, E. (1997) *Psychodrama: Group Psychotherapy as Experimental Theatre.* London: Jessica Kingsley Publishers.

Rorty, R. (1989) *Contingency, Irony and Solidarity.* Cambridge: The University of Cambridge Press.

Rowan, J. and Jacobs, M. (2002) *The Therapist's Use of Self.* Buckingham: Open University Press.

Rowson, R. (2001) 'Ethical Principles'. In F. Barnes and L. Murdin (eds) *Values and Ethics in the Practice of Psychotherapy and Counselling.* Buckingham: Open University Press.

Salas, J. (1993) *Improvising Real Life: Personal Story in Playback Theatre.* Dubuqua, Iowa: Kendall Hunt.

Salas, J. (1999) 'What is "Good" Playback Theatre?' In J. Fox and H. Dauber (eds) *Gathering Voices: Essays in Playback Theatre.* New Paltz: Tusitala.

Salas, J. (2004a) *An Interview with Jo Salas: Fe Day.* http://www.playbacknet.org/interplay/news/jofe.html 2006.

Salas, J. (2004b) 'Playback the Vote.' *Interplay ix,* 3, 7–9. This may also be found at: http://www.playbacknet.org/interplay/news/playbackthevote.html

Samuel, R. (1996) *Theatres of Memory. Vol. 1: Past and Present in Contemporary Culture.* London: Verso.

Sarbin, T. (1986) *Narrative Psychology.* New York: Praeger.

Sartre, J.-P. (2000) *Nausea.* London: Penguin.

Sawyer, R. K. (2000) 'Improvisation and the Creative Process: Dewey, Collingwood, and the Aesthetics of Spontaneity.' *Journal of Aesthetics and Art Criticism 58,* 2, 149–61.

Sawyer, R.K. (2002) 'Improvisation and Narrative.' *Narrative Inquiry 12,* 2, 319–49.

Schechner, R. (1988) *Performance Theory.* London: Routledge.

Schechner, R. (1993) *The Future of Ritual: Writings on Culture and Performance.* London: Routledge.

Schechner, R. (1994) *Environmental Theatre.* New York and London: Applause Books.

Schechner, R. (2002) *Performance Studies: An Introduction.* London and New York: Routledge.

Schmid, P. (1998) '"On Becoming a Person-Centred Approach": A Person-Centred Understanding of the Person'. In B. Thorne and E. Lambers (eds) *Person-Centred Therapy: A European Perspective.* London: Sage.

Shaw, R. (2003) *The Embodied Psychotherapist: The Therapist's Body Story.* Hove: Brunner-Routledge.

Smith, H. and Dean, R. (1997) *Improvisation, Hypermedia and the Arts.* Amsterdam: Harwood.

Spence, D. (1982) *Narrative Truth and Historical Truth.* New York: W.W. Norton.

Spinelli, E. (1994) *Demystifying Therapy.* London: Constable and Co.

Spolin, V. (1999) *Improvisation for the Theatre.* Evanston: Northwestern University Press.

Stanislavski, C. (1983) *Creating a Role.* London: Hapgood.

Stanislavski, C. (1995) 'Inner Impulses and Inner Action'. In R. Drain (ed.) *Twentieth Century Theatre: A Sourcebook.* London: Routledge.

Stern, J. (2000) *Metaphor in Context.* Cambridge, Mass.: The MIT Press.

Swallow, J. (2000) 'The Beginnings: Reflecting on 25 years of Playback Theatre.' *Interplay 11*, 2, 2.

Tange, M. (2002) 'Acting in Playback.' *Interplay 7*, 3, 6–8.

Taylor, C. (1991) *The Ethics of Authenticity.* Cambridge, Mass.: Harvard University Press.

The Collins Concise Dictionary (1988) London: William Collins.

Tottin, N. (2000) *Psychotherapy and Politics.* London: Sage.

Toukmanian, S. and Rennie, D. (eds) (1992) *Psychotherapy Process Research: Paradigmatic and Narrative Approaches.* London: Sage.

Tufnell, M. and Crickmay, C. (1990) *Body Space Image: Notes Towards Improvisation and Performance.* London: Dance Books.

Turner, V. (1969) *The Ritual Process.* London: Routledge and Kegan Paul.

Unsworth, B. (1996) *Morality Play.* London: Penguin.

Vettriano, E. (1999) 'The Playback Conference in York.' *The Prompt: The Newsletter of the Association for Dramatherapists* (Autumn).

Wilde, O. (1973) 'The Soul of Man Under Socialism'. In H. Pearson (ed.) *De Profundis and Other Writings.* Harmondsworth: Penguin.

Williams, K. (1981) *Culture.* Glasgow: Fontana.

Wyatt, F. (1986) 'The Narrative in Psychoanalysis: Psychoanalytic Notes of Storytelling, Listening and Interpreting.' In T. Sarbin (ed.) *Narrative Psychology.* New York: Praeger: 196.

Zapora, R. (1995) *Action Theatre: The Improvisation of Presence.* Berkeley: North Atlantic Books.

Zinder, D. (2002) *Body, Voice, Imagination: A Training for the Actor.* London: Routledge.

Subject Index

Author Index